EVERY LINING CLOUD

TOURING THE FOOTBALL GROUNDS OF THE WELSH PREMIER LEAGUE

Nathan Lee Davies

BLACKLINE PRESS

ISBN 9780956323897

www.blacklinepress.com
15 Lister Road IPSWICH IP1 5EQ
info@blacklinepress.com

To Grandad
Harold James Maddocks, 1925-2002

"A round man cannot be expected to fit in a square hole right away. He must have time to modify his shape."

Mark Twain

Acknowledgements

I'm a pretty useless individual.

Writing is one of only two things I can do successfully on my own without any help. The other – after many years of training – is masturbation, but we won't go into that.

The reasons why I'm such a basket case will become clear in the coming pages but, suffice to say, when I announced plans for this tour of Welsh Premier League football grounds and proposed book, it was probably written off as another pipe dream by those around me.

Eighteen months on, and after a lot of sweat and determination on my behalf, I'm finally ready to become a published author. Although I obviously deserve the majority of the credit, I recognise that I couldn't have completed this volume without the help and support of others.

No matter how lavishly I dress this section up, it's still going to turn into a dull list of faceless names for the majority of readers, but I need to express my sincere thanks to the many people who have assisted me, in one way or another, over the past eighteen months.

Let's get on with it.

I was first charged with the energy to begin such a harebrained project after finally watching *Dave Gorman's Googlewhack Adventure* on DVD. I probably purchased this production in about 2005, but it remained unappreciated at the top of a wardrobe for five years until I was laid up in bed and needed something to make me laugh. Not only did Gorman succeed in his job as a comedian, but he also delivered an energetic performance that inspired me to stop watching the uniquely inventive schemes of others and try one of my own.

At the age of 31, Gorman decided it was time to be taken seriously as an artist, grew a beard and set to work on his first novel. Unfortunately, his honest intentions were scuppered when he discovered that novel writing is actually quite difficult, and someone emailed to inform him that his website – www.davegorman.com – contained a "googlewhack". This term describes what happens when two words are entered into the Google search engine and it comes back with only one hit. Gorman's particular googlewhack was "Francophile Namesakes".

Gorman now had a distraction and the planned novel took a back seat as he became obsessed with his new googlewhacking hobby. This led him on a worldwide tour to track down other people responsible for similarly unique combinations of words. He eventually spent his publisher's advance on the crazy quest, without writing the promised novel, and had to create his *Googlewhack Adventure* show to pay them back.

In so doing, he managed to kick-start my chaotic mind – although my disorganised dreams were still in need of structure and support. Step forward Matt Smith of Blackline Press who contacted me after reading a series of blogs on my now defunct personal website.

I'd written about my culinary experiences at the OK Diner chain of traditionally American eateries, which are scattered around the A-roads of England and Wales. At the time, Matt was writing a book about cooked breakfast and asked if I'd be interested in submitting a chapter on a typically American offering. I jumped at the chance of getting my work published, but after rattling off a chapter for inclusion in *The Great British Breakfast*, I began looking for my next challenge.

I didn't have to look far.

EVERY SILVER LINING HAS A CLOUD Nathan Lee Davies

Blackline Press specialise in publishing books about football and specifically have an interest in groundhopping tours and challenges. I emailed Matt with my Welsh Premier League proposal and ever since he has been supportive and attentive. I haven't even met the bloke in person but can't speak highly enough of him and hope we join forces again in the future.

My family were a constant source of help and support, especially my dad and his partner, Paul Davies and Karen Haden, who accompanied me throughout the tour when they probably would've preferred to stay at home. They also paid for gallons of petrol, plenty of programmes and pies, as well as the odd bottle of beer, or ten. Dr Cassie Ogden (sister), Greg Ogden (brother-in-law), Elvie Lee Ogden (niece), Barbara Davies (mum) and Brian Wilson (mum's bloke) also deserve credit for providing encouragement and sticking by me in troubled times. My sister and her husband deserve extra credit for proof-reading these pages and giving me someone else to blame for any spelling mistakes or grammatical errors. In addition, Luke Ogden and Sara Ogden were on hand to translate and make sense of the indecipherable.

I've also depended on the kindness of strangers who've pointed me in the right direction, offered opinions through Facebook or Twitter or educated me through email. This section of names also includes those whose articles have been used to glean information; encouraging acquaintances, who've become friends; and others who'll probably never know that their names are in this book.

Looking back over the list of names that I've been maintaining, I'm not even sure who some of these people are but I obviously felt gratitude towards them at one stage so I'll take a deep breath and begin: John Acton, Billy Ashcroft, Katie Bartlett, Tom Bates, David Bergin, David Bigmore, Steve Blandford, Beth Bridewell, Matthew Burgess, Katie Bussman, Steve Buxton, Matt Cansick, Emma Cheshire, Mike Clarke, Rob Clement, Dave Collins, Oliver Cope, Jill Louise Coppock, Gareth M Davies, Tom Dickinson, Owen Durbridge, Neil

Dymock, James Edwards, Jamie Elliott, Ed Filugelli, Jaime Gill, Arfon Griffiths, Keith Griffiths, Keith Harding, Dr Katherine Harrison, Dr.A.K.Hignell, Andrew Howard, Chris Howells, Mel Ap Ior Thomas, Duncan Jardine, Matt Johnson, Scott Johnson, Bruce Jones, Dave Jones, Joey Jones, Mark Jones, Miranda Kempin, Patsy Kennedy, Robyn Kennedy, Mike Latham, Diane Lightfoot, Andrew Lincoln, Simon Lowe, Sarah Miloudi, Jane Monksfield, Jonathan Morris, NINDS – National Institute of Neurological Disorders and Stroke, David Rapson, Tony O'Reilly, Owen Pavey, Mark Pitman, Steven Rattray, Nigel Richards, Neil Roberts, Sam Roberts, Andy Searle, Rory Sheehan, Dave Smallman, Mike Smith, Phil Stead, Marc Tanner, Gemma Taylor, David Luther Thomas, Leah Webb, Graham Whittle, Hywel Williams, Matt Wilkinson and John Winterson.

My list of friends isn't so impressive but special mentions have to go to Steve Howarth, Valerie Leney, Verity Winn, Gareth Goodall, Rob Hopwood, Louise Hopwood, Leslie Rigby, Gail Matthews, Andrew Matthews, Joanna Parker, Liam Pritchard, Toby Owen, Adrian Chopin, Verity Enoch, Deborah Murray, Andy Evans, Ali Granger and Sarah Drane. Dr Brian Howman is actually my sister's friend but is a cool bloke who helped me resolve the punctuation nightmare that threatened my sanity prior to publication.

I've utilised many websites in my search for information on Welsh Premier League football. On the whole, coverage of the league is spectacularly poor, which made my job even more difficult, but there were some invaluable sites that provided me with desperately-needed nuggets of information.

The Welsh Premier will always struggle to improve and fail to invigorate potential supporters while the mass media continue to ignore and neglect the league, but sites such as the ones below are blazing an informative trail that others need to follow if the competition is ever to be opened up to a wider audience.

Official club websites:
www.atfc.org.uk
www.afanlidofc.com
www.airbusfc.com
www.balatownfc.co.uk
www.bangorcityfc.com
www.carmarthentownafc.com
www.the-nomads.co.uk
http://haverfordwestcounty.co.uk
www.llanelliafc.org
www.neathfc.com
www.newtownafc.co.uk
www.porttalbottown.co.uk
www.ptfconline.co.uk
www.saints-alive.co.uk

Unofficial club websites:
www.history.atfc.org.uk
www.carmarthentownafc.net
www.the-citizens-choice.co.uk
www.seasidersattic.co.uk

Competition websites:
www.welshpremier.com
www.welsh-premier.com
www.huwsgrayalliance.co.uk
www.welshleague.org.uk

Football Association of Wales:
www.faw.org.uk

Blogs:
www.markpitman1.com
http://ffwtbol.co.uk
http://llandudnojetset.wordpress.com

EVERY SILVER LINING HAS A CLOUD Nathan Lee Davies

http://theballisround.co.uk
http://lowerleaguemanager.com

Grounds:
http://footballgroundsinfocus.com
http://thegroundhog.wordpress.com
www.groundtastic.co.uk
www.welshgrounds.co.uk

Statistics:
www.statto.com
www.wfda.co.uk

Media:
www.bbc.co.uk/sport/0/football/welsh
www.dailypost.co.uk
http://blogs.dailypost.co.uk/northwalesfootball
www.flintshirechronicle.co.uk
www.leaderlive.co.uk
www.s4c.co.uk/sgorio
www.thisissouthwales.co.uk
www.southwalesargus.co.uk/sport
www.welsh-football.net
www.wsc.co.uk

Other:
www.ataxia.org.uk
www.corbettsports.com
http://golcymru.org
www.grammar-monster.com
http://grammar.quickanddirtytips.com
www.johnhartsonfoundation.com
www.ninds.nih.gov/disorders/friedreichs_ataxia/detail_friedreichs
_ataxia.htm
http://word2cleanhtml.com
www.wst.org.uk

EVERY SILVER LINING HAS A CLOUD Nathan Lee Davies

I suggest that anyone who wishes to follow the Welsh Premier League creates a new favourites folder and adds all the links provided above, which were all functional at the time of going to press. You should also bookmark http://en.wikipedia.org – the free encyclopedia that anyone can edit – absolutely anyone. As you can imagine, this leads to question marks over the reliability of what has been written, but with such a shortage of information via mainstream media sources these pages have been invaluable.

So that's about it. A thousand apologies if you feel you've helped but can't find your name above. I assure you that this is merely an error on my behalf and all contributions have been greatly appreciated. Now that I've finished working on this project and am ready for publication, I'm left wondering what lies in store for me next. Shall I attempt to write another book? Is it time to take that holiday of a lifetime to Las Vegas? Maybe I should return to writing regular blogs in cyberspace? Perhaps I could return to university and study for a MA?

I'm still unsure which route to follow, but until I decide, I'll just resume training in that other hobby of mine...

Warning

I don't want everybody to get it because first of all the office of humour is to offend, and if people are offended by it, then I think that's good. Why should everybody like you? To me, if everybody likes you, there's something wrong. You're doing something wrong.

Larry David in conversation with Brian Williams
Live from NY's 92Y

You'd never guess it, but I'm a quiet and polite bloke at heart, who wouldn't intentionally offend or upset anyone – especially those I'm close to. If I were to describe myself I'd opt for positive words such as "loyal", "honest", "caring" and "thoughtful" to reflect the upstanding member of society that I endeavour to be.

However, whenever this sensible soul is asked to express itself through the written word, it seems to be overcome by the devilish, irresponsible, angry and bitter side of my character. I've tried to quell this inner demon, but whenever he feels repressed, he seems to fight back with renewed determination to share his negativity, which is often shrouded in puerile humour. This is the poisoned mind behind the majority of the following pages.

Therefore, before joining me on my trip around Wales, I advise you to take a generous pinch of salt or, particularly if you're English, right-wing, a member of the monarchy, or a TNS fan, quickly develop a thick skin and sense of humour.

You've been warned.

GARBAGE
Only Happy When It Rains

I'm only happy when it rains
I'm only happy when it's complicated
And though I know you can't appreciate it
I'm only happy when it rains
You know I love it when the news is bad
Why it feels so good to feel so sad
I'm only happy when it rains

Pour your misery down
Pour your misery down on me
Pour your misery down
Pour your misery down on me

I'm only happy when it rains
I feel good when things are going wrong
I only listen to the sad, sad songs
I'm only happy when it rains

I only smile in the dark
My only comfort is the night gone black
I didn't accidentally tell you that
I'm only happy when it rains
You'll get the message by the time I'm through
When I complain about me and you
I'm only happy when it rains

Pour your misery down (pour your misery down)
Pour your misery down on me (pour your misery down)
Pour your misery down (pour your misery down)
Pour your misery down on me (pour your misery down)
Pour your misery down (pour it down)
You can keep me company
As long as you don't care

I'm only happy when it rains
You'll wanna hear about my new obsession
I'm riding high upon a deep depression
I'm only happy when it rains (pour some misery down on me) x5
(Pour some misery down on me) x4
I'm only happy when it rains (pour some misery down on me)
(Pour some misery down on me) x4

"Only Happy When It Rains" Written by Shirley Manson, Bryan Vig, Douglas Erickson and Steve Marker
© Published by Deadarm Music and Vibecrusher Music
Administered by Kobalt Music Publishing Limited

1
Kick-Off

EVERY SILVER LINING HAS A CLOUD Nathan Lee Davies

The question is this: what have I been doing? I'll tell you what I've been doing – nothing. I know what you're thinking. You're thinking that sounds pretty good. You're thinking that you might like to do nothing yourself. Well, let me tell you, doing nothing is not as easy as it looks. You have to be careful because the idea of doing anything, could easily lead to doing something, which would cut into doing nothing and that would force me to have to drop everything.

Jerry Seinfeld
Late Show with David Letterman
2001

It's an afternoon like any other. I'm transfixed by a medley of fonts, images and colours beaming through a 20-inch monitor while listening to a random selection of tunes via Windows Media Player.

I'm alone in my home office in north Wales and have spent the last few hours watching videos of amateur housewives who'd do anything for money and jealously scrolling through pictures of former classmates on Facebook who've made something of their lives.

As always, I try to fool myself into thinking I've been productive by checking my bank balance, reading a chapter of a book that I know I could've written better, before finding time to win an eBay auction for an item that will only gather dust in a kitchen drawer until the end of time. At least I don't have to alphabetise my CD collection. I did that last week.

To conclude this constructive hot streak, I've just shared a YouTube clip of a television commercial from the Eighties with my ten followers on Twitter. I can hear the laughter of ironic recognition from here as the Buzzcocks launch into a lively rendition of their 1977 classic, *Orgasm Addict*...

What am I doing with my life?

EVERY SILVER LINING HAS A CLOUD Nathan Lee Davies

I'm a 34-year-old Welshman with an ever-increasing beer belly, no direction and little purpose. I spent many years in academia, working to create a fulfilling future, but it was destined not to be. I could launch into successive paragraphs focussing on how life has been unkind to me, but I want to focus on what lies ahead, and you don't want to read about my moans and groans.

We'll therefore gloss over the depression, homesickness, unemployment, heartbreak, divorce, loneliness, homelessness and illness that have dogged the last decade – for the time being at least – to focus on how I intend to grow and develop as a person. I need to do this, and do it now, before it's too late. In twenty years time, I don't want to spend my days dribbling in a care home with only memories of wasted afternoons in my self-constructed prison to look back on, but how do I get out of this rut?

I have to focus on the things that stimulate me in a deeper and more spiritual manner than pixelated buxom beauties on the Internet, while searching for an acceptance and sense of belonging and purpose within a like-minded community. It would mean the world to me if I could start the day by looking into the mirror and understanding the confused timewaster who glares back at me with vacant eyes.

This is asking a lot, but it might just be possible if I combine my love of Wales, talent for writing and passion for the beautiful game while visiting all 12 football clubs that make up the Welsh Premier League (WPL) throughout 2011.

I'm not holding my breath for any magical answers, but surely it's worth a go and better than fucking myself to death...

***

EVERY SILVER LINING HAS A CLOUD Nathan Lee Davies

I realise I've probably just lost half of my readership after outlining the premise of this tome, but if you're still ploughing on, then let me assure you that it's my intention to avoid creating a dull and dry historical guide to the WPL, in favour of a humour-driven narrative that will feature autobiographical sections to tantalise, intrigue and titillate. Despite these entertaining aims, I recognise that the reader still needs some basic information to help put this trip in context and understand why I'd bother spending time and money I've not got on this bizarre scheme. I also need to remind myself so please bear with me.

The League of Wales was formed in 1992. Prior to this, Wales was almost unique in world football as despite the Football Association of Wales (FAW) being a FIFA member and, along with the other three home nations, holding a permanent seat on the International Football Association Board (IFAB), it didn't operate a national league. There were many reasons for this such as the inadequate road network throughout Wales and the fact that the major population hubs – Cardiff, Swansea, Newport and Wrexham – all boasted teams that had a proud history in the English Football League.

However, African and Asian nations felt that the FAW were taking advantage of their IFAB status and amidst growing pressure FAW secretary general, Alun Evans controversially announced in October 1991 that a new league would start at the beginning of the next season.[1] Twenty teams competed in the inaugural season and Cwmbran Town became the first national champions of Wales at the end of 1992-93.

---

[1] The League of Wales wasn't welcomed by everyone. This is neither the time nor place for an in-depth discussion of the legal wrangling that followed the FAW's decision to push ahead with the formation of a new league. Suffice to say it had massive implications, particularly for Welsh non-league clubs that wanted to remain in the English system. The "Irate Eight", as they were dubbed, consisted of Bangor City, Barry Town, Caernarfon Town, Colwyn Bay, Merthyr Tydfil, Newport, Newtown and Rhyl. A deeper examination of a troubled beginning for the League of Wales can be found at http://enwikipedia.org/wiki/Welsh_Premier_League

EVERY SILVER LINING HAS A CLOUD Nathan Lee Davies

Over the past twenty years, there have been changes in structure and sponsorship while a total of 38 different clubs have competed in the league. However, the biggest shake-up took place in 2010 when the membership was reduced from 18 to 12 clubs. This saw founder members Caersws and Connah's Quay relegated to the northern feeder league – known as the Huws Gray Alliance – along with Cefn Druids, Porthmadog, Rhyl and Welshpool. South Wales clubs – who use the MacWhirter Welsh League Division One as their feeder league – were unaffected.

We are therefore left with the so-called "Super 12" who have all achieved a valid FAW domestic club licence, which assesses clubs under specific criteria relating to administrative obligations, financial codes of practice and investment in young talent. This is not to mention the mandatory infrastructure criteria, which dictates that participating clubs should play at stadiums that boast a minimum 1,500 capacity with 500 covered seats, a minimum grade of floodlights, 13-person capacity dugouts and television broadcast facilities

These strict, sometimes stifling, regulations are deemed necessary as the FAW strives to slowly improve standards within the competition. Sporting prowess needs to be backed up by smart business acumen in the modern game, I'm afraid. This has led to some unpopular decisions and legal wrangles, but the FAW have a long-term vision and realise that a strong league cannot be built on unstable foundations.

The current format sees the Super 12 play each other twice before the league splits into top six and bottom six, with the clubs in those groups playing each other twice again to make a 32-fixture season. No club in the bottom six may finish higher than seventh, no matter how many points are gained during the split stage. Clubs finishing in third to seventh position will then take part in a play-off to determine who gains the third Europa League spot the following season. Should the Welsh Cup winners be amongst those clubs, the eighth placed club would be invited into the play-offs. Simple.

This will be a journey into the unknown for me as I'm ashamed to say I've never been to a game in the national league and I'm unfamiliar with vast sections of my own country. Over the course of the coming chapters, I'll travel the length and breadth of my homeland, engaging with my fellow countrymen like never before, to gain an understanding and appreciation of the game at this level. Hopefully, this will also allow me to be productive, positive and reflective about my own identity as a Welshman.

This is not a mere football odyssey but also a journey of self-discovery that'll begin just as soon as I've colour coded my boxer shorts...

Map

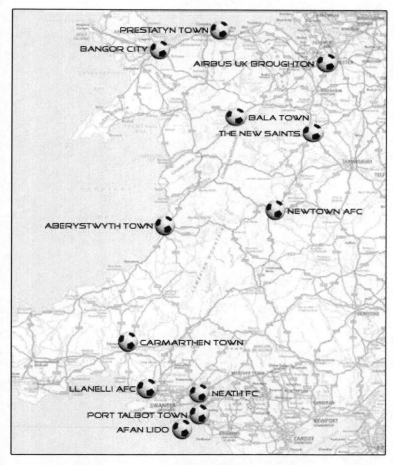

Due to poor north-south transport links within Wales, it was common for Welsh semi-professional football clubs to travel east to England for competitive matches.

In 1992, this all changed with the introduction of a national competition that forced Welsh football enthusiasts – or at least those not affiliated with the diffident exiles – to reacquaint themselves with frustrating back roads, while pissing in fields.

According to Google Maps, I'll travel 1773.8 miles to complete this tour. When you consider that these are long and winding Welsh miles spent behind tractors and day trippers, then this mission becomes a test of patience as well as stamina...

2
As Good as It Got

EVERY SILVER LINING HAS A CLOUD Nathan Lee Davies

My birth certificate says I was born in the town of West Bromwich, in the area of West Bromwich, in the County Borough of West Bromwich. So when people ask me why I support West Bromwich Albion Football Club, I explain that my decision was based on the only criterion anyone should ever use when choosing a football club – geography. You sit with a pencil, a ruler, and a map, identify the nearest professional football club to your place of birth, you buy a scarf with their name on it and that's that.

Frank Skinner
Frank Skinner
2002

I was born in Wrexham, north Wales.

***

I wasn't there. I was too busy eating mashed up banana, being entertained by strange looking puppets that lived on a street that no one knew how to get to and erecting unstable walls with coloured building blocks. It was the biggest match in Wrexham's history, yet my mum and dad couldn't see the benefit of their newborn baby being exposed to the talents of Mickey Thomas and Bobby Shinton, while listening to the Kop choir belting out expletives. I could only fill my nappy in protest.

Three decades later, I only have a dog-eared programme and a video cassette of flickering images – that seems to have been shot from the moon using a 16mm cine camera – to remind me that the game actually did happen. If only my parents had appreciated my early efforts at constructing a sentence. I was only a few months old but I'd managed to spell out "Can you take me to the Racecourse?" on my fuzzy felt board. Instead of rewarding me with a trip to the Third Division encounter between Wrexham and Rotherham United, I was given a thirty-minute lecture on the difference between the auxiliary verbs "can" and "may".

EVERY SILVER LINING HAS A CLOUD Nathan Lee Davies

On reflection, my folks could've been trying to protect me from the pain and disappointment that had consumed Wrexham supporters' only months earlier. With two home games of the 1976-77 season remaining, Wrexham only needed a point to secure promotion to the Second Division for the first time in their history. Two defeats later and with another season in the third tier beckoning, even the more upbeat Racecourse regulars began to believe that perhaps there was an element of truth in the myth that the club, players and management didn't want promotion.

Before fans had a chance to dry their tears of despair that summer, manager John Neal left for the bright lights of Middlesbrough, took star striker Billy Ashcroft with him and triggered a flood of transfer requests. I could sense the clouds of depression hanging over my hometown. Red Ted's permanent stitched grin began to droop, and even the appointment of club legend Arfon Griffiths as player-manager did little to lift his spirits.

Indeed, the sadness of my stuffed toy seemed to be justified when Wrexham started season 1977-78 with a whimper. With just one win in their first seven games, the Robins found themselves languishing in eighteenth position in the Third Division table. Griffiths took decisive action by signing Dixie McNeil for £60,000, from Hereford, and goalkeeper Dai Davies was recruited from Everton – for a bargain £8,000 – as he tried to save his children from a disturbing tendency towards lenition of stop consonants. "I am not a Welsh nationalist, but the little girl was beginning to get a Liverpool accent," said the Welsh-speaking keeper.

"Deadshot" Dixie scored on his debut and Wrexham went on a thirteen game unbeaten run to top the league table for the first time in four years. Even the *Match of the Day* cameras were on hand to record the 2-1 victory against Colchester, but it was the cup exploits of Arfon's men that really made the nation sit up and take notice. Top-flight opponents Bristol City were knocked out of the League Cup as Wrexham reached the quarter-finals, and they also managed to secure a place in the last eight of the FA Cup after claiming the scalps of Bristol City (again) and Newcastle United. Eventually, it took Liverpool and Arsenal to knock the Welshmen out of the respective competitions.

Thankfully, these cup shenanigans didn't interfere with Wrexham's league form, and seven straight victories in March helped earn Griffiths his fourth manager of the month award of the season. Off the pitch, ground improvements were given the go-ahead and two seven-inch records were released in tribute to the club's success, both of which were used instead of nursery rhymes to lull me to sleep. Who needs Humpty Dumpty when you've got the Brymbo Male Voice Choir extolling the achievements of Arfon's men in painfully contrived rhyme?

As the season drew to a close, Wrexham faced relegation-threatened Rotherham United on the back of five games without a win. Nevertheless, if the Robins could beat the Milllers, they'd ensure promotion to the second tier for the first time in their history. In preparation for this massive game, Arfon took his players to the Costa del Llandudno for a ride on the donkeys and a tram ride up the Great Orme. Whatever happened on the north Wales coast certainly helped to quash the tension and banish the jitters as Wrexham returned to the Racecourse to destroy Rotherham in emphatic fashion and finally escaped from the Third Division.

According to the yellowing pages of my history books, 16,586 fans crammed into the Cae Ras to watch Mickey Thomas, John Lyons, Graham Whittle (2) and Bobby Shinton give the home side a five-goal advantage at the break. It was such a fine display that even the referee – Mr. Bert Newsome – joined the rest of the ground in a standing ovation. Battling Rotherham pulled one back in the second period before Whittle completed his hat-trick and Cartwright added a seventh. At the final whistle, the crowd erupted and spilled onto the pitch in never-to-be-forgotten scenes. At least for those who were there.....

EVERY SILVER LINING HAS A CLOUD Nathan Lee Davies

Not content with winning promotion, the high-flying Robins went on to secure the Third Division championship trophy, which gleamed brightly alongside the Welsh Cup, the Welsh Youth Cup, the Reveille Giant Killers Cup and none other than the Border Counties Northern Floodlit Cup. It seemed that the future would be bright and I thanked my lucky stars that I'd been born in time to enjoy the many decades of dominance that Wrexham were surely bound for in my naïve and innocent eyes.

Subsequently, my formative years were clouded with disappointment as four unspectacular seasons in the Second Division ended in consecutive relegations back to the basement division amidst falling attendances and financial worries. Ever since, we've been scrapping around the lower leagues, stared liquidation in the face, suffered relegation from the Football League, and the biggest indignity of all, appeared on Setanta Sports. Sure, there has been the odd cup upset and promotion season to remind people that football is still being played in Wrexham, but nothing to compare with the dazzling glory of the 1977-78 season.

I live in hope.

The New Saints 3 Bangor City 2

Principality Welsh Premier League
Saturday, 19 March 2011
15:30

Park Hall / Neuadd Y Parc
Attendance: 617

What better place to start a tour of Welsh football grounds than with a trip to Oswestry – a market town that sits just five miles on the wrong side of the Anglo-Welsh border in Shropshire, England? This journey is supposed to be reconnecting me with my homeland, but here I was, preparing to spend the afternoon in foreign climes...

On reflection, I suppose it is appropriate for me to begin this book in the borderlands as I grew up in a border town and would argue that it's impossible to understand and appreciate the mental build-up of any Welshman, including me, without mentioning England and the English.

In my opinion, the most accurate description of Welsh attitudes towards our immediate neighbours appears in a book called *Xenophobe's Guide to the Welsh* by John Winterson Richards. In this entertaining and perceptive book, he notes:

> If the English did not exist, the Welsh would have to invent them. To a very great extent, the Welsh define their national identity in terms of the English:
>
> "The English are X, so we are not."
> "The English like Y, so we do not."
> "The English dislike Z, so we absolutely love him/her/it."
>
> Some people say that the Welsh have a love-hate relationship with the English but they are, in fact, 100%

wrong. For a start, there is precious little love involved. Yet hate is also conspicuous by its absence which is surprising, given that the English conquered the country through treachery, killed its last native ruler in a particularly nasty manner, and over a period of several hundred years comprehensively looted its natural resources.

The Welsh attitude to the English may be more accurately summed up as 10% resentment, and 90% pity. The resentment is not personal - it is a standard Welsh reaction to anyone who is, for any reason, better off (a Welshman will never accept that anyone can succeed where he fails without having some dishonest advantage).

The pity is also a standard Welsh reaction, in this case for anyone who has the incredible misfortune not to be Welsh.

It was with this in-built mingling of quiet disgust and pity that I huffed and puffed my way through Oswestry – past obscenely named pubs, such as "The George", and pedestrians wearing England football shirts. I felt slightly queasy, so visited a small café for a coke and to reflect on the circumstances that led Welsh football to spill over the border.

Llansantffraid FC was formed in 1959 to represent the miniscule Welsh village of Llansantffraid-ym-Mechain. With a population of only 1000, dreams of Welsh Cup wins and European football seemed laughable, although it soon became clear that this was a well-run club intent on progression. During their time in the Montgomeryshire Amateur Football League, the Saints clinched the championship seven times and lifted the League Cup on nine occasions between 1963 and 1993.

However, this ambitious club was destined for bigger and better things and in 1990 Llansantffraid began a meteoric rise through the newly structured Welsh pyramid that culminated in promotion to the League of Wales at the end of 1992-93. After establishing themselves in the top flight, they went on to record a breathtaking Welsh Cup final victory over hot favourites Barry Town in 1996.

As Welsh Cup winners, little Llansantffraid qualified for the European Cup Winners Cup and inevitably started attracting financial opportunists. Enter Mike Harris, the owner of Total Network Solutions, a large company based in the Oswestry area. He pounced on the success of Llansantffraid and bought the club, with the insistence that it changed its name to Total Network Solutions Llansantffraid FC, turning a wonderful fairytale into a commercial tool. Under their new moniker, they met the Polish cup winners KS Ruch Chorzow and earned a 1–1 draw at the Racecourse, Wrexham before losing 0–5 in Poland in front of 7,000.

Predictably, it wasn't long before the name of Llansantffraid was dropped completely and Total Network Solutions FC became the first example in the United Kingdom of a football club renaming itself after its sponsor's name only. With subsequent strong financial backing, the club was able to employ a full-time playing staff, challenge the dominance of Barry Town and consume debt-ridden WPL rivals Oswestry Town in 2003.[1]

From afar, this seemed an odd, cross-border pairing but the shifting sands that form the club's identity were shaken yet again with British

---

[1] In the summer of 2003, the FAW approved the merger between TNS and Oswestry.

However, on the eve of the 2003-04 season, UEFA threw a spanner in the works on the grounds that the two clubs were based in different countries.

On appeal, UEFA reversed its decision having reviewed the history of the development of football in England and Wales and noting Oswestry's role in the founding of the FAW and regular participation in the Welsh Cup from 1877. If European football's governing body can get their heads around such a union then I guess I should too.

EVERY SILVER LINING HAS A CLOUD Nathan Lee Davies

Telecom's capitalist consumption of Total Network Solutions in early 2006. As a result, the unique sponsorship arrangement lapsed at the end of the 2005-06 season and it became necessary to find a new name for the club. "The New Saints of Llansantffraid and Oswestry"was agreed upon as appropriate to the clubs' history – Llansantffraid were always known as "the Saints' and Oswestry had strong connections with Saint Oswald – while handily retaining the initials "TNS". A new club badge was also developed at the same time, featuring a dragon to represent Llansantffraid and a lion representing Oswestry Town.

This strange amalgamation originally played at Llansantffraid's home of Treflan, or the Recreation Ground as it was sometimes called. This was a modest ground that had a capacity of 2,000, including seating for 1,000, but wasn't capable of enclosure or upgrading to meet the Welsh Premier's criteria for season 2009-10 and beyond. In addition, it was unable to meet UEFA standards for the staging of European ties, which meant that TNS were forced to play home Champions League and UEFA Cup ties at Newtown's Latham Park, Wrexham's Racecourse and even the Millennium Stadium in Cardiff.

As a result, TNS controversially crossed the border and moved to Park Hall Stadium, Oswestry in 2007. Cash strapped Town had used this council-owned athletics stadium, but after the club's financial problems and the merger with TNS, the ground fell into disrepair and was purchased by Mike Harris. After redevelopment at a cost of more than £3 million with a £445,000 grant from the Football Foundation, Park Hall was brought up to the required standard. I was looking forward to finding out if the money had been put to good use.

So here I was in England, preparing to watch The New Saints entertain Bangor City at their Park Hall home. It was a crucial top of the table clash between the top two teams in the WPL. Bangor had been in the driving seat all season and had threatened to run away with the title, but their form since January had been so bad that ahead of the game TNS were only six points behind City, with a game in hand. A home win would blow the title race wide open – it promised to be a great introduction to Welsh Premier football...

After following long and winding roads to the middle of nowhere, I found myself sitting outside a leisure centre doubting whether or not I was in the right place and hoping I wasn't. The structure in front of me was named the Venue – a £3 million development including a ten-pin bowling alley, bar, restaurant, sauna, spa pool, children's play area, player changing rooms and training facilities. This is a well-equipped establishment of the sort that can be found in out of town retail parks across the country. Unfortunately, the Venue does not neighbour JJB Sports or Deichmann Shoes, but merely serves to hide a bland and sterile football ground that sits in a land dip behind it.

The athletics circuit that once surrounded the pitch has been removed and the stadium is now dominated by the arse end of the aforementioned leisure centre. The bland building runs almost the entire length of the near touchline and includes a small balcony from which members of the press and assorted dignitaries are offered excellent views. Directly beneath the prawn sandwich brigade is an uncovered, hard standing area for commoners. Beside this space is a block of 1,000 seats with a canopy cover running adjacent to the other half of the pitch.

The remaining three sides of this uncharismatic ground offer uncovered hard standing, uninspiring floodlights, hideous Perspex dug- outs – positioned directly opposite the Venue – and nothing else to speak of at all, except for the highly controversial FIFA approved plastic pitch.

No away team had beaten TNS at Park Hall all season so the surface clearly gives Mike Davies' men an advantage. Critics argue that players often lose their footing, are apprehensive about making tackles, and that the ball doesn't bounce in the same way it does on grass. This artificial surface has even been compared to a hockey pitch in the past.

EVERY SILVER LINING HAS A CLOUD Nathan Lee Davies

There are two sides to every argument though. While TNS seem to be gaining an unfair advantage on a sporting level, there are those who would argue such an arrangement makes perfect business sense – home games are rarely postponed, the pitch can be hired out to the local community, and there is little maintenance needed. When it comes to TNS, business arguments always win the day...

As kick-off approached, I flicked through the matchday programme – a highly professional 32-page effort, which is mirrored by an excellent official website that is a credit to the club and the league. It was while reading a page entitled "Oswestry Snippets", by Mike Clarke that I began reflecting on my attitudes. This page was a look back at Oswestry Town games against Bangor City from 1959 and 1960. Initially, I was disgruntled by the lack of similar Llansantffraid memories to provide balance. I regarded this as disrespectful to the Welsh origins of the club, but after reading that Oswestry, Bangor and Rhyl all used to play in the Cheshire League, I began to consider boundaries and identity, and question whether or not I should be so precious about lines on a map. After all, I support a Welsh club that plays in an English League...

The two best teams in Wales (sic) lined up before me and the referee got the big game underway. Bangor boast the largest fan base in the WPL and were cheered on by a healthy travelling support of approximately 250. It wasn't long before they were celebrating the first goal of the afternoon, courtesy of Chris Jones on three minutes.

As we entered the 20th minute, I considered asking the St John's Ambulance men for a neck brace to help me keep up with the long balls that were being aimlessly exchanged, but any pain that I was suffering was quickly forgotten as TNS stuck twice in three minutes to turn the game on its head. The atmosphere should have been electric, but attendances to watch such an artificially created club have always been poor. There is very little potential for noise from a few elderly Englishmen and a group of clueless nuclear families trying to find the entrance to the leisure centre.

EVERY SILVER LINING HAS A CLOUD Nathan Lee Davies

The second half continued with TNS in complete control and only a combination of poor finishing, competent goalkeeping and sheer good fortune stopped the home side increasing their lead. A touchline fracas saw TNS boss Mike Davies sent to the stand but with 15 minutes left, Craig Jones embarked on a 40-yard run that saw him glide through the Bangor backline before planting a 12-yarder into the net. Game over. Or was it?

Suddenly the tide changed and Bangor began showing the class and fighting spirit that had made them unbeatable over the first half of the season. With five minutes remaining, TNS goalkeeper Paul Harrison made a fingertip save from a Bangor free-kick, but Chris Jones was on hand to head home the loose ball. The away support was reignited and urged their side forward, but it was too little too late and the Saints held on to close the gap at the top to three points.

It had been an exciting, incident packed game of football, but the overall quality was extremely poor and reminiscent of Sunday league stuff in parts. As a result, I was looking forward to watching *Match of the Day* later that evening to see proper athletes showboat their skills in front of adoring masses. It was bound to be more entertaining than the dross I had just witnessed, even if Fulham or Stoke were featured.

As I crossed the border back into Wales, I considered that I still had eleven more matches to endure and to enjoy them I would have to stop making such unfair comparisons with the English Premier League – the richest league in the world. All teams at this level – except TNS – are part-timers and it is unrealistic to expect breathtaking pieces of skill or free-flowing passing moves in a league that is still in its infancy. Instead, I should be focussing my attentions on the potential for development and growth that each Welsh Premier club will need to utilise if the League as a whole is to improve and grow more popular.

At the end of the day, it cannot be denied that The New Saints are an ambitious and well-run club in a good catchment area with the necessary financial backing to move forward and prosper. However, for all this, they still play on the wrong side of the border.

Poor buggers...

TNS
Park Hall

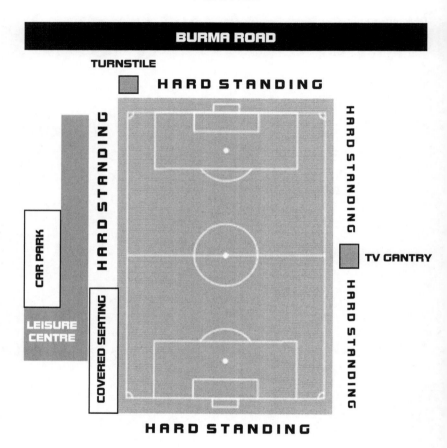

BURMA ROAD

TURNSTILE

HARD STANDING

HARD STANDING

HARD STANDING

CAR PARK

LEISURE CENTRE

COVERED SEATING

HARD STANDING

HARD STANDING

TV GANTRY

HARD STANDING

- Please note that in July 2012, TNS opened a new 500-seat stand at the opposite end of the stadium from Burma Road.

3
Tick Follows Tock

EVERY SILVER LINING HAS A CLOUD Nathan Lee Davies

Neurotic comedian Alvy Singer is anxiously waiting for his date outside the Beekman Theatre, New York. He is glaring at his watch, scratching his head and appears uneasy. Finally, during an awkward altercation with two enthusiastic men, who recognise him from television appearances, a taxi pulls up and Annie Hall jumps out to a warm welcome from Alvy.

"Jesus, what'd you do, come by way of the Panama Canal?"

The stressed couple rush towards the ticket booth of the theatre with Annie in a bad mood and Alvy blaming it on her menstrual cycle. They approach the ticket clerk.

ALVY: H'm has the picture started yet?
TICKET CLERK: It started two minutes ago.
ALVY: (*Hitting his hand on the counter*) That's it! Forget it! I – I can't go in.
ANNIE: Two minutes, Alvy.
ALVY: (*Overlapping Annie*) No, I'm sorry, I can't do it. We- we've blown it already. I – you know, uh, I-I can't go in in the middle.
ANNIE: In the middle? (*Alvy nods his head yes and lets out an exasperated sigh*) We'll only miss the titles. They're in Swedish.
ALVY: You wanna get coffee for two hours or something? We'll go next...

The pair continue to argue outside of the theatre much to the embarrassment of Alvy.

ALVY: Well, I'm sorry, I-I can't...I-I-I've gotta see a picture exactly from the start to the finish, 'cause-'cause I'm anal.
ANNIE: (*Laughing now*) H'h, that's a polite word for what you are.[1]

---

[1] *Annie Hall* (1977), by Woody Allen and Marshall Brickman, MGM.

Airbus UK Broughton 0 Carmarthen Town 0

Principality Welsh Premier League
Saturday, 02 April 2011
15:30

The Airfield / Y Maes Awyr
Attendance: 339

For reasons I'm not ready to reveal just yet, I don't drive.

As a result, I'm relying on family members to transport me around my homeland as I attempt to complete an unlikely quest. My dad, Paul, is the ideal man for the job. As a former long-distance lorry driver, he is confident behind the wheel and good with directions. This man would also do anything for his only son and I'm happy to take advantage of this, with my only reservation being his notoriously bad time-keeping skills, which inevitably clash with my neuroticisms and desire for precision.

Airbus UK Broughton play at the Airfield and this neat little ground is situated a mere 20 minutes from my Wrexham base. The kick-off for this match was set for 15:30, so I asked my dad to pick me up an hour beforehand to give us enough time to find the venue, take some photographs, visit the club shop and buy a burger or two from the food bar, before the players took to the pitch.

***

He waits; that's what he does.
And I tell you what: tick followed tock followed tick followed tock followed tick...

Surfer
Guinness TV commercial

EVERY SILVER LINING HAS A CLOUD Nathan Lee Davies

I knew he wouldn't be on time. Why break the habit of a lifetime? Dad finally arrived at 15:00 so at least there would be enough time to reach the ground before kick off, wouldn't there?

Who was I trying to kid? I was getting dizzy as we completed our third lap of the roundabout, desperately trying to find a football field in this small Flintshire community. With a name like the Airfield you would've thought we'd find the ground amongst the many aerospace buildings congregated to our left, but for some reason my dad decided to break all manner of traffic laws by speeding through a no-entry sign and proceeding the wrong way down a one-way street. At the end of this narrow thoroughfare, my dad pulled over to ask a clueless old bint for directions to the football ground, but the decrepit pensioner could only direct us to a public field where bored parents pretended to enthuse over an under-12's kick about.

I glared at my watch and uneasily scratched my head. We were running out of roundabout exits and by the time we chanced upon the right one, parked in the deserted club car park and began the short trek to the ground, it was 15:29. The ground was in sight. We only had to cross the road and we'd make it. I looked to my left and looked to my right before hastily heading towards the inviting turnstile that stood just 20 foot away. That's when it happened...

The unmistakeable, high-pitched reverberations of the referee's whistle signalled the start of the game before I'd entered the ground. I'd signed up to visit all 12 Welsh Premier football grounds and this meant watching the beginning, middle and end of all matches. I couldn't lie to myself. I turned back towards the car, dejected, deflated but proud that I'd kept to my anal and irrational principles.

Better never than late.

***

EVERY SILVER LINING HAS A CLOUD Nathan Lee Davies

I arrived home and switched on the television. The match I should have been attending was being played out before my eyes.

Since the beginning of the 2010-11 season, Welsh language broadcaster S4C has televised a live Welsh Premier League clash every Saturday afternoon as part of the channel's flagship football series *Sgorio*. The show also provides a comprehensive results service from the WPL and beyond, including the English Premier League and Football League.

Sgorio coverage is produced by independent television production company Rondo Media. A comprehensive website accompanies the television coverage and can be found at www.s4c.co.uk/sgorio.

The *Sgorio* team is made up of ex-Arsenal striker John Hartson, who joins fellow former Wales international Malcolm Allen as an expert summariser, while well-known sports reporter and commentator Dylan Ebenezer switched from the BBC to S4C to add his input.

Welsh football hero Hartson revealed he turned down offers from Sky and ESPN to work as a Welsh language pundit on S4C. "I've chosen S4C because I feel it's going places," he said.

"I feel very privileged to have been given this wonderful opportunity to work with S4C. This is why I rebelled as a kid about going to a Welsh school and this is where it's come in handy for me as I can speak the language.

"It's a very exciting time for everybody involved in the new format. From my playing days I remember the buzz from appearing on TV and I feel the live games will give the players an extra boost.

"There's lots of talent in the Welsh Premier League, players who could be playing at a higher level. I know that from watching several games, especially since I've been retired.

EVERY SILVER LINING HAS A CLOUD Nathan Lee Davies

"Having played all my football out of Wales I always kept a close eye on what was going on in the Welsh Premier and I'm very excited about the season ahead."

Sgorio is a professional, Welsh language production that everyone involved with should be proud of, but I'm embarrassed to admit that I rarely used to tune in, for the simple fact that I couldn't understand a bloody word being spoken. Thankfully, all that has changed as non-Welsh speaking viewers can now access English commentary by pressing the red button. It's an invaluable tool for the linguistically deprived.

It's widely accepted that Welsh is the language of heaven, but the Welsh Language Board indicated in 2004 that only 611,000 people – 21.7% of the population – were able to speak Welsh. I can only assume that the rest of us are going to hell in a handcart.

I have tried to learn this complex language through various college courses and reading materials, but I struggle to develop and maintain the necessary grammatical and pronunciation skills when everyone around me in Wrexham speaks English – or at least tries to. You are just as likely to hear Polish or Portuguese being spoken in my hometown, so it seems I am fighting a losing battle when striving to develop and maintain my linguistic roots.

No wonder I struggle with my identity when I can't even speak my own language despite years of practice and enough wasted phlegm to cause a tsunami in Abergele. I envy fluent Welsh speakers and wish I could tap into this part of my heritage, but then again, if my parents, grandparents and great grandparents didn't speak this ancient lexicon, maybe I am looking in the wrong place in my search for a connection with my culture. Perhaps I should just accept that I am an anglicised Welshman, with an overwhelming love and loyalty to his homeland that survived the rape of his language?

EVERY SILVER LINING HAS A CLOUD Nathan Lee Davies

My self-centered deliberation was punctured as the referee blew the final whistle at the Airfield. I'd been a stone's throw away from these footballers earlier in the day and, as John Hartson summed up the afternoon unintelligibly, I wished I'd taken my opportunity and given them all a good stoning to save my fellow countrymen from enduring this turgid goalless draw.

4
I do like to be beside the seaside

EVERY SILVER LINING HAS A CLOUD Nathan Lee Davies

Sunny Prestatyn
By Phillip Larkin

Come To Sunny Prestatyn
Laughed the girl on the poster,
Kneeling up on the sand
In tautened white satin.
Behind her, a hunk of coast, a
Hotel with palms
Seemed to expand from her thighs and
Spread breast-lifting arms.

She was slapped up one day in March.
A couple of weeks, and her face
Was snaggle-toothed and boss-eyed;
Huge tits and a fissured crotch
Were scored well in, and the space
Between her legs held scrawls
That set her fairly astride
A tuberous cock and balls

Autographed *Titch Thomas,* while
Someone had used a knife
Or something to stab right through
The moustached lips of her smile.
She was too good for this life.
Very soon, a great transverse tear
Left only a hand and some blue.
Now *Fight Cancer* is there.

EVERY SILVER LINING HAS A CLOUD Nathan Lee Davies

The seaside town of Prestatyn has always been a favourite of mine. Situated on the Denbighshire coast to the east of Rhyl, this resort was a home-from-home for me during my formative years. I could often be found in this imaginary paradise constructing modest skyscrapers from sand or demolishing all competitors on the crazy golf course. Why live in the world when you can live in your head?

My strong sense of fantasy and detachment from the mundane always thrived in this relaxed environment where my only enemy was my *Transformers* digital watch. My robot in disguise seemed to race alarmingly through the hours before signaling home time to my disbelieving eyes. It was with a heavy heart that I'd leave this sunny haven of mine, toss my stimulating daydreams into the Irish sea and clamber into a brown Austin Allegro heading for Wrexham, where the sobering realities of my childhood lay in wait.

Up until the age of 10, I was a fit and healthy child and even played football, albeit as unused substitute, for my local team of snotty ragamuffins. However, it was around this time that my school teacher pointed out that I lacked co-ordination while running and I suddenly became conscious of every shaky footstep. Unfortunately, so did the bullies.

Secondary school was a nightmare. I didn't have a clue what was going on with my body, but it was becoming increasingly difficult to walk in a straight line. I used to stagger about as if inebriated, much to the amusement of everyone else. My confidence plummeted as I was constantly ridiculed by pupils and teachers alike; even perfect strangers would stop me on the street to ask if I'd been drinking or taking drugs. The only place where this didn't happen was Prestatyn. It was a place full of carefree tourists where I could achieve anonymity and give my mixed-up mind the opportunity to conjure escapist fantasies – for an afternoon at least.

Therefore, I was looking forward to returning to this less tacky and cleaner version of Rhyl, even though my empty life has gradually eroded, been scrawled upon and generally lost its clean lines of innocence and hope since my last visit – much like the poster in Phillip Larkin's poem.

Bastion Gardens, home of Prestatyn Town FC, is a wayward drive from the crazy golf course where I'd putted my way to imaginary glory many years ago. Some of the biggest names in golf had succumbed to my youthful prowess. Seve Ballasteros described me as "a master at overcoming the feared windmill obstacle" after I'd outputted him for the third year in succession. However, my glory years were now a thing of the past; I'd returned to the coast to focus on a totally different sport.

Prestatyn Town 2 Port Talbot Town 0

Principality Welsh Premier League
Saturday, 09 April 2011
14:30

Bastion Gardens / Gerddi Bastion
Attendance: 201

Prestatyn moved to Bastion Gardens in 1969 when their previous ground was sold off for development. For many years the new ground was relatively undeveloped with the only buildings being the dressing room block, a tea bar and storage rooms. The pitch was simply roped off and no other spectator facilities were available. Small improvements were made over the years, such as the installation of posts and rails around the pitch, brick built dugouts, and even the erection of rickety old bus shelters acquired from Prestatyn Town Council.

As we entered a new century, Prestatyn matched the strides they were making on the field of play with improvements to the ground, such as the replacement of the bus stands with a more modern structure, which provided seating for 200 and covered standing for another 150. In addition, turnstiles were unveiled, dressing rooms were redeveloped and extensive landscaping work carried out.

However, the biggest changes came in the summer of 2008 when, having clinched promotion to the Welsh Premier League, the committee and a band of dedicated volunteers were left with just eight days to bring the ground up to the required criteria.

After working around the clock, the miracle was achieved – floodlights were installed, a turnstile block was built, 200 extra seats were added, a press box erected and the whole ground was tidied up and painted. Further updates and improvements have since been made to meet the higher criteria demanded in the Super 12 and the result is a 2,000 capacity ground.

There are 546 covered seats – originally from Shrewsbury Town's Gay Meadow – running along one of the touchlines to make up the Martin Walsh Stand. However, the three rows of plastic seats are set at a low level, and any decent view of the action that might be obtained is further hampered by the supporting poles that appear at the front of the stand at regular intervals.[1] The rest of the ground is made up of hard standing but credit should be given for an excellent supporters' club, and for the construction of a disabled enclosure, which provides sheltered viewing for six spectators and their carers.

It was a sun-baked afternoon, so I chose to watch the game near the dugouts, directly opposite the Martin Walsh Stand. I read my 36-page programme in the shade offered by the TV gantry and police control box but felt a little cheated by the afternoon's offering. I was disappointed with the absence of any manager's notes while the popular, regular column written by a local wag had been shelved to make way for extra news items copied and pasted from the Internet. The final fourteen pages simply resembled a local business directory. Having said this, all the important information and statistics were here and for £1.50, I couldn't really complain.

The Seasiders were in fine form and had been proving the doubters wrong all season. Following the demotion of Rhyl to the Huws Gray Alliance in 2010, Prestatyn had emerged from their shadows to become the pride of Denbighshire, qualified for the top six, were fresh from a credible 1-2 away win at Bangor City and were now on the verge of European qualification for the first time in their history. Such success tasted even sweeter, given the fact that Prestatyn were celebrating their centenary season.

---

[1] The Martin Walsh Stand backs onto Prestatyn Cricket Club's ground – the appropriately named Beach Close.

EVERY SILVER LINING HAS A CLOUD Nathan Lee Davies

This impressive, yet unexpected, success had proved the downfall of player-manager Neil Gibson, who was "replaced"' by former Liverpool and Wrexham striker Lee Jones at the end of March. In a puzzling reshuffle, Gibson was moved upstairs to become director of football with his side on course for their highest ever finish in the Welsh pyramid. It didn't make any sense to me but similar surprise appointments were made in the previous weeks by Airbus UK Broughton and TNS. The Wingmakers appointed Darren Ryan as first-team manager and handed Craig Harrison a new title, while the Saints gave Mike Davies a supposed elevation to allow Carl Darlington senior responsibility for first-team affairs.

Upon further investigation, it seems these clubs were forced to make management changes by strict European licence requirements. Managers leading clubs into Europe were required by the FAW to hold a UEFA Pro Licence. Gibson didn't have one. Jones, who had managerial experience at Caenarfon and Cefn Druids, did. It was a similar story at the other clubs.

Lee Jones was barking orders to his team and pacing around the technical area like an old hand, while midfield dynamo Gibson inspired those around him as he'd done all season. I couldn't help but wonder who was actually in charge and who'd picked the team. At the end of the day, all that mattered was that Prestatyn Town met the ludicrous European licence requirements, but it'll be interesting to see how long this odd couple work together once the club's European dreams are over.

Sandie Shaw blasted out "Puppet on a String" in my subconscious mind as I sought to concentrate on the match being played in front of me.

This was only my second game at this level and even though there were fewer goals and less drama, I enjoyed it far more than the top of the table tussle at Park Hall as both teams played an attractive passing game. The home side were the most effective. Lee Hunt scored in each half to ensure Prestatyn moved six points clear of Port Talbot Town and strengthened their grip on fifth position, which would guarantee a home draw in the end-of-season European play-offs.

After a post-match pint, I was leaving the cosy confines of the supporters club when I was knocked flying by a gang of excited infants running towards the shaven-haired star of Prestatyn's season with pens, programmes and notebooks in hand. Hunt's brace left him with 25 goals to his name in all competitions during a prolific campaign, but I couldn't help wondering if he'd ever beaten Seve Ballasteros at crazy golf...

Prestatyn Town
Bastion Gardens

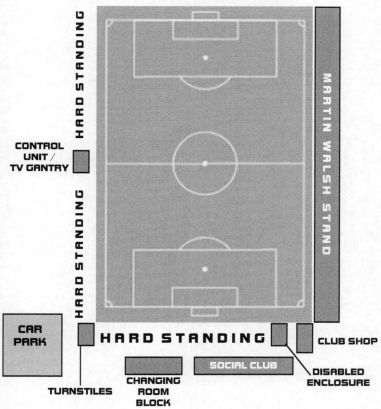

HARD STANDING

HARD STANDING

HARD STANDING

HARD STANDING

CONTROL UNIT / TV GANTRY

MARTIN WALSH STAND

CAR PARK

HARD STANDING

CLUB SHOP

SOCIAL CLUB

DISABLED ENCLOSURE

TURNSTILES

CHANGING ROOM BLOCK

5
Floating in the Cloudy Sky

EVERY SILVER LINING HAS A CLOUD Nathan Lee Davies

I staggered across a hectic car park, underneath threatening grey clouds, towards my date with destiny. Proud parents clutching a Moses basket of hope and potential gazed lovingly into each other's eyes as they emerged from the building I was heading towards. The young mother had clearly been up all night, but the emotional rollercoaster that her tear-stained face suggested she'd been riding was now ending with smiles, balloons and relief. After carefully strapping their bundle of joy into a rust-ridden Ford Cortina, the father released a bright red balloon marked with an unfathomable Chinese symbol and watched as it was consumed by the dark skies hanging over Alderhey Children's Hospital. I continued to wobble onwards, but before I could reach my desired destination, the heavens opened...

***

The specialist was talking at a rate of knots, but I wasn't listening. I could only think of how much he looked like Matthew Corbett and wondered if it would've been any easier if he'd employed his cuddly puppet friends to tell me that I was suffering from a progressive, genetic condition of the nervous system known as Friedreich's Ataxia. I concluded that it would only have added to the confusion as Sooty is only capable of a whisper while Sweep speaks in a squeaky dialect of his own.

I retuned into the unglamorous reality provided by the specialist as he mapped out the rest of my life using medical terms and unattractive words such as "wheelchair", "diabetes", "slurred speech", "heart disease" and "curvature of the spine".

Apparently, only one person out of every 50,000 in Britain suffers from this cruel condition, which traps and maintains a healthy and active mind in an eroding and useless body. Just half an hour earlier, I'd been hoping to hear about a trapped nerve that could be released with a simple operation and allow me to get my football career back on track. It wasn't to be. I'd have to live with the fact that the cards life had dealt me had just been reshuffled.

It was a lot to get my head around as despite reassurances from Dr Corbett that Britain was becoming more accessible and appreciative of disabled people's needs, I had enough social awareness to realise it meant a frustrating future, fighting stereotypes, avoiding pigeon holes and struggling to be heard...

***

On the dismal journey home from Alderhey, I was faced with impersonal reams of medical jargon that were supposed to educate and inform me about the disease I was fighting (see Appendix A). Instead of ploughing through this inaccessible nightmare, I chose to indulge myself with the inventive prose of Dave Lovett – chief football reporter for the *Wrexham Leader* – as I was more concerned with the battle for promotion from Barclays Division Three than whatever was going on inside my body.

I finished reading the match report of Wrexham's 3-1 home win over Walsall as the trusty Allegro entered the concrete confines of one of the Mersey Tunnels. While we progressed through the poorly-lit passageway, I allowed myself two minutes of contemplation about what I'd just been told, wiped a tear from my eye and focussed my attentions on the road ahead, which I hoped would eventually lead to bright sunshine and light.

Emerging from the underpass, I was greeted by dark and depressing rain clouds with the only splash of colour coming from that same red balloon I'd seen at Alderhey earlier. It was threatening to follow us all the way home until it was finally engulfed by the brume over Ellesmere Port. By this point though I'd managed to programme the Chinese symbol inscribed upon it deep into my memory, pledging to one day discover its true meaning...

Bangor City 2 Llanelli 5

Principality Welsh Premier League
Saturday, 16 April 2011
14:30

Farrar Road / Ffordd Farrar
Attendance: 623

Almost twenty years later, I was stranded and disillusioned in a wheelchair at Farrar Road, Bangor – a depressing and decrepit arena, characterised by flaking paintwork, rusting metal and crumbling concrete.

Two wooden seated stands of differing designs looked treacherous either side of the players' entrance. One was being supported from the rear by weather-worn planks of wood that didn't exactly inspire confidence. These archaic stands are a messy mixture of dusty benches and plastic seats, with a total capacity of 506. Any extra and I imagine they'd collapse.

Opposite this rickety structure stood uncovered terracing and a portacabin on stilts masquerading as a television gantry. Behind the far goal there is more shallow standing room that is open to the elements, while the largest terrace is at the Farrar Road end, complete with peeling paintwork and obtrusive roof supports. Overall, 1,700 spectators can safely congregate inside this hovel.

I'm not normally so harsh on old grounds and usually appreciate the architectural excellence of our forefathers, who built atmospheric stadiums full of character and unique charm. Where possible, the precious heritage wrapped up in aging arenas should be respected, preserved and carefully developed, but alas, there is no room for sentiment in football anymore, and many clubs are ignoring their history to start afresh in soulless, out-of-town plastic palaces that do little to excite or inspire. No one is sadder about this than me, but

EVERY SILVER LINING HAS A CLOUD Nathan Lee Davies

Bangor City need to move if they're to grow and develop. It should come as no surprise that relocation from Farrar Road has been discussed for ten years now.

I drained the remnants of my 750ml bottle of water and, with kick-off fast approaching, decided to ask a steward where the disabled toilets were situated. In response to my question, I received a classic return look of panic, combined with bewilderment and embarrassment, as it dawned on the moustachioed bloke in the florescent coat that this was the 21st Century and the largest semi-professional club in Wales could not even offer these basic facilities. My bladder was full, so the steward looked for a private and accessible spot for me to relieve myself into a urinal. Unsurprisingly, he couldn't find one so I had to cross my legs for 90 uncomfortable minutes.

Bangor City have been based in this busy residential area since 1920, after being evicted from their previous cramped ground at Maes y Dref to make way for the establishment of allotments.

Although Farrar Road is now clearly unfit for purpose, it is important to recognise that it hasn't always been such a depressing dive. This quickly deteriorating old ground has undoubtedly hosted some wonderful occasions. For example, Bangor qualified for the European Cup Winners' Cup in 1962 and a capacity crowd of 8,000 crammed into this modest arena to see the Welsh Cup holders win 2-0 against Napoli. Farrar Road, the venue for two Welsh Cup finals in 1928 and 1953, also hosted an Atletico Madrid side full of international talent in the second round of the Cup Winners' Cup back in 1985. The part-timers from north Wales did Bangor proud that evening and only lost 0-2.

Loyal supporters of the club are therefore entirely justified in having an emotional attachment to their club's home, but such sentimental memories should not stand in the way of progress. It's difficult for a neutral, such as I, to appreciate why many fans are opposed to the club's imminent move to a new 3,000-capacity ground at Nantporth, with Farrar Road being redeveloped into an Asda supermarket. Indeed by the time this book is published, the Citizens should be settling into their new home – where everybody should be able to urinate in comfort.

To take my mind off my bulging trouser pistol, I turned my attention to the bulky matchday programme. The classic front cover included all the relevant match details and was followed by 39 pages of advertisements on heavy duty, glossy paper. This alone would've been disappointing for £2, but hidden in the centre of this brochure were 28 paper pages dedicated to football, including news, statistics, regular columnists and Welsh language items, without an advert in sight. I have to applaud this novel and innovative approach as while it is necessary for all clubs to attract advertisers for the programme, many do so to the detriment of the articles they are showcasing. No such problems here as the necessary adverts simply cocoon page after page of informative and entertaining terrace talk.

I was looking forward to this afternoon's game as it was a dress rehearsal of the Welsh Cup final. Bangor were hot favourites to win the trophy for the fourth year in succession after 22 consecutive victories in the competition, but today's game would surely have a bearing on the final, due to be played at Parc y Scarlets, Llanelli in just 22 days time. The winners would qualify for the 2nd Qualifying Round of the Europa League, but this afternoon both clubs were still chasing European qualification through the league.

Llanelli didn't get off to the best of starts after an exhausting four-hour coach trip from south Wales. Winger Sion Edwards gave Bangor the advantage from close range after only two minutes and, such was the dominance of Nev Powell's men during the opening 20 minutes, it seemed inevitable that this lead would be strengthened.

However, the weary travellers gradually shook off their coach-induced slumber and began to find their stride. Chris Thomas fired a warning shot that Bangor's Paul Smith did well to save, but it came as little surprise when a long ball out of the visitors' defence set up Craig Moses to finish confidently on 37 minutes. There was still time before the break for Llanelli's Corbisiero to hit the woodwork and underline their dominance.

As the players trudged towards the dressing rooms, I made the most of my vantage point alongside the players' tunnel to applaud the sweaty athletes for their first-half efforts. As the final few stragglers and substitutes left the field of play, my attentions were turning towards the nearby refreshment kiosk when a Llanelli substitute caught me by surprise.

"Enjoying the game, mate?"

I've been attending football matches at all levels for over 25 years and not once has a player asked me if I was enjoying the entertainment being provided. Professional footballers are now under so much pressure and have so little in common with those watching from the terraces that such friendliness is unheard of nowadays. Can you imagine a Manchester United player engaging with a random face in the crowd like a lifelong friend? It wouldn't happen. I appreciate there is a world of difference between games being played at Old Trafford and Farrar Road, but this was a crucial game between two of the top four sides in the league and the relaxed, friendly approach of the players, let alone the intermingling fans, made for a refreshing change. The same atmosphere has been a feature of all the Welsh Premier games attended so far and I like it.

My stomach grumbled and I noticed that a long and marauding queue had formed at the tea bar. Those in front of me seemed excitable and impatient like young children on Christmas morning waiting to open their presents. It was clear that something special awaited me at the end of the salivating line.

EVERY SILVER LINING HAS A CLOUD Nathan Lee Davies

I ordered a pie from the rudimentary menu and expected to be served with a bog-standard meat and potato effort encased in soggy pastry. To be honest, I was surprised to find that such a dilapidated ground even had cooking facilities, and didn't expect to be offered much more than a mangy cat in a bun. Instead, I was presented with a heavenly treat inside a tin foil casing. Basically this was a shepherd's pie with a thin layer of pastry at the base and sides that held thick chunky meat beneath a deep mashed-potato covering. This serving was demolished with plastic cutlery, but it deserved to be surrounded by silver service. It was the equivalent of being served a three-course meal prepared and created by a Michelin chef, but having to eat it on your knee in front of a black and white portable television in a caravan in Merthyr. It was a bizarre experience, but easily the best pie I have ever tasted at any football ground I've ever visited.

My stomach was full, satisfied and ready to burst. Unfortunately, so was my bladder. I was praying for an exciting second half to help me take my mind off waterfalls and hose pipes. Thankfully, Andy Legg's half-time team talk inspired his charges to build on the momentum they had shown before the break and they forged ahead with an unforgettable performance that started in the 47th minute with a Chris Thomas effort to give them the lead.

I'd kicked off my Welsh Premier tour by watching Bangor lose their grip on top-spot against TNS and I was proving to be something of a bad omen as Jason Bowen and a double from Rhys Griffiths shot the visitors into a deservedly unassailable lead. This was clearly not the same side that had started the season in breathtaking form by setting a new record in British football during the modern era.

City's 15 wins out of 15 from the start of the season beat the achievement of the famous double-winning Tottenham Hotspur side of 1960-61. Spurs previously held the record of 11 consecutive wins from the start of the season in the top flight of their national league. The Citizens remained unbeaten until January when prolific striker,

EVERY SILVER LINING HAS A CLOUD Nathan Lee Davies

Jamie Reed, was sold to York City for an undisclosed five-figure fee and the seemingly unassailable leaders lost all confidence.

The 23-year-old had been in great form. He'd netted 17 league goals that had played no small part in Bangor's early season success. York originally tried to sign Reed in November 2010, only to have a derisory offer rejected, but finally got their man at the beginning of 2011 after doubling their initial bid. Reed had netted 41 goals in 51 WPL starts for City, but the Minstermen lured him away from Farrar Road with a professional contract and the "glamour" of the Blue Square Premier.

It says a lot about the formative nature of the game in Wales that little York City can splash the cash and tempt the best players away from the national league in favour of the English non-league system. You can't blame an ambitious young footballer for wanting to further his career, but it's a shame that to do so, he has to leave the Welsh system.

To their credit, Bangor continued to plug away and pulled one back through powerful centre-forward Les Davies – AKA the Truck – but the result leaves them trailing TNS in the title race with dreams of championship glory, built on the goals of Jamie Reed, quickly fading. I've now watched Bangor City lose twice in the space of a few weeks and based on what I've seen there is little chance of them being crowned champions of Wales for the first time since 1994-95.

The referee blew the full-time whistle. I later learnt that the Llanelli substitute who'd been so friendly at the break was trying to find me to gauge my opinion on his side's blistering performance, but I was no where to be found. Instead of hanging around to engage in idle chit-chat with an anonymous amateur, I was racing through Bangor City centre on four wheels in search of a disabled toilet...

Bangor City
Farrar Road

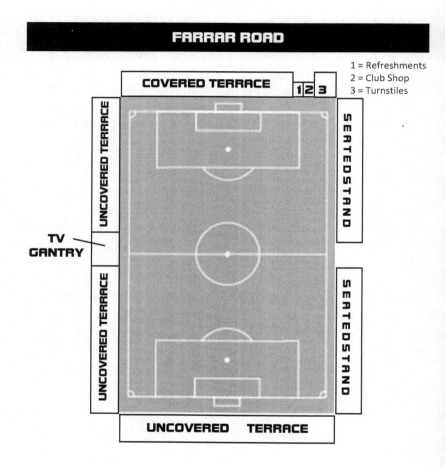

FARRAR ROAD

COVERED TERRACE

1 = Refreshments
2 = Club Shop
3 = Turnstiles

1 2 3

UNCOVERED TERRACE

UNCOVERED TERRACE

SEATED STAND

SEATED STAND

TV GANTRY

UNCOVERED   TERRACE

6
When We Win Promotion

EVERY SILVER LINING HAS A CLOUD Nathan Lee Davies

We arrived back in Wrexham at lunchtime. My parents weren't expecting me to return to school for double business studies and actively encouraged me to stay at home to discuss what I'd just been told. Apparently, I needed time to let it all sink in...

Balls to that.

I was just months away from my GCSE final exams and needed all the extra tuition I could get. Besides, I needed to make arrangements with my mates for that evening's big game at the Racecourse between Wrexham and York City – weather permitting.

Both sides were chasing promotion from Barclays Division Three with Brian Flynn's men in third position; just one place below the visitors from Yorkshire. I wasn't going to miss this game for anything – Friedreich's Ataxia or not.

It had been raining non-stop all day and the crunch clash was actually in doubt for a while. If the game had been postponed I would've had to cope with an evening of sober reflection, but thankfully conditions eased in time for the match and my much-needed distraction went ahead as planned, albeit on a mud bath of a pitch. The stormy weather didn't stop a crowd of 6,894 – the biggest home gate since the 1989 play-off final – from gathering to watch a match that heralded a new era – both for the football club and myself.

From the first whistle to the last, Wrexham ran the show. Even the frustratingly enigmatic Karl Connolly was in the mood and headed home after only a minute to settle any nerves. Steve Watkin then scored a second-half double (78', 88') to underline our dominance and lift us above York into second place, much to the excitement of everyone in the town. Even my usually emotionless parents looked as if they'd been crying when I returned home; probably at the realisation that Flynnie's Army were on the verge of rising from the doldrums.

EVERY SILVER LINING HAS A CLOUD Nathan Lee Davies

E-I-E-I-E-I-O
Up the Football League we go
When we win promotion, this is what we'll sing
We are the Wrexham, super Wrexham
We're gonna win the league.

***

It was a golden period in my life.

I had just been diagnosed with a debilitating disease, but for once in my life I was happy. Even though I was still stumbling around with all the grace of a cow suffering from bovine spongiform encephalopathy, at least I could finally understand my wobbly essence and plan for the future accordingly. I'd received the answers to questions that had been haunting me for most of my childhood and was left with one clear decision – sink or swim?

I had to face up to the fact that I was never going to score the winning goal in a FA Cup final, win a gold medal at the Olympics, or even keep out of the black on Bully's prize board. Indeed, a whole series of dreams and ambitions lay in tatters, but instead of dwelling on my limitations, I embraced my strengths and threw myself into my studies. The classroom was a level playing field for me; I absorbed and utilised information to ensure I gained academic advantages over the physically-fit airheads who surrounded me.

I was motivated by the fact that I didn't want to end up dribbling in a care home without any achievements to my name, so I suppose the eight GCSEs, three A-Levels and BA in American Studies from the University of Nottingham, which included a 6-month stint at the University of Illinois, should be considered a success. During that period, I also passed my driving test and performed a parachute jump from 11,000 feet that raised more than £1,500 for Ataxia UK.

EVERY SILVER LINING HAS A CLOUD Nathan Lee Davies

I apologise wholeheartedly for the self-congratulatory essence of these recollections. I realise you are not impressed and would rather read more self-indulgent bleating based around my growing pains and sexual frustration but such stories – there are many of them – are for another day. All you need to know at this point is that I was successfully evading pigeon holes and jumping hurdles put in my way by a hostile society that does not embrace or appreciate the contribution disabled people have to offer.

I was making positive progress by ignoring my disability and the effects of it. This didn't bother me while I was celebrating promotion, collecting diplomas, travelling the States, or jumping out of aeroplanes but, deep down, I knew it was only a matter of time before this cruel disease caught up with me...

Bala Town 4 Carmarthen Town 0

Principality Welsh Premier League
Sunday, 24 April 2011
14:30

Maes Tegid
Attendance: 352

I'd arrived in Bala ridiculously early. There was no sign of life at the ground, apart from an elderly gentleman Sellotaping a sheet of A4 paper to the exterior of the turnstiles. The amateurish sign, typed using Times New Roman in 20 point, indicated admission prices for the game. I couldn't help but think the sign would have been more effective if a different font, maybe Arial, had been used.

"Croeso i Maes Tegid. Diwrnod hyfryd, yntydi? Ydych chi wedi teithio'n bell?"

I stared back blankly at the smartly-attired chap, who was now wearing the roll of Sellotape around his wrist like a makeshift bracelet. I was still trying to learn Welsh at college but was struggling to grasp the basics. I had three options. I could tell the bloke that I liked ice cream, ask if he had any pets, reveal that I have a younger sister, or show my lack of understanding by shrugging my shoulders. I shrugged my shoulders.

"Rydym yn ddisgwyl lawer o gymorth heddiw."

I asked him if he had any pets.

"You don't speak Welsh, do you?" was the astute observation that he was forced to make in his second language. "You should've said something."

EVERY SILVER LINING HAS A CLOUD Nathan Lee Davies

Two Welshmen should be able to have a conversation in their own language, but I'd let the side down. Learning and practicing the Welsh language for four hours a week wasn't working. I just couldn't envisage myself speaking this beautiful language fluently. I suppose such a skill would take a while to develop, but I don't have enough patience and dedication to keep trying.

Anyway, now that we were speaking the same language my newfound friend began reciting Bala Town's recent history. Apparently, this was only Bala's second season in the top flight and they could consider themselves fortunate to still be amongst Welsh football's elite, despite finishing 2009-10 in a very credible 11th place in an 18- team league. The problem was that the FAW had decided to create the Super 12, relegate eight clubs and promote two clubs from the feeder leagues, meaning that relegation seemed inevitable. Nothing is ever straightforward in the developing world of Welsh football though and the powers that be ruled that the clubs that had won promotion didn't meet the required criteria to take their place among the elite for the 2010-11 season. Bala therefore survived by default.

This was proving to be another tough season. With only two games remaining Colin Caton's men were perilously positioned in 11th position. Only the long-since relegated Haverfordwest County kept them off the bottom of the league. With two clubs due to be relegated, Bala were in serious trouble but, rather frustratingly for a professional cynic such as myself, there was an unlikely glimmer of hope for the Maes Tegid faithful.

Newtown, the side above them, were five points better off after beating Aberystwyth Town the day previously but with two games remaining for Bala they could still reach safety. The Lakesiders had to win their final two games and hope Airbus could beat Newtown at the Airfield on the last day to ensure their top-flight status. Stranger things have happened.

EVERY SILVER LINING HAS A CLOUD Nathan Lee Davies

The committee member was proudly providing verbal profiles of current squad members when the large exit gate he'd been leaning against was suddenly opened by the groundsman, who'd just finished pegging the nets around the goalposts. I seized my opportunity and asked if it would be possible to enter the arena and take some photographs before the crowds arrived. My hosts were only too happy to let me wander freely around their neat and picturesque stadium, which had been nothing more than an unenclosed park ground when I last visited, less than a decade ago.

The journey to Bala had been spectacular. I hadn't seen as much natural beauty since that night I enjoyed a particularly filthy dream about Katherine Jenkins. It's obvious why this area is known as the Welsh Lake District as it's characterised by massive mountains, deep valleys, fast flowing streams, rivers, waterfalls, forests and the largest natural lake in Wales. The historic market town lies in the heart of this stunning National Park and is a stronghold of the Welsh language and Welsh culture. The main street is home to an array of independent shops, banks, supermarkets, cafes, restaurants and pubs.

Maes Tegid is located just off the main street, adjoining the town's senior and junior schools, and a large all-weather floodlit complex. The focal point is a large wooden pavilion in the turnstile corner of the ground, which houses the players' changing rooms and clubhouse, and also doubles up as a pavilion in the summer for the adjoining cricket field. This quaint structure looks like it should be positioned in the middle of a prairie in the American West, but instead sits alongside a football pitch in north Wales next to five small blocks of seats. Each of these stands holds four rows of covered, sky blue seats, resulting in a seated capacity of 504 in an overall ground capacity of 2,000. Some of the seats have been thoughtfully removed to provide sheltered accommodation for disabled patrons and an elevated viewing area for members of the written press.

EVERY SILVER LINING HAS A CLOUD Nathan Lee Davies

The opposite side of the pitch features uncovered hard standing, characteristic dug outs – as opposed to the modern Perspex monstrosities that seem to be en vogue – and a modern media centre and TV gantry. However, this impressive facility is somewhat overshadowed by the wondrous work of Mother Nature as Moel Emoel stands proudly in the near distance. Part of me was almost hoping for a tepid bore draw that would allow me to focus on the surrounding beauty without distraction from Mark Jones, Nick Harrhy or any of the other amateur cloggers.

Behind the far goal is uncovered hard standing at the base of a large grass embankment on which young families enjoy picnics in the Easter Sunday sunshine. Halfway up the bank stands a clutch of intertwined trees and through this copse is a partially-hidden white building of stately proportions. I've since discovered that this is a neo-Georgian house named Gwynfryn that is of considerable architectural interest. Built in 1931, the villa housed a veterinary surgery for many years and is still home to Bala's retired vet, Evan Davies. In addition, the house next to it was the birthplace of Christopher Timothy, who was the vet featured in the James Herriot book, *All Creatures Great and Small.*

The Town End of the ground offers more yet more hard standing and features a small covered enclosure, which resembles a bus shelter, but provides spectators with adequate shelter from the winter elements. There can be no denying that Maes Tegid is an idyllic and inspirational place to watch football. The fact that a town of fewer than 2,000 people can boast such a venue, and sustain Welsh Premier football, is a credit to everyone involved with the club.[1]

With time to spare before kick-off, I had a leisurely browse of the matchday magazine. This was a fairly standard, yet informative effort with a good amount of information on the visitors, statistics and even

---

[1] This was actually my second visit to Bala's ground. In 2006, I was just passing through the town, needed a piss, couldn't find a public loo, pulled up in the club car park, filled my urinal, opened the car door and created a puddle of urine on Maes Tegid. Ever since, Bala have enjoyed success and good fortune.

a couple of those half-arsed interviews with players and managers in which we find out that the menacing central defender listens to Justin Bieber or the star striker drives a Vauxhall Corsa. This particular issue informed me that manager Colin Caton's favourite footballer is Gazza, while the best ground that coach Steve Compton has been to is the Nou Camp in Barcelona. It's unclear whether he actually played here or just went on a behind the scenes tour, but after listing his former clubs as Wolves, Worcester City, Runcorn and Bangor City my money's on the all-inclusive tour.

This run-of-the-mill programme was elevated to must-read status by the excellent travel blogs that bluntly review grounds visited while following Bala. There is a page on a recent trip to the Airfield for a crucial League clash with Airbus UK Broughton and a hilarious article on their humiliating Welsh Cup fourth round exit to the students of University of Wales Institute, Cardiff (UWIC), of the Welsh League's third tier. Bala went into this game on the back of four straight defeats but were still expected to teach the students a lesson, so imagine the fury of those who had travelled for three and a half hours to watch their side lose 4-1 and get reduced to nine men in the process.

I closed the 36-page programme as the referee signalled the start of a cagey first-half, which was largely forgettable apart from a Shaun Kelly drive from the edge of the box that gave the home side the lead at the break.

During the second period, Bala were in complete control and Carmarthen offered little, but it wasn't until the game approached the last quarter that the home side asserted their dominance. On 73 minutes, Michael Hayes lobbed the visiting goalkeeper to double their advantage before substitute Ryan Marriott's angled drive ended the game as a contest. Carmarthen were being totally outclassed in front of a bumper holiday crowd. So much so, that it was hard to believe that the Old Gold had beaten Bala on three separate occasions during 2010-11.

EVERY SILVER LINING HAS A CLOUD Nathan Lee Davies

Eight minutes from time, Hayes converted a right-wing cross from close range for his second and Bala's fourth. The bloke I was sitting next to, clearly a regular at Maes Tegid, tapped me on the shoulder and, with a hint of desperation in his eyes, asked if I'd be attending next weekend's must-win game against already-relegated Haverfordwest County. The inquisitive supporter believed I was a lucky omen and that my very presence had conjured a season-saving performance that also went down as the club's biggest WPL home win. I assured him that the result had nothing to do with me, everything to do with the hapless Carmarthen defence, and even though I couldn't get to the game next week, I'd be listening out for their result. This was true, but I thought it wise not to mention that I'd be at the Airfield watching his club's relegation rivals battle for safety. It was going to be a tense final day...

As we prepared to bid a fond farewell to Maes Tegid, the elderly Welshman who had impressed and bedazzled me with his use of my native language shuffled towards me.

"I almost forgot," he hollered across the bustling car park. "I've got a five-year-old Golden Retriever named Gethin."

Bala Town
Maes Tegid

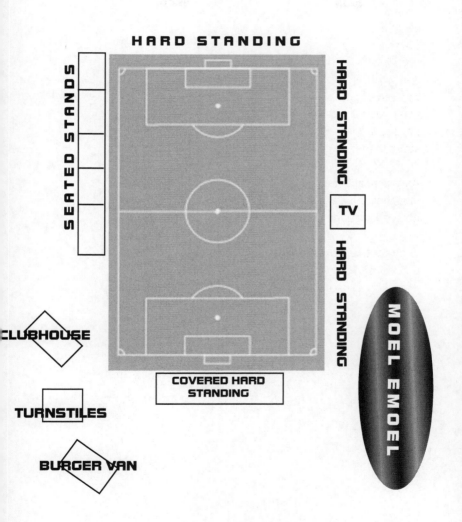

7
My Way

EVERY SILVER LINING HAS A CLOUD Nathan Lee Davies

I was sipping Jack Daniel's and Coke in the middle of the Atlantic ocean, while trussed up in a dinner jacket, listening to a Frank Sinatra tribute act and making small talk with Eric Pollard and Betty Eagleton from *Emmerdale*.

The previous paragraph may sound like the result of a bad acid trip, but it actually did happen. After graduating from university, I quickly landed a position with North Wales Newspapers as a features writer and as the most competent scribe in the whole organisation – not a hard job – I was quickly entrusted with important writing assignments. After only a few months behind my new desk, I was asked to write a centre-page advertising feature for Cunard after enjoying an all-expenses-paid cruise from Southampton to New York aboard the QE2.

Back on dry land, my daily routine included penning a controversially entertaining TV guide that resulted in floods of complaints and personal attacks. The problem was that I dared to criticise *Heartbeat*, or some other dead-end drama designed for the culturally naive or, even worse, recommended a programme that included bad language, nudity or both. I loved the fact that my words would often get underneath peoples skin and took it as a backhanded compliment if I managed to provoke a reaction from a brain-dead tabloid readership.

It wasn't all rewarding though. Afternoons would often be spent in deep resentment and frustration as I sub-edited the work of useless hacks and talentless contributors who'd never come into contact with a dictionary and had a reading age of five. Checking and correcting the work of others – especially imbeciles – was such a demoralising experience, especially for a perfectionist such as myself.

I would re-work paragraphs, deconstruct sentences and apply generous sprinkles of makeover magic to appalling articles that would've made more sense if they'd been written by the trained chimpanzees that used to sell us tea bags. After polishing such suspect articles, it seemed unjust to label the column with the original author's name when all traces of the original work had gone. Extra salt was rubbed into the wounds when you consider that much of this garbled nonsense was often produced by councillors, Members of Parliament, or law enforcers; people we're supposed to look up to. Unfortunately, I can't respect anyone who doesn't know the difference between "there", "their" and "they're".

Was I being too anal? I suspect that poor grammar and incorrect spellings shouldn't cause a deep depression, but I was also being asked to write sycophantic reviews of pandering hotels, restaurants and theme parks that were desperate for good publicity, whether they deserved it or not. I found it all very nauseating and artificial as I was being asked to curb my artistic flair and conform to the bland and sterile tastes of the mass market. I had my feet firmly on the journalistic ladder, but instead of developing this burgeoning talent, working on my NVQ, applying for work on the nationals and becoming a faceless clone, I chose to look elsewhere for happiness.

I realise now that my disillusionment with work and general resentment of the world around me was a by-product of my confused identity. I was now confined to a wheelchair and fighting tired stereotypes despite my academic credentials and promising career in journalism. The progressive nature of my condition increased my anxiety for the future, and I could not see anything positive in a future full of doctors, hospitals and care homes. Instead of confronting these issues and making peace with myself, I lashed out at everything else.

By this time, most of my friends were in serious relationships and talking about marriage while I was still engaged in a loveless tryst with my right hand and, to spice things up, an inflatable sheep. I'd never even been kissed without being charged and was still living with my parents, with little prospect of this bleak situation changing. I was desperate to escape my predicament, so I logged into an Internet chatroom for bored, lonely housewives and learnt to be careful what you wish for.

EVERY SILVER LINING HAS A CLOUD Nathan Lee Davies

To cut a long story short, I struck up a conversation with a large-breasted female of the species, discovered that we shared a passion for prawn cocktail flavoured crisps, handed in my letter of resignation – before we'd even met – and promptly moved to the Highlands of Scotland to set up home with a virtual fantasy figure and her three noisy children.

My brains had transferred from my head to my trousers.

Airbus UK Broughton 0 Newtown 3

Principality Welsh Premier League
Saturday, 30 April 2011
15:30

The Airfield / Y Maes Awyr
Attendance: 249

The scene was set for a thrilling climax to the league season with either Newtown or Bala Town being relegated from the top flight, along with Haverfordwest County, on a nerve jangling afternoon. I was looking forward to watching a decisive game in the end of season dog-fight and observing scenes of joy or despair as Newtown's destiny was helped or hindered by a bunch of wing makers. However, I hadn't accounted for the intervention of men in suits.

As previously stated, every club in the Welsh Premier League must hold a domestic licence. This precious piece of paperwork is reviewed and reapplied for every 12 months. At the beginning of April 2011, the FAW Club Licensing First Instance Body assessed 19 applications and granted ten. Of the successful applicants, nine were Welsh Premier clubs, while Llandudno of the Huws Gray Alliance were also awarded a licence.

However, Bala Town, Llanelli and Neath were unsuccessful in their bids. Llanelli and Neath were also denied their UEFA licences, which would enable them to take part in either the Champions League or Europa League should they qualify. Clubs aspiring for promotion to the WPL were also frustrated in their applications with Gap Connah's Quay, Cefn Druids and Flint Town United of the north and Afan Lido, Barry Town and Bridgend Town of the south being snubbed.

On April 28, just two days before the big match at the Airfield, an independent panel in Cardiff, heard appeals from the top flight clubs and those still hopeful of promotion. Llanelli and Neath sealed their passports for domestic and European football; MacWhirther Welsh League high-flyers, Afan Lido, had their domestic licence granted; but the biggest winners of the day were Bala Town. Not only were the Lakesiders successful in their appeal, but they also profited from the misfortune of others.

Gap Connah's Quay had been crowned as Huws Gray Alliance champions – a feat that usually leads to promotion to the WPL – but on this occasion they were controversially denied the licence and subsequent elevation that their on-field performances deserved. The Flintshire club were aware that their initial licence bid would be rejected as the floodlights at their Deeside Stadium ground didn't meet the required standard. However, after receiving funding from the FAW, work began to upgrade the lights and, following discussions with the governing body, the club understood that an appeal would have a strong chance of success – as long as the upgrade was completed in the intervening time. Connah's Quay kept to their end of the bargain, but access to the top flight did not follow.

Nomads chairman John Gray was understandably incensed and let off steam in conversation with David Bergin of the *Flintshire Chronicle*.

"We have asked a lawyer to look into it for us," he said.

"We are appalled at the actions of the FAW. We've always said the decisions these people make affect the club, the people who are part of the club, the young players in the academy whose funding is now under threat, but sometimes your face just doesn't fit."

"It's ridiculous. At the start of the season every team should know if they are playing for promotion or relegation.

"It should not be decided in a boardroom after the event, but on the pitch by the players.

"I don't know another system in Europe that operates in this fashion and I believe it must change. Whether we go up or not, we intend to fight this because the future of Welsh football depends on it."

On the other side of the fence, FAW domestic licensing officer Andrew Howard said he could not speak about the specifics of the Nomads case due to confidentiality rules, but defended the appeals panel.

"It is independent of the FAW and the clubs," he said. "It has lawyers, former policemen, even a judge on it and they look at the evidence before them and make a decision.

"Clubs know at the beginning of the season what the deadlines are and that they have to get their infrastructure in place before that date."

All this meant that Bala and Newtown were saved from the threat of relegation by default, only Haverfordwest County would be relegated and replaced by Afan Lido and my trip to watch Quay's local rivals take on Newtown had lost its potential for drama, excitement and emotion.

Airbus UK Broughton are based in Flintshire, which is uneasily close to the Wales-England border and the city of Chester. My outdated and inappropriate obsession with geographical boundaries – exposed during my earlier visit to watch TNS in Oswestry – is something I am desperately trying to eradicate from my mixed-up mind, but it may take some time. You'll have to bear with me I'm afraid.

Formed in 1946, the former works team have changed their name several times over the years in line with the company.[1] They have

---

[1] Over the years, this Broughton-based former works team has been known as Vickers-Armstrong, de Havilands, Hawker Siddeley, British Aerospace, BAe Systems and Airbus UK.

been established in the top division since 2004-05 when they were simply known as Airbus UK, with the name of the village being added from the start of the 2007-08 season.

At least I arrived at the Airfield before kick-off this time, which was something of an improvement. It was a mild afternoon, but a windbreaker was needed to protect against the stiff breeze that swirled around the venue. This is par for the course around here as beyond this neat little ground lies a fully functional and exposed airfield – the clue is in the stadium's name.

This spacious plot has a capacity of 1,500, including 519 seats. Lying on the edge of all the big factories and workplaces that comprise the Airbus site, the Airfield is surrounded by hard standing but also boasts three seated stands. The largest of these has six rows of seats and houses about 300 fans as well as including an enclosure on its roof from which television cameras monitor the action. This is a depressingly modern stand that suffers from four supporting posts at the front, which impair the view somewhat.

On the opposite side of the pitch is the clubhouse – a big brick building that includes the changing rooms, toilets and a further 100 covered seats, with provision for fans in wheelchairs. Unfortunately, the view from this cosy stand is ruined by more supporting posts, and fans that use the hard standing in front of and to the side of the structure – someone needs to tell these seemingly oblivious spectators that they don't make good windows for those who choose to sit in the stand. The dug-outs, club shop and refreshment stall are also located on this busy stretch of the stadium.

There is nothing but hard standing behind one of the goals, but things start to get interesting at the airfield end. The main runway is situated beyond a small seated stand that is only three rows deep and runs from one corner to the centre of the goal before making way for more hard standing. It is interesting to note that this stand has a bright red warning light attached to the roof, which is presumably used to keep tired and disorientated pilots from veering off course when coming into land. The runway really is that close to the stadium. Indeed, pre-match entertainment comes from planes landing and taking off, while even a dull goalless draw can be illuminated by running behind the stand to watch an aircraft arrive or depart.

Being in such close proximity to an important runway has also resulted in the installation of retractable floodlights that fold down onto brackets that support them. It is worth staying in the ground after the final whistle to see these towering lights being mechanically lowered. It is an unusual sight and one that any true groundhopper would appreciate.

With 30 minutes still to spare before kick-off, I wandered over to the club shop that is housed in a portacabin and made accessible by a ramp. I manoeuvred into the building and found a treasure trove of paraphernalia that included boxes crammed with assorted programmes from worldwide clubs plus various scarves, replica shirts, pennants, badges and probably a whole lot more that evaded my overwhelmed eyes. I didn't know what to look at first, but chose to focus on the cork boards that were littered with enamel badges and add to my collection of over 700 of these shiny lapels. Don't laugh. It stops me from trainspotting.

I resolved to take out a bank loan and return to this palace of delights as there was so much for me to paw my obsessive fingers over. If I hadn't been writing this book I would've forgotten about the game and asked if I could be locked in the shop for ninety minutes. This was the fifth WPL ground I'd visited, and this was by far and away the best club shop, which makes me wonder if clubs at this level are missing a trick. Developing your own line of merchandise is costly, but if this is backed up by old programmes found in attics and second hand replica shirts then clubs can create inviting and potentially lucrative side businesses for supporters to enjoy. I spent an extra £20 on badges that would otherwise have stayed in my wallet and this is an avenue of income that I feel other clubs should investigate further and follow the example set by Airbus.

I prised myself away from the shop in time for kick-off. Any stomach-churning tension that this fixture promised had disappeared due to the whims of decision makers, but there was still plenty to play for. A win could catapult Newtown up to a respectable ninth position while Airbus needed a point to guarantee a home draw in the European play-offs. The Wingmakers sat on top of the Conference play-off zone, but Aberystwyth Town were just two points behind them and ready to take advantage of a slip up by their rivals.

It's a pity no one pointed this out to the home team, who never found their stride and struggled against a strong Newtown side that was unrecognisable from the one that had looked doomed for much of the season. Quality football was at a premium though and there was little to get excited about. In fact, I spent the first 30 minutes flicking through the solid, yet unspectacular, 36-page programme.

There is a decent amount to read in this issue, but unfortunately this is the result of plenty of recycled material from other sources and articles on the club's history or pen pictures of the squad that are merely reprinted every issue. As it was the first time I'd read the magazine it did a reasonable job of holding my attention, but I wouldn't buy it on a fortnightly basis, even if it only costs £1.50.

I was impressed to read that the Dalkeith Airbus Supporters Club were not only sponsoring the match, but had also travelled down from Scotland especially for the game. That's dedication for you and just goes to show that even during bleak financial times some people still manage to have more money than sense.

This misguided group would definitely have been drowning their sorrows after Newtown's former AFC Liverpool striker Steve Jones took the game by the scruff of the neck and notched a hat-trick past a lacklustre defence with no response. The result meant that Airbus had only won one of their last six matches and would have to travel to Aberystwyth Town for their play-off quarter-final tie, after the Seasiders beat Carmarthen 1-0 at Park Avenue.

As we were leaving the ground, a voice over the loudspeaker announced that Bangor City had beaten The New Saints in the end of season title decider at Farrar Road, with the only goal of the game coming from Craig Garside after 68 minutes. This was enough for City to clinch their first national crown since 1995 in front of 1,707 fans – easily the biggest league crowd of the season.

A smile spread across my face. I was glad the league trophy was staying in Wales.

Old habits die hard...

Airbus UK Broughton
The Airfield

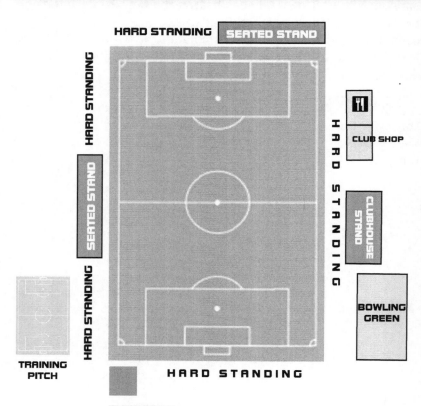

AIRFIELD

HARD STANDING SEATED STAND

HARD STANDING

HARD STANDING

SEATED STAND

HARD STANDING

HARD STANDING

CLUB SHOP

CLUBHOUSE STAND

BOWLING GREEN

TRAINING PITCH

HARD STANDING

TURNSTILE

- In August 2012, the Airfield was renamed the Hollingsworth Group International Airfield after the club signed a sponsoring deal with the Sandycroft construction firm.

8
A Bridge Too Far

EVERY SILVER LINING HAS A CLOUD Nathan Lee Davies

Haverfordwest County deserve an apology.

I should really have visited New Bridge Meadow at the end of 2010-11, but the Bluebirds were already cast adrift at the foot of the table and looked odds on to be replaced by one of many promotion chasing clubs who were confident of being granted the required domestic licence.

Subsequently, after consulting a map to reaffirm my decision, I conveniently ignored the league's whipping boys on the south-west coast. If you've learnt anything about me so far, you'll realise this misguided choice has bugged me ever since as I cannot truly say I visited every WPL ground during 2011. This will haunt me for all eternity, so I'm writing this micro-chapter to apologise to the Pembrokeshire club for ignoring them, and to recognise their historic involvement in the national league.

In 1992-93, Haverfordwest County became founder members of the League of Wales, but their stay was brief. After just two seasons in the new set-up, the Safeway supermarket chain made an offer to buy the club's historic Bridge Meadow ground. The proposed deal included the construction of a new ground, but this would leave County without a suitable venue for top-flight matches. After careful consideration, and with admirable foresight that is rare in modern day football, they decided to accept the offer and resigned from the League of Wales.

The whole affair was a runaway success as their three seasons in the Welsh League saw them finish as runners-up twice, before clinching the championship and promotion in 1997. Furthermore, the club was furnished with a new stadium that is considered as one of the best grounds in Welsh football. Unfortunately, I'm unable to comment on it at the moment other than to say this multi-purpose stadium has a capacity of 2,000 and was home to Haverfordwest during their dreadful 2010-11 campaign.

EVERY SILVER LINING HAS A CLOUD Nathan Lee Davies

The West spent much of the season in the relegation zone, recorded only five league victories, lost 72% of their matches and were embarrassed by a goal difference of -46. There was also chaos in the manager's office as long-serving Derek Brazil was surprisingly sacked in November 2010.

"After a disappointing start to the season, Haverfordwest County AFC have reluctantly decided to part company with their management team of Derek Brazil and Mark Evans with immediate effect," said a statement from the New Bridge Meadow.

"The directors have made their decision at this stage of the season in the hope that they will be allowing the next manager enough time to rectify a situation which, at the moment, sees the club staring relegation in the face.

"Derek Brazil has done sterling work at the club as a player and also over the last four and a half seasons as the manager.

"The directors are greatly indebted to the service he has given to the club. Mark Evans has been great support to his manager over the last three seasons and we thank him for the hard work he has done within the club too.

"The directors will be advertising the post of manager and are keen to fill the position as soon as possible."

The statement said nothing about the limited resources Brazil had to work with, or how the likeable Irishman guided an outfit with modest means to 10th, 8th and 7th finishing positions in the days of the 18-club Welsh Premier. It seemed that County had lost their long-term vision.

The club appointed 32-year-old Gavin Chesterfield as their new gaffer, but the former Barry Town boss was unable to arrest the club's poor form. After taking charge of only a handful of games, the young manager made a shock decision to quit – citing "travelling difficulties" for his departure. It seems I wasn't the only one who couldn't be arsed venturing to this part of the country.

Derek Brazil was then surprisingly reappointed in February, just three months after being dismissed, but couldn't save the club from relegation. The former Manchester United and Cardiff City defender didn't hang around to survey the damage though; following the final game of the season, he quit.

"Things did not work out as planned for me, or the club, in the nine games since I've returned and I need a blank sheet of paper and to start afresh," Brazil revealed to www.welsh-premier.com.

"It hasn't been a great season on and off the pitch, but I don't regret going back there, I just feel I need a new challenge next season."

I am sure the Bluebirds will learn from their mistakes, reorganise and be back in the WPL before too long, when I promise I'll move heaven and earth to visit New Bridge Meadow, complete the tour, update the book and silence the demons in my mind that taunt me about an incomplete mission...

Haverfordwest County 2010 -11

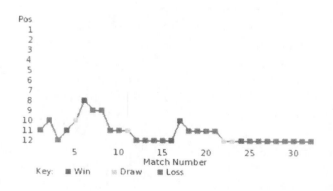

9
Half-Time

Loosemores League Cup

The Loosemores League Cup is a competition that is unappreciated by some, but seen as a realistic chance of winning silverware by others, much like the English equivalent.

Reserved for those clubs that play at the top of the Welsh pyramid, the League Cup has been staged in various guises and formats since the inaugural season in 1992-93. Since 1993 it has been sponsored by Cardiff-based solicitors Loosemores. In 2010-11, the tournament was played on a straight knockout format with teams playing each other on a two-legged basis, in a regional draw up to and including the semi-finals.

The northern section included Bala Town, Airbus UK Broughton, Prestatyn Town and Newtown while Aberystwyth Town, Neath, Carmarthen Town, Haverfordwest County made up the southern section. Bangor City and TNS of the north received byes to the quarter-finals while the same applied to Llanelli and Port Talbot Town in the south. With prize money of £10,000 for the winners, clubs had every incentive to compete for this trophy apart, it seems, from Bangor City.

While proving to be unbeatable in the league and on course for qualification to the far more lucrative Champions League, City felt they could do without the midweek distraction of a two-legged League Cup semi-final against TNS. Subsequently, Nev Powell angered many by fielding substantially weaker teams that embarrassingly slumped to a 12-1 aggregate defeat against the full-time professionals from Oswestry. The aggregate score was the highest in the competition's 19-year history, eclipsing Carmarthen's 10-3 rout of Llanelli in 2004.

Meanwhile in the south, Llanelli made it to the final with a 4-1 aggregate win over Aberystwyth Town. These results were resolved

EVERY SILVER LINING HAS A CLOUD Nathan Lee Davies

in November with the final due to be played in January at Aberystwyth Town's Park Avenue. Players and supporters of both sides were already at the ground, when referee Brian James surprised and frustrated everyone by deeming the rock-hard surface unplayable, just 90 minutes before kick-off.

After one of the worst winters on record caused countless postponements and a subsequent administrative nightmare, the final was eventually scheduled to take place at the beginning of May at Park Avenue. Just 48 hours after losing their championship crown to Bangor, The New Saints picked themselves up to win the Loosemores League Cup for the third year in succession.

It was certainly a match worth waiting for. It seemed that TNS were heading for a routine victory. Aeron Edwards netted on the stroke of half-time and this advantage was doubled through Chris Sharp – son of former Everton legend and ex-Bangor boss Graeme – on 73 minutes.

Llanelli kept plugging away though. Chris Holloway headed home at the far post to give Andy Legg's men a chance, but time was running out. With just three minutes left on the clock, Craig Moses sent the Llanelli fans wild with a magnificent 30-yard equaliser for the Reds.

There was still time for more drama though and when Sharp grabbed his second of the afternoon with only a minute of normal time remaining it seemed certain that the League Cup would be heading back across the border. Llanelli fans were no-doubt preparing for a solemn drive back to south Wales when Jordan Follows unleashed a 20-yarder to take the game into extra-time. It was truly sensational stuff.

Extra-time was a largely one-sided affair with Llanelli proving dominant, but a stunning effort from TNS midfielder Scott Ruscoe, just 14 seconds before the end, sealed their dominance of a competition they have now won five times.

Welsh Cup

The Welsh Cup is one of the oldest cup competitions in the world, having been competed for since 1877-78. The winning team qualifies for the following season's Europa League (previously teams qualified for the European Cup Winners' Cup, which was discontinued in 1999). The 2010-11 final was between Llanelli and Bangor City.

The Reds from south Wales were looking for their first-ever win on their third appearance in the final, which would be staged just down the road from their Stebonheath Park home at Parc y Scarlets rugby stadium, Llanelli. This was certainly a fitting venue for this showpiece contest, with its 14,850 capacity, but it should be remembered that Carmarthenshire is not the easiest part of Wales to reach. Indeed, Bangor fans faced a six-hour train journey to reach their destination, while their rival fans merely needed to add an extra five minutes to their usual matchday routine.

Newly crowned WPL champions Bangor were chasing a record-equaling fourth successive triumph in their fifth final in six seasons. They were also defending an incredible run of 23 Welsh Cup ties without defeat, which helps to explain why so many Bangor fans made the exhausting journey from north Wales to cheer on Nev Powell's men. Indeed, estimates suggest they easily outnumbered Llanelli fans in the 1,719 crowd.

The two sides met in the 2008 final when they conjured a classic afternoon of drama that will go down in folklore as one of the most explosive and entertaining encounters in the competition's history. Llanelli were favourites back then and, under the guidance of Peter Nicholas, were aiming to complete a domestic treble after a season to remember.

This clash was held at Latham Park, Newtown, and a day of drama started as early as the fourth minute when City's Peter Hoy saw red

EVERY SILVER LINING HAS A CLOUD Nathan Lee Davies

for a dangerous challenge on Llanelli's Craig Jones. Bangor then took the lead with a goal from livewire Ashley Stott and led at the break as they made light of the one-man advantage held by Llanelli.

Peter Nicholas' men obviously had a stern talking to at the break. The second half was only a few minutes old when Llanelli's Rhys Griffiths scored the equaliser and followed this with a second on the hour that seemed to seal the result. Bangor refused to give up hope though and were boosted when Llanelli's Wyn Thomas was dismissed for foul and abusive language. Time was running out though and it wasn't until the final seconds of normal time that Chris Seargeant snatched a 2-2 draw and sparked a delirious, but violent, pitch invasion by Bangor troublemakers. Several Llanelli players were confronted and goaded by the mindless minority, while Peter Nicholas claimed some were physically struck.

Once order had been restored, the match continued into an equally eventful extra-time, which saw Bangor run out 4-2 winners. Llanelli's frustration boiled over and they were reduced to nine men when Rhys Griffiths was shown a red card for alleged use of an elbow.

The 2011 final was a less volatile affair, dominated by the Reds from Carmarthenshire. Bangor were always on the back foot at Parc y Scarlets, falling behind to first-half headers from Rhys Griffiths and Craig Moses.

Alan Bull reduced the arrears early in the second half, but Llanelli were not to be denied as Griffiths took his total to 29 for the season and Chris Venables completed an emphatic 4-1 scoreline.

"Bangor won the league, but this was our day today and we'll be celebrating tonight," said player-manager Andy Legg.

UEFA Europa League play-offs

The following couple of paragraphs require your full attention and may result in a headache.

Llanelli finished the Welsh Premier season in fourth position, but were spared the bother of the end of season play-offs by reaching the Welsh Cup final against Champions League qualifiers Bangor City.

With runners-up TNS also guaranteed a Europa League entry, it was left to third-placed Neath and fifth through eighth-placed sides Prestatyn Town, Port Talbot Town, Aberystwyth Town and Airbus UK Broughton to compete in the inaugural play-offs for the second Europa League spot available via league placement.

That wasn't too bad, was it? Actually, these play-offs succeeded in maintaining the interest and attention of supporters all season long with an almost complete obliteration of meaningless league matches. In turn, this led to a tremendous increase in attendances with an average of 343 supporters passing through the gates during 2010-11. This was a massive jump on the previous season's average of 276, and almost 15% higher than the previous record average of 300, set in 2003-04.

Two teams from the Conference section of the split league were the first to do battle. Seventh placed Aberystwyth Town faced Airbus UK Broughton who qualified in eighth position thanks to Llanelli's cup run. The match took place at Park Avenue, with the Black and Greens having home advantage due to their higher league finish.

The odds were stacked in the home sides favour, but it was Airbus who stole the initiative through an Ian Sheridan penalty after 21 minutes. It wasn't until the second half that Aberystwyth came to life. They sealed a trip to face Neath at the Gnoll in the semi-final, courtesy of goals from Ashley Stott (60') and James McCarten (85').

EVERY SILVER LINING HAS A CLOUD Nathan Lee Davies

The other semi-final saw Prestatyn Town host Port Talbot Town at Bastion Gardens. This was a repeat of one of the league games I'd attended in April. The Steelmen had a score to settle and looked set to make up for their 2-0 defeat the previous month. The away side's early dominance saw them take a deserved lead through Lee Surman's 29th minute header, but they couldn't conjure a decisive second goal despite their superiority in possession. With six minutes left, the almost inevitable happened when Prestatyn managed to claw level, against the run of play, through a Lee Hunt penalty. Just four minutes later, an unlikely turnaround was complete when a left-wing corner was forced in at the far post by David Hayes.

Meanwhile at the Gnoll, third-placed Neath comfortably beat Aberystwyth Town 2-1. Craig Hughes (32') and Paul Fowler (34') put the Eagles in control and the lead could have become unassailable, but for a hatful of missed chances, including a second-half Lee Trundle penalty saved by Stephen Cann in the Aber goal.

James McCarten cracked home a stunning free-kick for the visitors with only a minute remaining, but it was too little, too late. Neath held on to ensure they would host Prestatyn at the Gnoll in the Welsh Premier's first-ever Europa League play-off final.

The match certainly lived up to its billing and was a fitting end to a thrilling season. The majority of the 988 crowd were still searching for their seats when Neath took the lead with just 12 seconds on the clock. Chad Bond played a neat one-two with Craig Hughes and fired home from 18-yards to stun the large group of fans who'd travelled from north Wales. Such an early setback could have led to a total collapse, but Neil Gibson's side rolled their sleeves up and drew level on 25 minutes when Lee Hunt latched on to a long throw from Jack Lewis in thunderous style.

The scores remained level at the break, but the game turned when Neath boss, Andy Dyer, made a 53rd minute substitution. Dyer took off Craig Hughes and replaced him with Andrew Hill – the clubs longest-serving player – and it took him less than two minutes to make an impact. Prestatyn only partially cleared a corner and Hill headed home the resulting cross to send the Eagles soaring. The Seasiders continued to battle away, but with just six minutes remaining Hill was again on hand to seemingly secure a Europa League spot.

Prestatyn rallied and refused to give up on their European dream by producing a late onslaught, which led to Jon Fisher-Cooke pulling one back in the second minute of added time. Alas, time was about to run out and Neath qualified for Europe for the first time in their short history. It was just rewards at the end of a season in which they'd finished 18 points ahead of their opponents.

Two-goal hero Andrew Hill said scoring the goals which took Neath into Europe for the first time was like a dream.

"Nine years ago when Andy [Dyer] took over he phoned me up and said come and play for Skewen in the third division of the Welsh League.

"To achieve this now and for me to score the two winners is a dream really."

Manager Dyer was equally thrilled:

"This is what it's all been about," he said.

"It all boils down to this. The boys' performance was a little bit inconsistent but we've dug in there and Andy – our legend at the club – has scored two.

"The league table doesn't lie at the end of the day, we've finished third and we've deserved it. The league has got the best four teams representing it in Europe."

Principality Welsh Premier League 2010-11
Final League Table

Pos	Team	P	W	D	L	F	A	GD	Pts
1	Bangor City **(C)**	32	22	4	6	80	44	+36	70
2	TNS **(EL)**	32	20	8	4	87	34	+53	68
3	Neath **(EL)**	32	16	10	6	62	41	+21	58
4	Llanelli **(EL)**	32	15	8	9	58	41	+17	53
5	Prestatyn Town	32	10	10	12	44	46	-2	40
6	Port Talbot Town	32	8	12	12	37	48	-11	36
7	Aberystwyth Town	32	11	9	12	42	54	-12	42
8	Airbus UK B'ton	32	11	8	13	53	52	+1	41
9	Newtown	32	8	11	13	40	55	-15	35
10	Carmarthen Town	32	10	5	17	39	64	-25	35
11	Bala Town	32	10	3	19	40	57	-17	33
12	Haverfordwest **(R)**	32	5	4	23	30	76	-46	19

Women's Welsh Premier League

The Women's Welsh Premier League was only founded in 2009 and was originally contested between eight teams, divided into two conferences — four teams from north Wales and four from south Wales. Both Conference winners then met at a neutral venue to decide who was crowned Women's Champion of Wales and earned the right to represent Wales in the UEFA Women's Champions League.

The teams played each other on a double round-robin basis. The first match to take place in the league was contested at Aberystwyth's Park Avenue on 24 September 2009. The home side defeated Llanidloes Ladies 2-0 in front of 367 supporters.

EVERY SILVER LINING HAS A CLOUD Nathan Lee Davies

Swansea City became the inaugural champions after facing Caernarfon Town in the final at Haverfordwest's New Bridge Meadow and romping home 4-0.

Season 2010-11 was only the league's second full-term and although the north-south format remained in place there was an increase in the number of competing teams, which rose from 8 to 10 teams, 5 per regional conference. Aberystwyth Town, Caernarfon Town, Llanidloes, Llandudno Junction and Wrexham made up the northern section while the south was represented by Caerphilly Castle, Newcastle Emlyn, Swansea City, Trefelin and UWIC.

Northern Conference

Pos	Team	P	W	D	L	F	A	GD	Pts
1	Caernarfon Town Ladies (Q)	8	6	1	1	20	8	+12	19
2	Llanidloes Ladies	8	5	1	2	17	10	+7	16
3	Wrexham Ladies	8	3	2	3	11	10	+1	11
4	Aberystwyth Town Ladies	8	2	2	4	7	11	-4	8
5	Llandudno Junction Ladies	8	0	2	6	5	21	-16	2

Southern Conference

Pos	Team	P	W	D	L	F	A	GD	Pts
1	Swansea City Ladies (Q)	8	7	1	0	32	8	+24	22
2	UWIC Ladies	8	6	1	1	24	10	+14	19
3	Caerphilly Castle Ladies	8	4	0	4	24	14	+10	12
4	Trefelin Ladies	8	2	0	6	10	26	-16	6
5	Newcastle Emlyn Ladies	8	0	0	8	3	35	-32	0

For the second season in succession, the play-off final was contested between Caernarfon Town and Swansea City, though this time the match took place at Victoria Park, Llanidloes. The change of venue didn't alter the result though as Swansea Ladies won 1-3 to book another trip to Europe.

The above is a description of women's football by a male chauvinist pig without any reference to swapping shirts, sweaty sport bras, after match showers, or the problems of playing with period pains, while knowing they should be at home preparing dinner for their hungry families.

I'm obviously coming down with something...

Summer news round-up

As well as the usual close season transfer shenanigans and a couple of surprise faces riding the managerial merry-go-round, which you'll read about later, there were also a few more substantial stories of interest to connoisseurs of the game at this level.

The Welsh Premier League AGM took place in June, when Afan Lido were officially welcomed into the top flight for 2011-12, replacing relegated Haverfordwest County. In addition, a couple of small alterations were made to the rulebook. It was decided that a maximum of seven substitutes – increased from five – will be allowed from August 2011; two of whom still had to be under the age of 19. It was also decided that a maximum of four loan deals per season (three at any given time) would be allowed between member clubs of the WPL, irrespective of the transfer windows.

***

Llanelli's Rhys Griffiths won the player of the season award for 2010-11, voted for by WPL managers. The Golden Boot winner – for the sixth consecutive season – picked up the prize ahead of Michael Johnston of Bangor and Craig Jones of Neath.

Neath winger Chris Jones scooped the young player award. Jones finished ahead of TNS defender Danny Holmes and Prestatyn's Kai Edwards.

Bangor's Neville Powell won the manager of the year prize, for a second successive season, beating former Neath boss Andy Dyer and Llanelli's Welsh Cup winning manager Andy Legg to the honour.

EVERY SILVER LINING HAS A CLOUD Nathan Lee Davies

***

The Welsh Premier's first season of Super 12 and European play-offs saw an attendance increase of nearly 25% on 2009-10, suggesting that the new format has been a success.

An average of 551 spectators watched the four play-off fixtures, bringing the league's average gate for the whole of the campaign to a highest-ever figure of 343, compared with just 276 in 2009-10.

The biggest winners were Neath, who attracted a club-record crowd of 988 to the Gnoll for the Europa League play-off final. The attraction of Trundle, O'Leary and Co during the season saw gates rise to an average of 584 – a 164% improvement on the previous campaign.

Meanwhile, a record Farrar Road crowd for the domestic league era of 1,707 watched the Citizens' title showdown with The New Saints, bringing the total of supporters passing through the turnstiles to 12,751, a leap of 74.4% on last season.

Gates also increased at Airbus UK Broughton (29.4%), Carmarthen (7%), TNS (4.6%) and Port Talbot (0.6%), but there were significant falls elsewhere.

Nearly 28% fewer fans passed through the gates at Bala's Maes Tegid, while Llanelli recorded a 24.6% decrease at Stebonheath Park.

Newtown's relegation struggle resulted in a 20% drop at Latham Park while the other losers were Aberystwyth (12.9%), Haverfordwest (12.6%) and Prestatyn (0.8%).

The previous highest average attendance in the domestic league of 300 was recorded in season 2003-04.

***

EVERY SILVER LINING HAS A CLOUD Nathan Lee Davies

The New Saints won the inaugural FAW Futsal Cup in Cardiff and qualified for the UEFA Futsal Cup in August.

Futsal is a variant of the beautiful game that is played indoors on a smaller pitch and between two teams comprised of five players each. Unlimited substitutions are permitted. Futsal also features a smaller ball with less bounce than a regular football. The rules create an emphasis on ball control, passing, improvisation, creativity and technique.

Attracting young Welsh footballers to this game can only be a good thing as it's popular in countries such as Brazil, Spain and Portugal and helped to develop the skills of Ronaldo, Robinho, Kaka and Cesc Fabregas, to name but a few. Futsal is a fast-paced, skill-oriented game and the much-maligned FAW should be applauded for encouraging its practice throughout Wales.

The young Saints team beat GAP Connah's Quay 7-4 in the final and claimed a prize of £1,500 and a place in Europe.

***

The WPL will run an Under-19 Northern League for the 2011-12 season as a further development to the FAW Academy system.

This is an important step as southern youngsters have been able to compete for their clubs in a youth set-up for many years but northern academy graduates are plunged straight into first-team football, a jump that is regarded as too great for the majority by managers and the technical advisors at the Welsh Football Trust.

Six teams will compete in the inaugural league, which will help youngsters hone their skills before stepping up to the first team. Aberystwyth Town will join TNS, Airbus UK, Bala Town, Prestatyn Town and Bangor City in the new set-up, with Newtown opting not to enter a team in the first year.

EVERY SILVER LINING HAS A CLOUD Nathan Lee Davies

***

It was concerning to learn that Welsh Premier clubs had been piling-up tax debts despite conditions in the domestic licensing system that stipulate all such debts should be paid in full when due and not deferred. Realistically, this was never going to happen as clubs strive to grow in the midst of a global economic crisis, but according to the people at www.sportingintelligence.com, WPL clubs owed £71,733 in direct tax and £4,482 in indirect tax at the end of the 2011 tax year, compared to a £42,583 direct tax debt for the previous year. Unsurprisingly, the FAW declined to comment on the rise, but I sincerely hope they are looking at ways to address the situation and not merely burying their heads in the sand.

***

The New Saints became the first Welsh Premier club to launch a dedicated App for the iPhone. Although I'm a 34-year-old technophobe, I was delighted by such news as it shows a sophisticated understanding of consumer culture and the key role of new technologies in fans' relationship with their clubs.

The App features the latest news from TNS, links to the TNS and Venue websites, the club's Facebook page, YouTube channel and Twitter feed, as well as a dedicated fan wall.

I sincerely hope the rest of the Welsh Premier clubs follow this idea and develop their own Apps as it's important to utilise every available promotional tool to attract the next generation of supporter.

***

It's all been going on at Newtown during the close season as Mike Jones stood down as chairman, and just hours later manager Andy Cale and assistant Lee Williams also confirmed their decision to leave the club.

EVERY SILVER LINING HAS A CLOUD Nathan Lee Davies

"My vision for the future of the club is clearly not shared by the board of directors and my position has become untenable," said Cale – the league's most successful manager after five title successes as TNS boss.

"I worked with the lowest budget in the Welsh Premier League last season and the players have been magnificent. They responded to the changes that were needed to take the club forward and the management and squad were completely behind the chairman in ensuring the short and long term future of Newtown FC.

"But those aims are clearly not shared by all members of the board of directors and without their full support it is impossible for Lee and myself to continue.

"We have the basis of a very strong Welsh Premier League side at the club and I was confident that we could press on to becoming a top six club next season. But the board has decided that a further overall reduction in expenditure is required and the management team has to respect that decision.

"I wish the club, the players and the supporters every success in the future and thank them for their support. Working with Mike Jones has been a privilege and along with Lee Williams I wish him well for the future."

Bernard McNally, a holder of the UEFA Pro Licence, was appointed as the new Newtown manager. It's his first foray into Welsh football after coaching in Romania, India and England. In addition, Elwyn Preece became the new chairman at Latham Park.

***

Prestatyn Town unveiled a new badge as they embark on their second century of existence.

EVERY SILVER LINING HAS A CLOUD Nathan Lee Davies

The old round badge will be consigned to history and a new "shield and scroll" style emblem will be used on the club's shirts from the start of the season.

Media officer Mark Jones explained: "An awful lot of supporters loved the centenary logo which was basically the town crest with writing around it," he said.

"The new design has taken elements of that and parts of the old badge and I hope that in time it will come to be seen as "our" badge. The old circle with the dragon standing on what was supposed to be the top of the world had gone to look a bit tired and needed a revamp.

"As we go into the second century of our existence it is nice to have something fresh and interesting," he added.

The new badge features blue and yellow to represent the sea and sand of the shoreline, oak leaves to reflect the hillside, and the castle and Welsh dragon which have adorned the crests of many organisations in the town, perhaps most notably Prestatyn High School.

The year of formation (1910) has been added and the bilingual motto "Penderfynol – Determined" remains.

***

TNS were involved in a bright marketing initiative organised by Welsh Football Trust club development officer Tim Broome.

The Oswestry-based club joined forces with Aberystwyth Town and Newtown to share marketing ideas and increase awareness of their clubs and the Welsh Premier League in general.

One of the first initiatives is the introduction of a joint season ticket deal, which will enable free-entry on production of a season ticket at any of the three grounds throughout the season.

EVERY SILVER LINING HAS A CLOUD Nathan Lee Davies

"The aim is for clubs to become the hub of their community encouraging more support from a wide range of organisations," said Broome.

"We hope to organise similar workshops with all Welsh Premier League clubs in the near future.

"We see Welsh Premier clubs being at the forefront of club development in Wales and these meetings will start to reinforce that message."

***

The Welsh Premier League's headline sponsorship deal with the Principality Building Society ended after five years and, at one stage, it seemed likely that the competition would be without a sponsor at the beginning of 2011-12. This led to much disgruntlement with the FAW's new full-time commercial team as member clubs would've been, at least, £5,000 out of pocket.

Fortunately, the FAW managed to dissipate the growing anger and frustration at the last minute with the announcement of a new three-year deal with north Wales-based bookmakers Corbett Sports.

"We're absolutely delighted to get a sponsor in the current climate," said league secretary John Deakin.

"Corbett is a company I've spoken to in the past and in fact we came close to contracting them as an official betting partner a few years back but it didn't materialise.

"I don't think the clubs will be disappointed with the financial package this gives them."

Michael Corbett, managing director of Corbett Sports, added: "We are thrilled to have the opportunity to support the Welsh Premier League and the member clubs across Wales.

EVERY SILVER LINING HAS A CLOUD Nathan Lee Davies

"Our company was founded in Flintshire in 1947 by my grandfather and we wanted to mark our 65th anniversary in 2012 by partnering with a truly national competition.

"Having spent my childhood watching local football across north Wales, a passion for sport has run through the Corbett family for decades and we believe in supporting Welsh football from the grassroots up.

"The league has vastly improved in recent years and with the help of Corbett Sports long-term investment, we believe the competition can continue to grow in stature and quality."

The league was sponsored in its first season by Konica Peter Llewellyn Limited of Swansea, but then went for nearly 10 years without any external financial support until J T Hughes Mitsubishi (2002-2004) and then Vauxhall Masterfit (2004-2006) moved in.

The Principality deal was the longest in the history of the league.

***

The BBC Sport website conducted a survey during the summer to determine the price of football throughout the leagues that matter to them – the four main English divisions and the Scottish Premier League. Clubs were asked for their cheapest and most expensive match day adult tickets, as well as the prices for a cup of tea, a programme, and a pie in order to work out the cost of football for fans without season tickets. The survey showed that only 11 out of 104 clubs in England and Scotland will offer adults the chance to enjoy a day supporting their team for less than £20 during 2011-12.

After being overlooked by Auntie, the Welsh Premier League carried out its own research and the results showed that a bargain bundle of football entertainment can still be had in a league full of potential.

Indeed, it was noted that eight clubs in the Welsh Premier League can offer the full match day experience for less than £10.

					Cheapest day out
1	Afan Lido	£5.00	£1.50	£1.00	£0.60	£8.10
2	Port Talbot Town	£5.00	£1.50	£1.20	£1.00	£8.70
3	Newtown AFC	£5.00	£1.50	£1.80	£0.80	£9.10
4	Airbus UK	£6.00	£1.50	£1.00	£1.00	£9.50
5	Llanelli AFC	£5.00	£2.00	£1.50	£1.00	£9.50
6	The New Saints FC	£5.00	£2.00	£1.50	£1.00	£9.50
7	Bala Town	£6.00	£1.50	£1.50	£0.80	£9.80
8	Bangor City	£5.00	£2.00	£2.30	£0.60	£9.90
9	Carmarthen Town	£7.00	£1.50	£1.20	£0.80	£10.50
10	Aberystwyth Town	£7.00	£1.50	£1.50	£0.80	£10.80
11	Prestatyn Town	£7.00	£1.50	£1.50	£0.80	£10.80
12	Neath FC	£7.00	£2.00	£1.40	£0.60	£11.00
	AVERAGES	£5.83	£1.67	£1.45	£0.82	£9.77

Of course, the standard of football is not as high in the WPL as it is in the four principal English leagues, or even the Scottish Premier, but it's a burgeoning environment that is developing season upon season and I feel lucky to be backing a league without pretentions, pampered players or ludicrously inflated ticket prices.

***

It had been a largely positive close-season, with many positive initiatives being launched and signs that Welsh football is slowly building and thinking of the future. On the eve of the new campaign, the league's new sponsors, Corbett Sports, issued their championship odds for 2011-12 and made TNS favourites to win the title at 2/1.

2010-11 champions, Bangor City, were available at 21/10, whilst Neath – who had spent the summer working hard to establish their status as a full-time club in the Welsh Premier – were at 5/1.

TNS 2/1
Bangor City 21/10
Neath 5/1
Llanelli 11/2
Port Talbot 20/1
Prestatyn Town 25/1
Aberystwyth Town 33/1
Airbus UK Broughton 33/1
Bala Town 33/1
Newtown 33/1
Afan Lido 50/1
Carmarthen Town 50/1

I'm not much of a gambling man, which is a good thing when having an addictive and compulsive personality. Subsequently, I wouldn't like to guess who'll win the title, but I'm definitely looking forward to find out during the season ahead...

<u>10</u>
Fool on the Hill

EVERY SILVER LINING HAS A CLOUD Nathan Lee Davies

The next train at Platform 12 is the 14:51 Virgin Trains service to Birmingham New Street, calling at Haymarket, Carlisle, Penrith, Oxenholme, Lancaster, Wigan North Western, Warrington Bank Quay, Crewe, Stafford, Wolverhampton and Birmingham New Street.

I'd been travelling since 6am but still hadn't escaped an arctic Scotland. The Scotrail service steadily crawled out of Inverness, snaked through the snow-capped Cairngorms and, after hours of wintry bleakness, finally crossed the Forth Rail Bridge towards civilisation.

Like most train stations, Edinburgh Waverley is a bitterly cold place that is regularly assaulted by bitter winds, rushing under bridges and across concourses to savage the bones of weary travellers. On this occasion though, my bruised and battered heart was warmed by the fact that this would be my last visit to these parts. I clutched my one way ticket tightly. Armed with a ham and mozzarella baguette and a modest Gola holdall full of my prized possessions, I was ready to continue my final journey back to where I belong, via Crewe and Chester, after an eight-year absence.

As the Virgin Super Voyager shuttled southwards, I stared into space with a furrowed brow. I reflected on my time north of the border and wondered what the future had in store for me now that my marriage had imploded in such spectacular fashion.

Everything had started well enough. We rented a large four-bedroom bungalow, overlooking the Moray Firth and Fort George – an 18th century fortress, which continues to be used as a garrison. My new abode was positioned at the top of a steep hill and cut off from the rest of the village, which was a welcome novelty for someone who had always lived at the centre of busy communities. I embraced the isolation while my step-children, then aged ten, eight and six, seemed to instantly accept me as a father figure. In addition, I was enjoying regular sex with a kind and caring partner, who overlooked my disability and just so happened to have big tits. I was in my element.

The honeymoon period didn't last for long though. It wasn't as easy as I thought to find employment with the local media in Inverness as I was a stranger to the area and didn't understand the insular and hostile regional psyche. Even when an opening became available, it would've been detrimental to the whole family if I'd started work as we were better off on benefits. I was hundreds of miles away from home in a foreign land, without any friends, prospects or hope.

I tried to keep myself busy with a sponsored tour of football grounds that raised over £1,500 for Ataxia UK, wrote some articles on a freelance basis and tried to develop my own website without any technical expertise. It was a frustrating time of emptiness and depression. To make matters worse, I failed to put up a fight when I was wheeled down the aisle at Inverness Registry Office in 2005.

I was just doing what I was told and going through the motions. My confidence and self-respect had disappeared and I was wholly reliant on my wife to act as my personal secretary and full-time carer. Our relationship was in a rut and I was heading towards a spiritless oblivion before discovering that my wife's legs were as spreadable as Clover margarine and open to all comers.

Even though I didn't deserve the heartbreak of being lied to and cheated on, maybe I should be thanking the Highland heffalump for giving me the shake I needed to wake up, gain control of my life and build myself a brighter future. I now only wish she hadn't waited eight years to play away.

We are now approaching Wrexham General. Change here for a better life.

The boy was back in town…

Llanelli 2 Dinamo Tibilisi 1

Europa League, 2nd Qualifying Round, 1st Leg.
Thursday, 14 July 2011
18:50

Parc y Scarlets
Attendance: 552

Welsh clubs have a proud record in Europe. Cardiff City, Swansea City and Wrexham were frequent participants in the old European Cup Winners' Cup, which they qualified for through the Welsh Cup. Unfortunately, this route was closed off to them in 1995-96, after they opted to continue in the Football League, rather than join the League of Wales – but not before enjoying their share of continental success.

Cardiff reached the semi-finals of the now discontinued trophy in 1967-68, while Wrexham won through to the quarter-final stage in 1975-76. Famous Welsh victories in Europe include Cardiff conquering the mighty Real Madrid 1-0 at Ninian Park in 1971, Swansea's 17-0 destruction of Sliema Wanderers of Malta, over two legs in 1982, and Wrexham's thrilling aggregate triumph against FC Porto in 1984. There were many more memorable European moments for these clubs, but they put themselves in exile by snubbing the national league, so this is not the place for romantic recollections of their continental successes. Instead, we'll focus on the achievements of those clubs who remained loyal to the FAW and supported the national competitions.

Inaugural champions of the League of Wales in 1992-93, Cwmbran Town were the first club from the domestic league to compete in Europe. They played in the Champions League preliminary round against Cork City and actually beat their Irish opponents 3-2 at Cwmbran Stadium, before losing the away leg 2-1 and being knocked out on the away goals rule.

Subsequent campaigns have bought little success although there are signs of slow improvements being made in recent seasons. Supporters must be realistic and patient – not qualities usually associated with football fanatics – as standards gradually develop and improve. However, there is no escaping the fact that a cursory glance at the statistics below support the ignorant views of those who believe the WPL is a waste of time and that its clubs are not worthy of taking the European places on offer to the FAW.

[*European results table overleaf*]

European Results

YEAR	COMP	RND	CLUB	AGG	OPPONENT	H	A
1993-94	CL	P	Cwmbran T	4-4	Cork City (IRL)	3-2	1-2
1994-95	UC	P	Inter Cardiff	0-8	Katowice (POL)	0-2	0-6
	UC	P	Bangor City	1-4	IA Akranes (ICL)	1-2	0-2
	CWC	P	Barry Town	0-7	Žalgiris Vilnius (LTU)	0-1	0-6
1995-96	UC	P	Afan Lido	1-2	RAF Jelgava (LAT)	1-2	0-0
	UC	P	Bangor City	0-5	Widzew Lodz (POL)	0-4	0-1
	ITC	G4	Ton Pentre	0-7	Heerenveen (NED)	0-7	
			Ton Pentre	0-4	Békéscsaba (HUN)		0-4
			Ton Pentre	0-3	Leiria (POR)	0-3	
			Ton Pentre	0-2	Næstved (DEN)		0-2
1996-97	UC	P	Newtown	1-7	Skonto Riga (LAT)	1-4	0-3
	UC	P	Barry Town	2-1	FC Dinaburg (LAT)	0-0	2-1
	UC	Q	* Barry Town	4-4	BVSC Budapest (HUN)	1-3	3-1
	UC	1	Barry Town	4-6	Aberdeen (SCO)	1-3	3-3
	CWC	Q	Llansantffraid	1-6	Ruch Chorzow (POL)	1-1	0-5
	ITC	G4	Conwy United	0-0	Charleroi (BEL)	0-0	
			Conwy United	0-3	Zaglebie Lubin (POL)		0-3
			Conwy United	1-2	SV Ried (AUT)	1-2	
			Conwy United	0-4	Silkeborg (DEN)		0-4
1997-98	CL	Q1	Barry Town	0-6	Dynamo Kiev (UKR)	0-4	0-2
	UC	Q1	Inter Cardiff	0-8	Celtic (SCO)	0-3	0-5
	CWC	Q	Cwmbran T	2-12	National Bucuresti (ROU)	2-5	0-7
	ITC	G2	Ebbw Vale	0-0	Grazer AK (AUT)	0-0	
			Ebbw Vale	0-4	Hrvatski Dragovoljac (CRO)		0-4
			Ebbw Vale	1-2	Bastia (FRA)	1-2	
			Ebbw Vale	1-6	Silkeborg (DEN)		1-6
1998-99	CL	Q1	Barry Town	1-10	Dynamo Kiev (UKR)	0-8	1-2
	UC	Q1	Newtown	0-7	Wisla Krakow (POL)	0-0	0-7
	CWC	Q	Bangor City	0-3	Haka (FIN)	0-2	0-1
	ITC	1	Ebbw Vale	1-9	Kongsvinger (NOR)	1-6	0-3
1999-00	CL	Q1	Barry Town	2-3	Valletta (MLT)	0-0	2-3
	UC	Q1	Cwmbran T	0-10	Celtic (SCO)	0-6	0-4
	UC	Q1	Inter Cardiff	1-2	Gorica (SLO)	0-2	1-0
	ITC	1	Aberystwyth T	3-4	Floriana (MLT)	2-2	1-2
2000-01	CL	Q1	TNS	2-6	Levadia Maardu (EST)	2-2	0-4

118

EVERY SILVER LINING HAS A CLOUD Nathan Lee Davies

Year	Comp	Round	Match		
	UC	Q	Barry Town 0-5 Boavista (POR)	0-3	0-2
	UC	Q	Bangor City 0-11 Halmstads BK (SWE)	0-7	0-4
	ITC1	1	Cwmbran T 0-2 Nistru Otaci (MDA)	0-1	0-1
2001-02	CL	Q1	Barry Town 3-0 Shamkir (AZE)	3-0	1-0
	CL	Q2	Barry Town 3-9 Porto (POR)	0-8	3-1
	UC	Q	Cwmbran T 0-5 Slovan Bratislava (SVK)	0-4	0-1
	UC	Q	TNS 0-6 Polonia Warsaw (POL)	0-2	0-4
	ITC	1	Carmarthen T 0-3 AIK Solna (SWE)	0-0	0-3
2002-03	CL	Q1	Barry Town 0-6 Skonto Riga (LAT)	0-5	0-1
	UC	Q	TNS 2-12 Amica Wronki (POL)	2-7	0-5
	UC	Q	Bangor City 1-2 Sartid Smederevo (SRB)	1-0	0-2
	ITC	1	Caersws 1-3 Marek Dupnitza (BUL)	1-1	0-2
2003-04	CL	Q1	Barry Town 2-4 FK Vardar (MKD)	0-3	1-2
	UC	Q1	TNS 0-7 Manchester City (ENG)	0-2	0-5
	UC	Q1	Cwmbran T 0-6 Maccabi Haifa (ISR)	0-3	0-3
	ITC	1	Bangor City 2-6 Gloria Bistrita (ROM)	0-1	2-5
2004-05	CL	Q1	Rhyl 1-7 Skonto Riga (LAT)	0-4	1-3
	UC	Q1	TNS 1-4 Osters IF (SWE)	0-2	1-2
	UC	Q1	Haverfordwest 1-4 Hafnarfjördur (ICL)	0-1	1-3
	ITC	1	Aberystwyth T 0-4 FC Dinaburg (LAT)	0-0	0-4
2005-06	CL	Q1	TNS 0-6 Liverpool (ENG)	0-3	0-3
	UC	Q1	** Rhyl 4-4 FK Atlantas (LTU)	2-1	2-3
	UC	Q2	Rhyl 1-3 FC Viking (NOR)	0-1	1-2
	UC	Q1	Carmarthen T 5-3 Longford Town (IRL)	5-1	0-2
	UC	Q2	Carmarthen T 0-4 FC Copenhagen (DEN)	0-2	0-2
	ITC	1	Bangor City 1-4 FC Dinaburg (LAT)	1-2	0-2
2006-07	CL	Q1	TNS 0-2 MyPa-47 (FIN)	0-1	0-1
	UC	Q1	Llanelli 2-1 Gefle IF (SWE)	0-0	2-1
	UC	Q2	Llanelli 1-6 Odense BK (DEN)	1-5	0-1
	UC	Q1	Rhyl 1-2 FK Suduva (LTU)	0-0	1-2
	ITC	1	Carmarthen T 1-8 Tampere United (FIN)	1-3	0-5
2007-08	CL	Q1	TNS 4-4 Ventspils (LAT)***	3-2	1-2
	UC	Q1	Carmarthen T 3-14 Brann (NOR)	0-8	3-6
	UC	Q1	Rhyl 3-3 Haka (FIN)****	3-1	0-2
	IT	1	Llanelli 6-6 Vetra (LTU)*****	0-3	1-3
2008-09	CL	1	Llanelli 1-4 Ventspils (LAT)	1-0	0-4
	UC	Q1	TNS 0-2 FK Suduva (LTU)	0-1	0-1
	UC	Q1	Bangor City 1-10 FC Midtjylland (DEN)	1-6	0-4
	IT	1	Rhyl 3-9 Bohemian (IRL)	2-4	1-5

EVERY SILVER LINING HAS A CLOUD Nathan Lee Davies

Season	Comp	Round	Result		
2009-10	CL	Q2	Rhyl 0-12 Partizan Belgrade (SRB)	0-4	0-8
	EL	Q1	Llanelli 1-3 Motherwell (SCO)	0-3	1-0
	EL	Q1	TNS 2-4 Fram Reykjavik (ICL)	1-2	1-2
	EL	Q2	Bangor City 0-3 Honka Espoo (FIN)	0-1	0-2
2010-11	CL	Q2	TNS 4-1 Bohemian FC (IRL)	4-0	0-1
	CL	Q3	TNS 1-6 RSC Anderlecht (BEL)	1-3	0-3
	EL	Q1	Llanelli 4-5 FK Tauras (LTU)	2-2	2-3
	EL	Q1	Port Talbot T 1-7 TPS Turku (FIN)	0-4	1-3
	EL	Q2	Bangor City 3-2 Honka Espoo (FIN)	2-1	1-1
	EL	Q3	Bangor City 3-10 CS Maritimo (POR)	1-2	2-8
	EL	Q4	TNS 2-5 CSKA Sofia (BUL)	2-2	0-3

CL Champions League UC UEFA Cup EL Europa League IT InterToto Cup CWC Cup Winners' Cup
* Barry 4-2 on pens ** Rhyl on away goals ***Ventspils on away goals
****Haka on away goals ***** Vetra on away goals

Table provided courtesy of www.welsh-premier.com

These results don't inspire much confidence or hope for the future...

[*The chapter continues overleaf, but use the blank space below to reflect on the results above and ponder how far Welsh clubs can ever expect to progress in Europe. Alternatively, just fill this gap with a doodle of the last piece of genitalia that you had in your mouth. It's up to you*]

EVERY SILVER LINING HAS A CLOUD Nathan Lee Davies

Three Welsh Premier clubs now qualify for European competitions, plus the winners of the Welsh Cup. The WPL champions enter the Champions League while the runners-up, play-off winners and Welsh Cup winners compete in the Europa League.

On this occasion, I travelled to south Wales to watch the semi-professionals of Llanelli compete in the second qualifying round of the Europa League as Welsh Cup winners. They faced tough opposition in the form of FC Dinamo Tblisi of Georgia – formerly one of the most prominent clubs in Soviet football before their country broke away from the collapsing Union to form their own national competition, the Umaglesi Liga.

Dinamo dominated the domestic scene, were champions for the whole of the 1990's and produced some of the finest Georgian players such as Temuri Ketsbaia, Kakha Kaladze, Shota Arveladze and Giorgi Kinkladze. Ahead of this game, the so-called Brazil of the Caucasus had an impressive haul of 13 Georgian league titles and nine Georgian Cup successes. In addition, they had qualified for Europe on 29 occasions. Opponents don't come much tougher at this stage.

The match was being played at Parc y Scarlets, which is home to both the Scarlets and Llanelli rugby union teams, with drainage work making the football club's Stebonheath home unavailable. At this stage I must confess to knowing very little about rugby and caring even less. I realise that this is not very stereotypically Welsh of me, but I just can't grasp the rules and learn to appreciate the art of egg chasing. The only good thing that I can see about this sport is that we can compete with, and often beat, England. Any excuse to bathe in national pride against a common enemy must be celebrated, but this is all the "sport" can offer me.

As someone who struggles to understand and appreciate the importance of rugby in south Wales, I expected to find a ground that only minimally met UEFA regulations. Imagine my surprise then when

EVERY SILVER LINING HAS A CLOUD Nathan Lee Davies

I arrived at a shiny new stadium that boasts a capacity of 14,870. Apparently, it opened in November 2008 at a cost of £23 million and replaced Stradey Park, the home of Llanelli's rugby teams for almost 130 years. It reminded me of the time I caught a glimpse of the glitzy Country Music Awards live from Nashville – complete with red carpet, screaming fans and paparazzi – and realised that just because I'm not interested in something, it doesn't mean others aren't.

The stadium was designed by the Miller Partnership – specialist sports stadia architects who also designed Murrayfield, the home of Scottish rugby. Having previously been known by the provisional title of Pemberton Stadium, this impressive all-seater development had also hosted the Welsh international football team, Scarlet FM's 2010 Fireworks Extravaganza featuring "big" *X-Factor* names Marlon McKenzie and Lloyd Daniels, and even the Saturdays. All this, plus it's been the venue of choice for the last three Welsh Cup finals, but still the rugby arena had somehow managed to escape my notice.

My eyes were finally open. For the first time I had evidence that the stereotype flogged by Max Boyce was actually true. In many parts of Wales, rugby is religion and Parc y Scarlets has been built as a fitting place of worship. The approach to the main stand is known as the "Ray Gravell Legends Walkway", and is paved with bricks naming each Llanelli RFC and Scarlets player to have played for Wales. A statue of Ray Gravell is erected outside the stadium. I'm sure he was a talented bloke, but I'd never even heard of him. This was my first visit of the year to south Wales and already I was feeling like a stranger in a foreign land.

I entered the plush South Stand and took the lift up to the disabled viewing platform, which was accessible via an executive lounge complete with buffet and liquid refreshments. I dodged men in expensive suits as I whizzed past photographs of men playing catch with an oval shaped ball and wheeled out onto a large area in the middle of the stand specially designated for fans in wheelchairs. It was perfectly central to the halfway line and although I've been to over 100 football grounds across Britain I can say, without doubt, that this rugby stadium provided me with the best view of a football match that I'd ever had, with fellow fans sitting in front, to the sides and behind me. I was at the centre of things for once.

This impressive stand also houses a club shop, ticket office, gym and changing rooms, along with public eating and drinking areas. In addition, there is a large sports bar named after Delme Thomas and a museum named after Ken Jones. I am clueless but assume they used to play rugby and therefore achieved God-like status amongst those strange creatures from south Wales.

The other three stands are quieter but equally impressive and all have a slight curvature to allow for better views. In the past, I may have focused squarely on the bland similarities that this stadium has with all the other depressing new builds that are devaluing the beautiful uniqueness and variety of ground architecture in Britain but, almost halfway through my tour, it was nice to relax and enjoy an unbeatable view, safe in the knowledge that I could relieve myself in one of the many disabled toilets at any time.

Pissing would have to wait though as the match was about to get underway. Llanelli's part-time players lined up against illustrious and skilful opponents, who were representing a club that had beat FC Carl Zeiss Jena of East Germany to lift the European Cup Winners' Cup in 1981.

However, the Georgians were probably just as nervous and intimidated going into this game, as Andy Legg's men were the subject of a UEFA investigation and fined 3,000 euros in the aftermath of last season's pulsating Europa League exit at the hands of Lithuanians FK Tauras. Master marksman Rhys Griffiths and Craig Moses were both red-carded in the second leg, while defender Martyn Giles was also reported for violent conduct after the final whistle. Chris Holloway had received his marching orders in the first leg at Stebonheath Park, but it should be noted that such poor discipline was uncharacteristic and the referee's performance was the source of some concern.

Speaking after the defeat in Kaunas, Andy Legg said: "I'm absolutely delighted with my players I thought they were outstanding and I'm very disappointed for them.

"It's not up to me to criticise the referee [Goran Spirkoski], but in my opinion he's got both decisions [the two sending offs] completely wrong.

"It doesn't help when the opposition are throwing themselves around the pitch and holding their face pretending they've been smacked.

"We didn't do that, we're an honest bunch of players and I'm very disappointed with the opposition."

All this meant that Llanelli were without Rhys Griffiths, who had four European goals to his name, Chris Holloway, Martyn Giles, Craig Moses and Chris Venables, through suspension, while frontman Chris Llewellyn missed out through injury. Responsibility for restoring Llanelli's reputation thus fell to a mixture of youngsters, new signings and fringe players. Supporters needn't have worried though. As soon as the referee blew his whistle, this unlikely collection of players turned on the style and produced an unbelievable performance. Reputation counted for nothing.

It took only eight minutes for 21-year-old Jordan Follows to latch onto an inviting through ball from Antonio Corbisiero and calmly slot the ball past the Georgian giant in goal. Dinamo could only muster a few long range efforts in response, while the part-timers looked confident and in control. They passed the ball around nicely and were unfortunate not to add to their lead before the break.

A fairytale was unfolding before me, but while the brave battlers of my homeland prepared for the second instalment of an epic contest, it was time to close the storybook and open the 32-page programme that I'd paid £2 for earlier that evening.

It was an excellent read that was produced in difficult circumstances. This was the first issue of the programme that Neil Dymock had worked on as editor following the sad passing of media officer Hugh Roberts, who'd been in charge for the previous 20 seasons. After his death, the club received notification that Hugh's publication had been awarded "Best Welsh Programme" by the Soccer Club Swap Shop, but the newly-formed team of contributors have picked up his mantle and produced an enjoyable read that is a fitting tribute to his memory.

According to a double-page tribute by Barrie Thomas of the *Llanelli Star*, Hugh Roberts was a proud Welsh speaker, so I'm glad he didn't witness my utter bewilderment as I was presented with a page written in Georgian and Welsh. As far as I could make out, this was a warm welcome to those connected with Dinamo Tblisi, but I'm not sure why the same message also appears in Welsh. I'm almost certain they don't speak a lot of Welsh in Georgia. My head was overloaded with consonants, so I guiltily turned the page and my back on my mother tongue once again.

There was an excellent article on previous Welsh trips to Georgia, with the return leg in mind. I discovered that this wasn't the first time Dinamo had faced Welsh opposition in European competition as in 1976 they were drawn against Cardiff City in the first round of the Cup Winners' Cup. The Bluebirds beat Dinamo 1-0 at Ninian Park, but the away leg didn't go according to plan.

The trip began with a lengthy flight from London to Moscow and then on to Tblisi. These cautious travellers took no chances on the 5,000 mile trip and flew with a chef and plenty of provisions, including steaks, bread, water, vegetables and 400 tea bags.

EVERY SILVER LINING HAS A CLOUD Nathan Lee Davies

Apparently the menu on the flight from Moscow to Tblisi comprised of two boiled sweets and a cup of mineral water. I'd love to put a contemporary footballer on such a flight to see how he'd cope without any modern-day luxuries such as video games, MP3 players or iPad's; I'm cruel like that.

Tickets were like gold dust for this match as it was the first to be played at the newly-refurbished National Stadium. Over 300,000 fans applied for tickets, which were priced from 75p for the cheap seats to a hefty £1.65 for a decent view, but only 100,000 were eventually allocated – a mere 20% over the official capacity. The majority of these cramped fans returned home happy after a 3-0 Dinamo win, but at least the Cardiff players and management could reflect on their exit over a nice cup of tea and a carrot from Welsh soil.

Back at Parc y Scarlets, I was expecting a backlash from the East Europeans, but it never materialised and the second half continued in much the same vein as the first with the Reds in ascendance. On 51 minutes, there was more cause for celebration thanks to man of the moment Follows, who capitalised on a defensive mix-up by Dinamo to run clear on goal and curl a wonderful left foot shot into the top corner.

I wish I could say that the crowd went wild, but it was more like a generous gathering of locals and a vocal pocket of twenty dedicated Georgians. In total, there were only 552 fans huddled together in the main stand, while the other three sides of the ground were closed. Llanelli were putting on a wonderful show on a famous night and their efforts deserved far greater support.

As the game drew to a close, the pressure from the visitors was increasingly intense and Ashley Morris produced a miraculous save from a shot in the six yard box to maintain the Reds' advantage. Unfortunately, Tblisi didn't have to wait much longer to grab a precious away goal as with only nine minutes left, Lloyd Grist was caught the wrong side of his man and after a tussle in the penalty area, the referee awarded a penalty. David Odikadze confidently dispatched the spot-kick to boost the visitors' chances of a second leg comeback.

The Reds could've folded in the face of such disappointment but chose to regroup and press forward in the hope of stretching their slender advantage – it was no more than their performance deserved. In the final seconds of added time, winger Craig Williams looked certain to restore the two-goal advantage, but Dinamo goalkeeper Giogi Loria used his 6'6" frame to get his fingertips to a cheeky chip and push the ball wide.

Victory was briefly celebrated by the vociferous few who'd bothered to turn up and I was left to hope, beyond hope, that the players and officials of this minute club would get the praise and recognition that such a scoreline deserved. It was a great result for Welsh football in general, with thirteen of the fourteen Llanelli players used hailing from Wales, including a trio of youngsters who'd come through the academy ranks at Stebonheath.

"To beat a club with the stature of Dinamo Tblisi is an outstanding achievement," said player-manager Andy Legg after the match.

"I'm really chuffed for the lads and it doesn't really mater what happens in the second leg – they can go out there and hold their head up high and give it their best shot.

"They've got nothing to lose."

***

The omens weren't good from the start.

Andy Legg's squad assembled at Gatwick but were forced to leave without their physiotherapist, Chris Miller, who was grounded after losing his passport. The Reds management had to arrange cover with a local Tbilisi based physio instead.

Things didn't improve at the Boris Paichadze National Stadium either, where the Reds were simply outclassed.[1] The luxury of being able to call upon Rhys Griffiths, Chris Holloway and Chris Venables made little difference as they slumped to a 5-0 defeat in front of an 18,000 crowd.

Football at this level is about more than just results though. It's about community, commitment and charity. In this respect, all involved with Llanelli AFC can be proud of their efforts in representing Wales. Ahead of the match, club officials visited the Tsisartkela (Rainbow) Day Centre for underprivileged children in Tbilisi to donate gifts.

Working children is a recent problem in the Georgian society and is a result of economic hardship, forceful displacement and migration faced by groups of children in the large cities. They work from morning till night as "loaders" – sellers trading in cigarettes and other items. These children are thus left without schooling and proper development.

The centre aims to assist such children, aged between six and 16, by providing the micro-environment for meaningful development, education and entertainment. It has been running since 2002. British Ambassador Judith Gough was present to see Llanelli officials present the children with football shirts and scarves. Extra gifts, mainly books, educational aids and medicines, were bought from donations from Llanelli players and supporters, which raised 1,000 Georgian Lari (nearly £400).

Ambassador Gough said: "I am delighted to see Llanelli AFC in Tbilisi

---

[1] In 1995, the National Stadium was renamed as the Boris Paichadze National Stadium. Paichadze was a legendary former Georgian football player who scored 105 goals in 190 games for Tblisi, according to Wikipedia.

and wish them success in the match tomorrow. I'm also very grateful for the charitable work they do and I hope they and the children will enjoy this day. Centres such as Tsisartkela do a vital job and it is important that we support them."

Llanelli AFC has a proud tradition of doing charity work in various countries over the last five years. They have visited orphanages in Lithuania (twice) and Latvia, and have funded a holiday for a group of Scottish children. Furthermore, children from Latvia and Lithuania have visited Wales as guests of the club.

Llanelli manager Andy Legg said: "It is a small gesture towards the hospitality we receive in the places we visit in Europe. To see the smiles on the children's faces brings home how lucky we are as a club to be playing in such a European competition as the Europa Cup, while we hope that when the children grow up they will have learned and developed at the centre to give themselves the opportunity to continue to develop as adults and make a contribution to Georgian society."

***

On the face of it, Welsh football was in a pretty appalling state. The national team had sunk to an embarrassing 114th in the latest FIFA world rankings and none of the Welsh Premier clubs competing in Europe had survived past July. In addition, Champions League representatives Bangor City suffered a record-breaking defeat in Finland and the critics were having a field day.

YEAR	COMP	RND	CLUB AGG OPPONENT		H	A
2011-12	CL	Q2	Bangor City 0-13 HJK Helsinki (FIN)		0-3	0-10
	EL	Q1	Neath 1-6 Aalesunds FK (NOR)		0-2	1-4
	EL	Q1	TNS 2-1 Cliftonville (NIR)		1-1	1-0
	EL	Q2	Llanelli 2-6 Dinamo Tbilisi (GEO)		2-1	0-5
	EL	Q2	TNS 3-8 FC Midtjylland (DEN)		1-3	2-5

EVERY SILVER LINING HAS A CLOUD Nathan Lee Davies

Such disappointing scorelines make easy work for lazy journalists, who are only too eager to pour scorn on a fledgling national league.

However, supporters of the Welsh Premier League should not be reading the knee-jerk reactions of the mass media, but the more reflective and considered thoughts of insightful writers, such as Dave Jones of the *Daily Post,* or serial blogger Mark Pitman, who both argue that the picture is not quite as bleak as it appears.

Jones covers football at all levels throughout north Wales and considers statistics when defending the record of Welsh Premier clubs in Europe. He points out that during the first five campaigns (1993-94 to 1997-98), our teams could only muster three wins in 40 matches in Europe – a dismal win percentage of 7.5. This has subsequently improved over the last five seasons (2007-08 to 2011-12) and our boys have recorded nine victories in 48 games – a win ratio of 18.75%.

While conceding that the record of Welsh Premier clubs in Europe is still statistically poor – just 21 wins in 168 matches – Jones argues that things, overall, have been getting better in recent years, and believes that the quality of opposition faced in 2011 must be taken into account.

For example, Bangor competed really well against an exceptional HJK Helsinki side, who regularly record high scores in the domestic competition they dominate. The 0-3 "home" defeat at Rhyl's Belle Vue ground was undeserved and they competed well for the first 45 minutes in Helsinki, despite trailing 2-0. It was just one bad half, where they conceded eight goals, which ended up making things look a lot worse than they were. The part-timers from north Wales had succumbed to a squad full of professional athletes and internationals, underlining the need for greater financial investment in the Welsh game.

EVERY SILVER LINING HAS A CLOUD Nathan Lee Davies

Meanwhile, Mark Pitman highlights the progress made by TNS in recent seasons. Their previous results in Europe had earned the full-time side a place in the seeded pot for the opening round of this year's UEFA Europa League, the first time a club from the Welsh Premier League had earned this right. This also meant that for the first time, a club from the national league went into the opening round match as favourites to progress, which they did after beating Cliftonville

Neath – who were undergoing the transition to a full-time operation at the time – also competed well against a team that was full of international players. They actually took the lead in Norway, through a Lee Trundle free-kick, before FK Aalesund replied with four goals ahead of the second leg in south Wales. This return match saw the Eagles perform superbly well, create enough chances to threaten a comeback and were unfortunate to lose 0-2. This was far from a disgrace.

Jones concludes that no club from our national league is ever going to win a European competition and the best we can hope for is progression through a round or two, a good payday and some decent quality pre-season practice. This is probably true, but I'm a dreamer and hope that one day, albeit in the far future, the progress and improvement that is being made, will lead to European glory for a Welsh Premier club.

Just don't hold your breath...

Parc y Scarlets

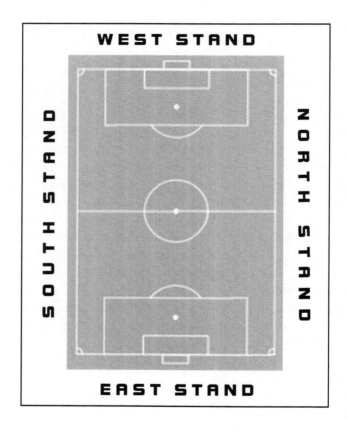

11
Cheers

EVERY SILVER LINING HAS A CLOUD Nathan Lee Davies

I've never been much of a family man. Why people occasionally gather with others they don't like merely because they share the same gene pool is beyond me. It's another form of pigeon-holing, and I'll continue to resist being boxed up and categorised with these virtual strangers for as long as I live. There are a few exceptions to this rule though, and as I arrived back where I belong I was happy to find my dad was waiting for me; breaking the habit of a lifetime and arriving on time.

I was exhausted after an arduous journey and looking forward to a good night's sleep in a warm and comfortable bed. The problem was that it was already 8pm and I didn't have a clue where I'd be spending the night. At this stage, I faced the very real prospect of drifting off to sleep underneath the stars beside the gin-soaked tramps that occupy local bus shelters and eat scraps of discarded food outside McDonalds that even the pigeons avoid. Still, it was preferable to lying beside my soon-to-be ex-wife and her volcanic arse.

The problem was that I needed an accessible place to lay my head, but none of my immediate family could provide such a luxury. I needed a building without steps that featured wide doorways and an accessible bathroom complete with the requisite monkey bars and emergency alarm in case of a fall. A 42" plasma TV and a copy of *The Bare Wench Project* – starring Penthouse Pet of the Year (1993) Julie Strain as the Bare Wench – would've been nice, but as I'd spent much of the train journey reading up on how to maintain a fire in an oil drum, it's fair to say I was prepared for the worst.

I retired to the pub to consider my options. I didn't choose any old pub though. I chose the Turf – on the corner of the Racecourse Ground. I was home.

The Cae Ras had been a venue for sporting events, including horse racing and cricket, since the early nineteenth century. Sportsmen and disillusioned punters found refreshment in a building called the Turf Tavern, built between 1840 and 1844, though that building was knocked down and replaced by the current one in the 1860s. This pub has history; prior to the completion of the Mold Road Stand in 1999, it was renowned for being contained within the Racecourse with a viewing balcony that overlooked the pitch.

In the mid-1990's, I often frequented the alehouse before and after big games as well as during Wednesday afternoon breaks from college when my mates and I would crowd around the pool table as we potted for high stakes – 20p or a packet of pork scratchings. The pub boasted a lounge for the serious drinkers at the front of the building that I rarely ever frequented, and a livelier recreational area to the rear, complete with the aforementioned pool table, dart board, 20" colour TV, and jukebox. I was also impressed by the countless scarves and pennants that adorned the walls – but there was a problem.

This was 1995 and the smoking ban in pubs was a mere pipe dream for campaigners, so when you stepped foot in any drinking establishment, but especially the Turf, you had to wade through thick clouds of cigarette smoke that had discoloured the walls, ceiling and decorative memorabilia with a dirty yellow tint. If I'm ever diagnosed with a smoking related disease, I'll know where I contracted it. To make matters worse, the jukebox hadn't been updated since 1978, so the only half-decent tunes that ever emanated from this dilapidated machine were "Hotel California" by the Eagles or "Wrexham is the Name" – a stirring anthem sung to the tune of "Men of Harlech", in recognition of the club's golden era, which led to promotion to the second tier of English football, European success and famous victories in domestic cup competitions. The song is extremely stirring to Wrexham fans and preferable to anything else the jukebox had to offer, unless you fancied a dry slap from one of the many tattooed and bejewelled knuckleheads who frequented this joint.

I'm happy to report that the Turf has since had an extensive makeover by Marston's Brewery and is now a clean and pleasant environment in which to enjoy a pint, shoot some pool, throw darts, watch sport on a widescreen TV or select decent tunes from an updated jukebox. The problem was that the adjacent football ground now hosted substandard non-league football and the club was in disarray – since 2002 it had been plagued by political struggles and underhand dealings in the boardroom, as well as a period spent in administration with the very real threat of liquidation.

Suddenly supporting Wrexham had become a chore. I'd always used football as a release from the pressures and strains of my stressful personal life, but now I was being asked to sign petitions, join protests and raise money for a club in crisis. I simply had too many problems of my own to worry about preserving football at the Cae Ras for future generations. Cheering on legends such as Mickey Thomas, Joey Jones or Gary Bennett used to help me forget my problems, but I couldn't get as enthusiastic about acne-ridden teenagers hoofing long-balls against Eastbourne Borough. All in all, the shambles that I returned to was unrecognisable from the club I left behind in 2001, which mirrored my own fall from grace.

"Dakota" by the Stereophonics blasted out of the loudspeakers as I sipped a Diet Coke and longed for a return of the shit pub – good football days, which beat the current combination hands down, however much I enjoyed browsing the stain-free memorabilia that adorned the walls.

My attentions returned to the more pressing concerns of my sleeping arrangements. After dropping a series of heavy hints, my dad kindly offered to bankroll a few nights at a local hotel to allay my immediate fears, but the long term future still worried me as my sister and brother-in-law joined us in the pub.

I've always been close to my sister and I was happy to see her, but I could tell she had something on her mind. Conversation was stilted; she looked white as a sheet and was decidedly edgy. Her husband wasn't much better. There was something afoot and with my recent run of luck I was preparing myself for more negative news that could tip me over the edge. A one-way ticket to Switzerland was looking more appealing with every passing second...

"I'm pregnant. You're going to be an uncle."

I'd only been home for half an hour, but I already had a reason to look forward to the future with hope in my heart.

Maybe this family lark isn't too bad after all.

Afan Lido 0 Prestatyn Town 1

Corbett Sports Welsh Premier League
Saturday, 13 August 2011
14:30

Marston's Stadium / Stadiwm Marston's
Attendance: 188

.

Despite only being formed in 1967, rapidly rising to become founder members of the League of Wales and lifting the inaugural League Cup in 1992-93 and again in 1993-94, it had been six years since Afan Lido had last hosted top flight football at their modest home. On the 9th April 2005, Lido beat NEWI Cefn Druids, with the game's only goal scored by Karl Reynolds, to give themselves a lifeline in their battle against relegation. Unfortunately, it was not enough as three successive away defeats, combined with a three point deduction by the FAW for fielding a suspended player, eventually led to their relegation from the 18-team league.

Lido hadn't exactly bowed out in a blaze of glory, but their return was greeted with much enthusiasm. Despite only finishing as runners-up in the Welsh League to Bryntirion Athletic, who hadn't even applied to play in the WPL, the Aberavon outfit had been granted a FAW domestic license to become one of just three clubs to gain promotion from the south Wales feeder league in over a decade.

Kim Bowley had been manager of the Seasiders for just over a year, but despite winning promotion in his first full season, Bowley was thanked by being sacked and immediately replaced with Andy Dyer. That's right, the man who'd been in charge at Neath for nine successful years was surprisingly sacked by the Eagles for reasons that were never made clear.

A club statement was released by Lido, which read as follows:

EVERY SILVER LINING HAS A CLOUD Nathan Lee Davies

An opportunity became available to speak to Andy and the outcome of those discussions has resulted in him being appointed manager with immediate effect.

We would like to thank the outgoing management team of Kim Bowley and Vince Lewis for their hard work carried out over the last few seasons and in gaining promotion last term. We are extremely grateful for their valuable contribution over that period and are hopeful both remain at the club in some capacity.

Andrew comes to the club having gained experience over the last few seasons with Neath, taking them to a third place finish last year and a place in Europe for the first time. Andrew has a Pro Licence which complies with both UEFA and domestic licence criteria. Andy brings his assistant, Ray Pennock, with him.

Dyer, who'd been recognised for his achievements with Neath, as one of three FAW nominations for manager of the season for 2010-11, now had survival on his mind in very different surroundings.

My dad was losing his rag as we drove around the gloomy landscape of south Wales in a circle. We stopped to ask for directions and received precise instructions that led us to the GenQuip Stadium, home of Port Talbot Town, who were playing away against Airbus UK Broughton. The old man almost burst a blood vessel, but I assured him it was a good sign as Lido play less than half a mile away from their rivals in the neighbouring district of Aberavon. We didn't have far to go.

Twenty minutes later, we were circling the Marston's Stadium in search of an entrance. The unimaginative floodlights and oppressive perimeter fencing could be seen between the dull and lifeless houses that scream depression and do nothing to inspire visitors, let alone residents, but there was no sign of a car park or turnstiles. I was getting thirsty for colour by the time we stumbled on the entry point and rushed into the ground to be invigorated by splashes of red and white after our depressing journey around dreary streets.

The Marston's Stadium is plonked on the edge of a estate and is nestled between houses and obscured by a retail park. There is not much to boast about in this 4,200 capacity ground, which includes two stands at either side of the pitch and hard standing behind both goals.

The main stand is a standard collection of covered seats, which does little to intrigue, unlike the older structure directly opposite. Three rows of seats are covered by a corrugated iron roof, through which a step ladder rises up to the required television gantry. The dug-outs are positioned in front of this stand, so spectators have to contend with three supporting posts as well as managers and substitutes bobbing up and down between them and the pitch. The back of the stand is painted in magnolia with AFAN LIDO spelt out in large red letters, making it pleasing to the eye.

I was enjoying an investigative circuit of the ground when I met a steward, dressed in a compulsory orange florescent jacket. Like everyone I met that afternoon, he was charmingly friendly and clearly wanted me to enjoy myself in his corner of the world. He was concerned that I'd have to abort my imaginary lap of honour due to the obstructive presence of a floodlight along the path I was travelling on. Pointing to the controls on my electric wheelchair, he tried to reassure me:

"If you get stuck up ahead just toot your horn and I'll come to your rescue."

It was a tight squeeze between the floodlight, the edge of the path and the steep grass embankment, but I made it, which was almost a pity after such a kind offer. It had meant a lot to me as it was a sincere gesture without a trace of condescending tones. Such warmth was found all around the ground from the humorous old dear who offered me the first pie to be sold at Marston's Stadium, to the alluring young lady who promised to lead me to the club shop.

I followed her into the Lido social club – a typical bar area complete with garish carpet and heavy velvet curtains. The fruit machine chimed a lively jingle as I followed the shapely arse to what I imagined would be a back room full of merchandise for me to spend my money on. Instead, my guide ducked behind the bar and began rummaging underneath the lager pumps before pulling out a small, dusty cardboard box and dumping it on the bar.

"This is the club shop," she said, most sincerely.

I peered into the tired box to find a handful of badges and a screwed up piece of paper from the days of dot matrix. I immediately recognized the glitzy shards of enamel from my own collection of pins, but decided that I'd have to buy one after all the trouble my new friend had gone to. I also wanted to show my support for a small-scale football club that may not have the most impressive infrastructure, but more than make up for it by creating a welcoming and friendly atmosphere, free from pretentions.

Am I being patronising? I don't mean to be and neither do I want to offer unnecessary criticism but, as Roy Walker insisted on reminding me through my formative years, I must say what I see. With this in mind, I turned my attention to the matchday magazine.

At first glance the programme seemed professionally produced, glossy and colourful. All the essential information was included amongst evidence that the commercial team had been successfully spending the summer months selling advertising space to boost the coffers and raise enough funds to ensure the club could afford to fulfil forthcoming fixtures. Such practicalities take precedent over the time-consuming chore of compiling an entertaining magazine bursting with illuminating articles. I understand and accept this, but cannot, under any circumstances, forgive sloppy spelling or a blatant disregard for punctuation.

Even if the editor's first language is Welsh, which I doubt from the distinct lack of Welsh employed in these pages, this doesn't excuse the shambolic use of English in Andy Dyer's programme notes:

> Can first of all i-welcome prestatyn and Gibbo to the Lido for what is our first welsh prem game in 6 years, and a huge game it is for this club too. We are back wear this club belongs and are fighting for our first 3 points of the season.

Where do I start?

Surely, we should be expressing ourselves clearly and precisely in whichever language we choose to use, but I'm afraid this is not the case here. I'm not criticising Andy Dyer, as his talent clearly lies in other areas, but someone at the club – the tea ladies even – could've checked his notes before they went to print. It's basic junior school stuff.

My anal frustrations were at boiling point, so it probably wasn't the best time to read "Pen's Page", in which we were promised a light-hearted view of life at Afan Lido, complete with needless exclamation marks over half a page. To open the season, Pen decides to simply list the nicknames he has decided to force upon the unsuspecting players during 2011-12. In typical playground fashion they're rather predictable: Chris Pridham is Prids, Andy Hill becomes Hillo and the footballer formerly known as Andrew Mumford is transformed into Mumf. Pen must have spent hours dreaming up such original monikers, but now it was time to close the programme in despair and watch Orange Face, Trigger, Jock and company take on Prestatyn.

EVERY SILVER LINING HAS A CLOUD Nathan Lee Davies

I'm not in a position to comment on the quality of football in the regional feeder leagues as I haven't ever watched a game at that level, but the polished performance of Afan Lido suggests that there are clubs of quality playing in the MacWhirter Welsh League, which has to be an encouraging sign for Welsh football. Having said that, Dyer had been busy in the transfer market and had made no less than 11 new signings to strengthen his squad, including three of his former players, who were released from Neath; Llanelli youngster Declan John; and Port Talbot Town midfielder Liam McCreesh.

Prestatyn lined up without last season's top goal scorer Lee Hunt, who'd made a surprise summer move to Bala Town after notching sixteen league goals for the north Wales Seasiders last term – including two in the game I'd seen against Port Talbot at Bastion Gardens. I was interested to see how the visitors would cope without Hunt as they'd been quiet in the transfer market and had no obvious replacement. They were also without the influential duo of Gareth Wilson and Paul O'Neill, through suspension and injury, so it seemed that they'd have a tough afternoon in store.

So it proved. It took only eight minutes for Lido to hit the back of the net, but Hoody (Jonathan Hood) had his effort ruled offside before Prestatyn's Dave Roberts, a summer signing from Newtown, was called upon to perform heroics between the sticks with smart saves from Creeshy (Liam McCreesh) and Golden Nugget (Leon Jeanne). The home side also hit the bar through Jonah (Mark Jones) before Prestatyn found their feet and started to assert themselves.

On the half hour, Ross Stephens was sent clear on goal with only the goalkeeper to beat, but couldn't quite keep his feet on the greasy surface and made a right tit of himself with a chance that Hunty would've buried. However, his blushes were spared when a neat ball in from the right dropped to Dan Evans, who took his time to place an angled drive beyond the keeper's reach to give the north Walians an undeserved half-time lead.

EVERY SILVER LINING HAS A CLOUD Nathan Lee Davies

Lido started the second half full of determination and Town were indebted to their new shot stopper once again as Jeanne's crisp shot forced Roberts to react quickly to smother the ball successfully. Soon after, the impressive Jeanne hammered another effort a foot wide.

Disaster struck for the away side on the hour when Martin Beattie received his second yellow card, and with ten minutes left it looked like Lido would level after Roberts brought down Hood in the box. Jeanne picked up the ball and faced his rival for the man of the match award from 12 yards to decide who would walk away with a bottle of corked wine.

It was the debutant keeper who came out on top as he saved Jeanne's tame spot kick to leave Lido rueing missed opportunities. Before the referee blew the full time whistle there was still time for the luckless Jeanne, Mark Jones and substitute Tyrone Topper to go close, but the ten men of Town held on for three unlikely points.

Half an hour later I was enjoying a Budweiser in the Afan Lido social club. The lounge area was full to capacity and there seemed to be more people crushed into this drinking hole than were watching the match. I'd managed to get a prime position, directly in front of a generous widescreen television, which was showing *Gillette Soccer Saturday* to frustrated followers of Andy Dyer's side. There was not much interest shown as Jeff Stelling informed us that Stilian Petrov had been shown a yellow card at Craven Cottage or that Yeovil Town had added a third from the penalty spot against Oldham, but I was secretly happy that Wrexham were beating Cambridge United 1-0 at the Racecourse.[1]

I felt a little guilty for missing my home town club in action on the opening day of the season, but it was something that had to be done

---

[1] For the life of me, I still can't understand why a WPL club were showing *Gillette Soccer Saturday* ahead of S4C's live coverage of the day's late kick-off between Bangor City and Llanelli, at Farrar Road. The home side got revenge for their Welsh Cup final defeat with a thrilling 3-2 victory.

as I needed to finish the tour I'd started and develop the ideas that had been floating around my head for eons into something solid. I was being selfish, but my need for creative productivity was just as great as Wrexham's need for promotion back to the Football League. I was putting myself before the club, which is something I wouldn't have dreamt of doing as a teenager. I guess I'm maturing at last.

My guilt and sense of regret was compounded by the events of the previous week, in which Wrexham fans from all over the world showed true spirit, loyalty, and dedication to the club by digging deep into their personal savings to raise the £100,000 demanded by Conference chiefs to demonstrate the Reds' financial ability to meet their league commitments for 2011-12. This was above and beyond the call of duty and is a tribute to a fantastic set of supporters.

Still, I had every reason to be proud of myself as I celebrated the halfway point of my tour of WPL grounds. Research and writing had been going well and I was looking forward to an overnight stay in Llanelli before a trip to the Gnoll to watch Neath take on Aberystwyth Town in the Sunday fixture. I'd enjoyed a great game of football at a friendly club and was now drinking alongside freshly showered semi-professionals, who mingled with fans in a convivial atmosphere.

One man I was definitely happier than was former QPR and Cardiff City winger Leon Jeanne who cut a lonely and pensive figure as he stared into a refreshing glass of fruit juice at the bar. He looked to have the weight of the world on his shoulders after missing a penalty on his debut. Supporters were patting him on the back and trying to encourage him, but he clearly blamed himself for Lido's pointless start to the campaign. This was a shame as he was their best player by far and will be integral to Andy Dyer's hopes of keeping the club in the top-flight based on this performance.

The vidi-printer began to churn out a series of full-time results when it decided to break my heart by informing me that Cambridge midfielder Conal Platt had notched an injury-time equaliser with the help of a wicked defection.

I joined the Golden Nugget by the bar and ordered a double whisky...

Afan Lido
Marston's Stadium

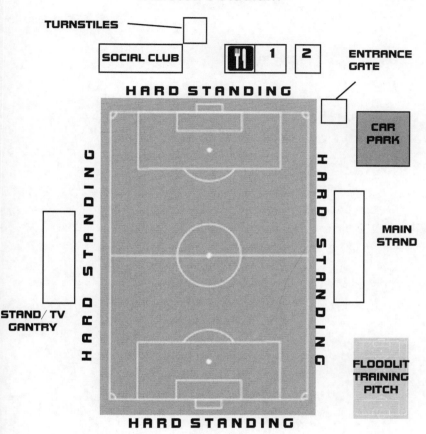

TURNSTILES

SOCIAL CLUB

🍴 **1** **2**

ENTRANCE GATE

HARD STANDING

CAR PARK

HARD STANDING

HARD STANDING

MAIN STAND

STAND/ TV GANTRY

FLOODLIT TRAINING PITCH

HARD STANDING

1) CHANGING ROOMS
2) EXECUTIVE LOUNGE/MEDIA UNIT

12
Dead End Street

EVERY SILVER LINING HAS A CLOUD Nathan Lee Davies

And in the end, it's not the years in your life that count. It's the life in your years.

Abraham Lincoln
16th US President (1861-1865)

I woke up on my 32nd birthday in Room 301 of the Ramada Plaza hotel, Wrexham, knowing that I had a host of problems to overcome before I could even contemplate cramming some much needed life into my empty years. I wiped small stones of debris from my half-closed eyes, took a deep breath and began an extensive rebuilding process, while bearing in mind the fact that things often have to get a lot worse before they get any better...

I'd arranged a breakfast meeting in the hotel bar, but I wouldn't be donning a suit and tie to discuss the exchange rate mechanism over a plate of smoked salmon and an Espresso Macchiato. Instead, I was scruffily adorned in an old Miami Dolphins sweatshirt and a pair of faded jeans as I met with solemn-faced council officials, social workers and housing officers over a plate of burnt toast and a plastic cup of sour orange juice.

Under the circumstances, I didn't have much of an appetite anyway. There is something about having to declare yourself homeless that reduces the appeal of a hearty breakfast. Even the offer of one of a selection of variety box cereals failed to move me. I had lost my snap, crackle and pop, and just wanted a solution to my accommodation problems.

Ideally, I was about to be offered a two-bedroom bungalow near the Racecourse, but if this wasn't possible I was prepared to stay at the Ramada for a couple of weeks while details were ironed out. I didn't think I was being unreasonable and even expected some slight delays and inconveniences before securing a place of my own.

As I listened to the local bureaucrats drone on about legislation, financial assistance, planning permission and other dry topics, I could feel my hopes of a quick climb up the property ladder evaporating. It seemed that Wrexham Council were determined to mummify me in red tape as I had specific requirements that they just couldn't meet with a limited portfolio of suitable housing at their disposal. If I was a single parent, a drug addict or had just been released from prison then things might have been different, but, as it was, all I could do was just sit and wait for some poor bugger living in accessible accommodation to die.

I was already preparing myself for a new career as a serial killer, specialising in the murders of elderly gentlemen living in attractive council properties, when the conversation turned to my sleeping arrangements for the immediate future. I thought I could cope with an extended stay in the four-star hotel that had provided me with shelter the night previously. Attractive reception staff, room service and a varied selection of porn channels made such a stay appealing, but it wasn't cheap. Depending on the time of year, each night could cost between £60 and £100. This was far too expensive for a local council with a tight budget, so I suggested relocation to a nearby Travelodge – much to the amusement of unimpressed officials.

While I was depressed in Scotland, my condition deteriorated and my weight ballooned, which meant it was increasingly difficult and dangerous to get from my wheelchair onto a bed. Ever since losing the ability to bear weight on my legs, I'd been using a transfer board as a movement aid. This is a piece of polished wood that would be slipped underneath my arse and thighs to enable me to shuffle across, with support, from one surface to another. As I was getting heavier and less agile I required more support and was putting myself, and those helping me, at risk of injury.

My social worker was not impressed when he heard about this dangerous manoeuvre and, after seeing a demonstration, decided that I needed more support than my dad and his dodgy back could provide. As a result, he thought the only solution was to start using an electric hoist system to safely move me from one surface to the other. Such equipment is widely available in care homes, where there would be professional carers on hand around the clock to attend to my every need at the push of a button.

I freaked out. I'd never experienced personal care before. I'd always relied on my parents or ex-partners to assist me, but now I was facing institutionalisation before my time. It was humiliating enough to have to ask for help from those I was close to, but I would now have to have my bollocks washed by perfect strangers in a clinical environment. In between mouthfuls of brioche, I was reassured by the civil servants that my stay in residential care would be a brief one and I'd be permanently housed within six months. With no alternative option available, I'd have to grin and bear it.

What had happened to the confident young university graduate who was climbing the journalistic ladder at the turn of the century? Arrangements were made for me to move into Pendine Park care home at the end of the week and the meeting broke up. Notebooks were closed, breakfast crumbs were swept away and my fate had been decided by people I hadn't met an hour ago.

I returned to my room full of anxiety, confusion and depression. I was stuck in reverse without any guiding lights and little to look forward to. If it wasn't for my imminent qualification as an uncle, I don't know what I would've done.

There was a large red envelope in between the telephone and complimentary sachets of Nescafe on the bedside table. I held the sealed card up to the light that peered weakly through the window and squinted. It was just about possible to see a faint outline of two anonymous footballers from the seventies locked in an aerial challenge for a lofted ball underneath two mysteriously floating words: Happy Birthday.

I threw the card across the room and started to cry.

Neath 4 Aberystwyth Town 2

Corbett Sports Welsh Premier League
Sunday, 14 August 2011
14:30

The Gnoll / Y Gnoll
Attendance: 476

You've done too much, much too young

The Specials
"Too Much Too Young"
1979

TOO MUCH, TOO YOUNG (DAMMERS) ©1979 Plangent Visions Music Limited

Neath Football Club has only existed in its current form since 2005, when neighbouring Welsh League outfits Skewen Athletic and Neath decided it was in both clubs' best interests to merge. I could now launch into protracted paragraphs that trace the history and development of both clubs prior to the merger, but it's really not that interesting and the few that are bothered can launch a Google search to garner information, while the rest of us do something less boring instead.

Originally christened Neath Athletic, the new outfit played their Welsh League Division One home games at Llandarcy Park and enjoyed instant success, finishing their first season as runners-up. Champions Goytre United declined a step-up to the Welsh Premier League, so Neath could've won promotion at the first attempt if not for problems meeting the ground criteria. Athletic worked hard on making all the necessary improvements to their ground and in 2006-07, this off-field effort was matched by some sterling performances from Andy Dyer's men, who ensured a place in the top flight as champions with a league record 92 points.

EVERY SILVER LINING HAS A CLOUD Nathan Lee Davies

Their first season at the top of the pyramid saw the Eagles achieve a highly credible seventh position in the 18-team league. However, it was clear that the set-up at Llandarcy Park would make it impossible to meet new UEFA ground criteria, so the search for a new home began. After exploring their options, the club entered a ground share with Neath RFC at the Gnoll from the start of 2008-09. Here we go again. South Walians and their bewildering combination of rugby and football, with the newcomers cast as ugly bridesmaids to the glorious goddesses of Welsh sport. It's all foreign to me.

Speaking at the time, rugby club chairman Geraint Hawkes said: "By joining forces in a ground share agreement the clubs, Neath community and surrounding areas will benefit hugely.

"There are now genuine opportunities to develop the Gnoll as its historic, but ageing, facilities need to be extensively upgraded to accommodate both codes.

"The prospect of attracting European football is a truly exciting one, which will bring much needed revenue into the community.

"This is yet another chapter in Neath rugby's proud history and one that I feel is vital and in-keeping with our long term ambitions."

The Gnoll has been home to the rugby union side – known as the Welsh All Blacks – since the club formed in 1871. It has also hosted cricket and, more recently, rugby league. However, when the Eagles played Swansea City in a friendly to mark the beginning of their tenancy in July 2008, it was the first football match to be played at the venue. I was surprised by this as the historic stadium seems ideal for football, but the ghostly voices that echo around the Gnoll all reminisce about classic conversions, fantastic flankers and terrific tries. Whatever floats your boat, I suppose.

I spotted the Gnoll on the distant horizon thanks to an impressive set of traditional floodlight pylons on each corner of the ground that reminded me of the ones at the Racecourse, and brought back fond memories of illuminated midweek matches at my spiritual home. These majestic pillars of light were not in use on this pleasant Sunday afternoon in south Wales, but nevertheless they acted as superb guides when trying to find the ground. Who needs satellite navigation when you've got such aesthetically pleasing landmarks?

My floodlight fetish excited me from afar, but when I got closer and passed through the Gnoll's ornate gates, I quickly realised that this arena is far too big for Welsh Premier football. It is good that they have room to grow into, but it will be many years before they average four figures, let alone the 6,500 needed to fill the Gnoll.

As usual, today's gate was below the 500 mark, so only one side of the ground was open, comprised of two separate stands built over the top of the dressing room and club offices. The main section of seating is the original stand with its low multi-columned roof supporting a rickety TV gantry while an extra stand, of similar design, was added at a later date. These structures are complimented by blocks of temporary uncovered seats running along their base and covering a former paddock. In total, around 2,000 seats are positioned along this side of the pitch, while the players emerge from entrance doors between the two stands.

Along the opposite side of the pitch is a temporary, lightweight construction that holds around 1,000 seats, with a low canvas roof and several supportive columns to hinder the viewing public. To the left of this disappointing arrangement is the Town End of the ground, which is an impressive section of covered terracing, complete with sturdy crash barriers. It's probably not much to write home about in relation to famous terraces of world football, but I'd become accustomed to basic hard standing areas in the WPL, so this was a real treat for me. Behind the opposite goal is a smaller terrace that is open to the elements. All in all, I was quite impressed with the traditional elements that the Gnoll had to offer, but on closer inspection there was much to disappoint...

EVERY SILVER LINING HAS A CLOUD Nathan Lee Davies

As mentioned previously, I have a large collection of enamel badges. These emblems only cost between £2 and £3, but serve as good mementos of the day, while taking up less room than a bundle of musty programmes. The problem was that I couldn't find a club shop anywhere in the Gnoll and this apparent lack of commercial enterprise was confirmed by the programme seller.

Maybe, as I'd found yesterday, the social club was home to a dusty box of badges? Unfortunately, I was unable to find out as the licensed premises were situated in an inaccessible part of the ground, between the main stand and open terrace. Fellow fans were staggering up and down the small set of steps that led to the bustling bar area, but if I wanted to mingle with these like-minded psychopaths, I was expected to leave the stadium and access the main entrance from the street. This was a massive ball-ache with kick-off fast approaching, and not even the faint possibility of adding to my badge collection could entice me on this inconvenient and discriminatory jaunt. I would be forced to return home without a souvenir of my visit and, perhaps more worrying, I would have to watch Neath do battle with Aberystwyth Town while stone cold sober. It really was most frustrating.

Perhaps I'd find a merchandise catalogue in the lightweight 16-page programme? This anorexic edition favoured style over content; although it looked the part, it had very little to offer those interested in finding out more about Neath or their opponents. It was disappointing to find large white spaces on the few pages not filled with adverts, while it says a lot that I thought the highlight of this glorified pamphlet was the back page advertisement for Gnollfest 2011 – a music festival held at the Gnoll. This had been organised by the rugby club and featured a half-decent line-up including Terrorvision, the Bluetones and an extensive list of support acts. This additional talent was headed by a group called Marseille. I'd never heard of them either, until an illuminating piece of text informed me that this group features Neil Buchanan of *Art Attack* fame. I could barely wait to get home and find a video clip of the former *Finders*

Keepers presenter in musical action, but first I had a football match to watch.

As the players took to the field, an unfamiliar figure took to the Neath dug-out, following Andy Dyer's surprise dismissal in the summer. Dyer had achieved so much in such a short space of time. He twice led Skewen Athletic to promotion from the doldrums before taking charge of the newly-merged club and guiding them into the WPL. This was topped off with European qualification, following their play-off triumph over Prestatyn. Despite this incredible recent success – which came just six years after their formation – he'd left the club under a cloud in the summer and clearly felt he'd been stabbed in the back.

"I am extremely disappointed with the decision." Dyer told the *South Wales Evening Post*.

"The reasons that they have given me, which I won't reveal in the press, I totally disagree with.

"The success I have brought to the club can't be questioned at all.

"I have lined up some good signings and big pre-season friendlies, which will bring a small fortune, and I have left them in the best shape they have ever been in."

Passionate words, but justifiable to an outsider such as me. There is no arguing that Dyer had done a sterling job since joining Skewen Athletic in the third tier of the Welsh League, but his efforts now seem to have been airbrushed from the club's history, judging by the lack of appreciation shown in the programme and on the club's official website. I can understand the desire to move on under a new management team, but surely there should've been some recognition of his achievements, or at least an explanation for his departure.

Instead, it was Terry Boyle who found himself in charge. Boyle has a wealth of experience in Welsh football circles as an international defender and respected coach. With this appointment, the Eagles believed they had found the man to take the club to the next level.

"Boyle was one of a number of high-calibre applicants for the role but his success in working with young players and developing talent made him the stand out choice to take the job," said a statement on the Neath website.

Boyle added: "It's a pleasure to take the job at Neath. They have had a swift rise in Welsh club football, culminating in them qualifying for European football next season.

"They have a lot of talented lads at the Gnoll and I hope to use my experience in player development to challenge for the league title.

"There are exciting times ahead at Neath and I very much look forward to playing a part in those."

Peter Nicholas, formerly part of Dyer's management team, was installed as Boyle's assistant. The former Arsenal and Luton midfielder won 73 caps for Wales and managed Barry Town and Llanelli to championship successes in 2001 and 2006 respectively.

Neath had opted to be led by a duo that had masses of experience, as opposed to a bright, young thing bursting with ambition and a determination to succeed. Only time would tell whether or not they'd made the right decision, but hopes were high that Neath were in a position to challenge for the title given that the new management had injected some much needed youth into an ageing squad. Defenders Kai Edwards and Jack Lewis joined from Prestatyn, as well as promising striker Luke Bowen, who was snapped up from Port Talbot Town. These were just the pick of the new signings that would be orchestrated by more experienced campaigners, such as Kristian O'Leary and captain fantastic, Lee Trundle. Both have played in the

EVERY SILVER LINING HAS A CLOUD Nathan Lee Davies

Football League with Swansea City, but were persuaded to join the Neath revolution by Andy Dyer.

This looked an exciting mix on paper and proved just as effective on grass as the Eagles started the domestic campaign in style. In fact, Lee Trundle took just five minutes to put them in front from a free-kick on the edge of the area that was a perfect blend of skill and fortune. The former boyfriend of Atomic Kitten star Liz McClarnon – a poor man's Posh and Becks – expertly curled the ball around the wall, only to see it cannon back off the post and rebound over the line off the back of Steve Cann in the Aber goal.

It was a flying start for the home side and it got even better after 14 minutes, when Trundle was again on hand to head on a corner into the path of Paul Fowler, who doubled the lead. It was a great start for Neath who were fulfilling their close season promise with their captain running the show and standing head and shoulders above anyone else on the pitch. Trundle was the Lionel Messi of the WPL, and on this performance he could be as influential for Neath as Diego Maradona was for Napoli in the Eighties. I'm exaggerating a little, but you get the idea.

"Magic Daps", as he's affectionately known, could clearly still do a job in the Football League and had rejected moves to League One clubs Yeovil Town, Tranmere Rovers and Swindon Town. So what was he doing at Neath?

"The club showed a lot of ambition when I sat down and spoke to them," Trundle told BBC Sport Wales.

"I spoke to a lot of league clubs as well, but the things Neath said to me, the direction the club was moving and the things they wanted to achieve appealed to me.

"I know myself I can still play in the Football League and score goals – that's never been an issue with me.

EVERY SILVER LINING HAS A CLOUD Nathan Lee Davies

"Being in the Swansea area is massive for me as well.

"Although being a Liverpool lad, I've got Swansea in my heart and I still love Swansea as a club, so to stay here and give a chance for the Swansea fans to come over and support me when I'm playing here was another big thing for me."

A few years ago I would've lambasted Trundle for not showing ambition or failing to challenge himself at the highest possible level. Part of me still believes he chose the easy option, but this is now being countered by an understanding of the appeal of community and an appreciation of the value of roots, having neglecting my own for so long. Although the decision to return to the WPL seems to be motivated solely by personal reasons, there is no denying that Trundle has increased interest in the competition and his presence is encouraging an increase in standards.

Things got worse for the visitors on 18 minutes, when defender Sion James was dismissed by referee Dean John, following his second caution in a minute. Aberystwyth Town are no mugs though. They'd also had a busy summer and manager Alan Morgan had eight new faces in his squad, four of whom were making their full competitive debuts. They were obviously keen to impress as the expected collapse never materialised. Instead, the Black and Greens dug deep, kept their shape and pulled a goal back on the half-hour mark when defender James McCarten smashed a 30-yard free-kick into the bottom corner of the goal.

The comeback didn't last for long though as barely two minutes later, Luke Bowen – who'd enjoyed a successful season with Aber in 2009-10, notching 17 goals in 34 WPL starts – latched onto a misplaced pass from Anthony Finselbach in the middle of the park, raced forward and struck decisively to restore Neath's two-goal advantage at the break.

EVERY SILVER LINING HAS A CLOUD Nathan Lee Davies

I'd enjoyed an action-packed first period but now I had to spend 15 minutes drinking bottled water due to the obstructive steps to the social club when I would've killed for some alcohol. I was also beginning to get tired after an uncomfortable night's sleep in a Port Talbot Premier Inn. I'm sure the beds are very comfortable, but I couldn't tell you as there was no electric hoist to lift me out of my wheelchair and onto a cosy mattress, which meant spending the night fighting cramp in my reclined chair while trying to ignore the satisfied snoring of my dad in the bed beside me.[1]

Subsequently, I wasn't in a good mood. I was running on very little sleep and found myself deprived of alcohol by an inability to scale steps. Little did I know, as I washed down a rather ordinary burger with Scottish water from the Campsie Fells, but things were about to get even worse.

Nature called but I couldn't find any disabled toilet facilities. A steward confirmed that I was reliving my Farrar Road nightmare and would have to spend the second half counting down the clock. It really is an appalling situation that needs addressing urgently. Wheelchair users are being discriminated against and made to feel

---

[1] Although most hotels now cater for disabled guests by providing a low percentage of minimally accessible rooms, guests that need extra adaptations for a peaceful night are forgotten about.

Many of my friends from university are now based in London after putting their degrees to good use while I continue to struggle in the sticks. I sometimes meet up with them in the Capital and require an overnight stay after drinking to the early hours. This invariably means paying for a hotel room and sleeping in my chair as I'm only aware of three hotel rooms in the whole of central London with the ceiling track hoist system I need.

Things are slowly improving, with the emphasis on slowly. Credit must go to the Holiday Inn chain for installing these devices in various hotels nationwide, including Kensington, Bloomsbury, Heathrow, Cardiff and Birmingham. Meanwhile, Premier Inn have actually installed a hoist at London Stratford, and the Copthorne Tara, Kensington boasts two fully equipped rooms. However, it'll be a long time before such innovations are the rule rather than the exception.

For more information, visit **www.chuc.org.uk**

like second-class citizens who don't deserve to use the same amenities offered to the able-bodied. Surely there are legal requirements to provide accessible toilets for all paying spectators? If not, there should be. I didn't have time to dwell on the matter as it was time for the second period, so I tied a knot in it and endured a lengthy 45 minutes.

Neath's Kerry Morgan scored five minutes into the second period with a delightful chip over Cann to seemingly seal the victory at 4-1, but Town helped me focus attention away from the river of urine that was threatening to burst through the banks of my bladder, by refusing to throw in the towel. Indeed, the visitors were in the ascendency for the last half hour, with debutant Wyn Thomas reducing the deficit with a header from one of a series of corners. Chris Doran was by far the busiest goalkeeper for the rest of the game and even had his crossbar rattled, but the full-time outfit held on for a deserved victory.

So that was the end of my weekend in south Wales. I'd enjoyed two very different games at very different grounds, but to my surprise it was my accessible day in the cosy confines of the Marston's Stadium that I'd enjoyed the most, rather than the soulless struggles experienced at the Gnoll. The tiny, semi-professional outfit from Aberavon had provided for my every need in an intimate and friendly atmosphere, while the full-timers at Neath clearly had ideas above their station and were trying to grow up much too quickly.

I probably could've dwelt on my time in the beautiful south still further and drawn more conclusions about the future development of the WPL as a whole, but this wasn't the time for thoughtful deliberations.

I really needed a piss...

***

EVERY SILVER LINING HAS A CLOUD Nathan Lee Davies

After failing to get my hands on a Neath lapel to plug the obvious Eagle-shaped hole in my collection, I was struggling to sleep. My anal tendencies were haunting me once more. There was only one solution to my problem. I logged onto eBay, typed "Neath badge" into the search box, pressed enter and hoped for the best.

I received five matches to my search, including two rugby club crests, a plastic button badge advertising Neath and Port Talbot college, which was a bargain at 99p, a Neath & District Bowling League emblem and a piece of enamel with the unmistakeable football club crest engraved upon it. I clicked on the link and bought it immediately for £2.25 + £1.25 postage using the Buy It Now button.

The seller was named badgesdana123 and operated out of Bratislava, Slovakia. A few days later, I received the attractive badge in the post and marvelled at the wonders of the Internet. It really was an absurd situation. I'd been to the club's home ground and not found any merchandise, but eventually discovered my memento in Eastern European cyberspace. I realise we are only talking about £3.50, but every little helps.

Now that the club are running on a full-time basis, I hope they recognise the need to establish a commercial department of their own and develop some much-needed business acumen.

It's the only way they'll survive...

Neath
The Gnoll

TURNSTILES

COVERED TERRACE

TEMPORARY SEATING

MAIN STAND (NEW WING)

GNOLL PARK ROAD

PLAYERS TUNNEL

MAIN STAND (ORIGINAL)

DISABLED SECTION

UNCOVERED TERRACE

SOCIAL CLUB

13
Strange Ones

EVERY SILVER LINING HAS A CLOUD Nathan Lee Davies

The following was discovered in an unopened envelope by staff at the British Heart Foundation in the bottom of a bag of donated clothing, sometime in the future.

***

There's a place where the strange ones go
Where nobody here could know
They look down from the clouds and smile at
Everyone down below

I had hit rock bottom.

Being shoved into an unstylish room with urine stains on the carpet and barely enough room to swing a cat was not the triumphant homecoming I had in mind but circumstance had led me to the most undesirable room on the entire care home complex. I could barely hide my dismay despite being assured that the unit I'd be joining provides round the clock nursing care by a highly qualified and experienced team of nurses and care practitioners. That's what it said on the website anyway.

It wasn't the sort of environment that I was used to or enjoyed being in as I hadn't ever really faced up to my own disability and was nervous about the unpredictability of my mentally disabled neighbours. I wasn't in the right frame of mind to open my mind, or my heart, to others and I kept my door firmly shut at all times to let my ignorance breed and confidence wallow. After all, my stay would only be a short one according to my social worker…

After my initial compl

One fish finger and 14 chips. I counted.

Captain Birdseye.

Buster Merryfield.

Trevor Francis tracksuits

BUSH, BUSH, **BUSH, BUSH, BUSH, BUSH**

Identity - X-Ray Spex

identity is the crisis can't you see
identity identity

when you look in the mirror
do you see yourself
do you see yourself
on the TV screen
do you see yourself in the magazine
when you see yourself
does it make you scream

when you look in the mirror
do you smash it quick
do you take the glass
and slash your wrists
did you do it for fame
did you do it in a fit
did you do it before
you read about it

"Identity"
Written by Marianne Elliott-Said
Published by Maxwood Music Limited
Used by kind permission.

<html>

<body>

<p>This is a paragraph.</p>

```
<p>This is a paragraph.</p>
<p>This is a paragraph.</p>


</body>
</html>
```

2 + 2 = 5

SWEaty, unfUCKABle lardd--arse

...full protected sex. oral without protection, cum in mouth, french kissing, anal, facial...

Everything in it's right pla**C**e

```
are wonderfull!how do you say in welsh not at
allNathan says:hmmmmmmmmmmmmm - not surei will
searchzabagaz says:diolchNathan says:did u get
text last night?zabagaz says:yesbut i was already
sleepingheheso i saw it this morningNathan
says:sorry i sent it too latedid u sleep ok
anywayzabagaz says:yestoo  muchi was so tired
yestNathan says:not at all = ddim o gwblu here all
day?I have to tell u about the other project i am
working onzabagaz says:{tellll meeeee!Nathan
says:ataxia uk are giving 5000 pounds to a member
to travelzabagaz says:ahaNathan
says:http://www.ataxia.org.uk/page.builder/travel_
fellowship.htmlzabagaz says:hahah lolololo travel
fellowship like in the lord of the
ringhahahahaNathan says:hahahahahait has to be
```

```
used in a challenging wayso my application is to
go to...zabagaz. says:mmmmmtohahahahahahNathan
says:

http://www.stagecoachtrailsranch.com/and las
vegasone moloozabagaz says:Nathan says:backzagabaz
says:croesoNathan says:diolchdid I tell u
********zabagaz says:i think soNathan says:what r u
doing today? You have invited zabagaz to start
viewing webcam. Please wait for a response or
Cancel (Alt+Q) the pending invitation. zabagaz
says:applying and going to buy some thingsNathan
says:treats 4 urself i hope zabagaz accepted
your invitation to start viewing webcam. zabagaz
says:e fish for ****Nathan says:never mind -  u
should also buy urself somethingzabagaz says:i
dont usually buy treatseyyyyyyyyyyyyyyyyyyshow me
the smileaaahhahahaeyits strangei am still ur
spionhahahahahahahahahahai can see everything u
doahahahahahaahNathan says:hahahahai want to spy
on u toohahahahahazabagaz says:hahahaits strange i
have to call btcos i dont knCHNKWKS
```

, I would turn on *The Jeremy Kyle Show* to remind myself that, compared to some, I still maintained a semblance of dignity whil

STILL I WOKE UP SUCKING ON LEMON

```
                        jAMie's School dinners
```

Take a colour – like Picasso took blue – and fill your story with it. I don't mean use the word 'blue' whenever possible, but imply it through connection – summer sky, jeans, swimming pools etc. This will feel laboured but it's a way of getting in the habit of making connections. Helen Dunmore once wrote a story about a lighthouse and the colours red and white appeared regularly in various guises – blood, clean sheets, types of food.

@@@@@@@@@@@@@@@@@@@@@@@@@@@@@@@@
@@@@@@@@@@@@@@@@@@@@@@@@@@@@@@@@
@@@@@@@@@@@@@@@@@@@@@@@@@@@@@@@@
@@@@@@@@@@@@@@@@@@@@@@@@@@@@@@@@
@@@@@@@@@@@@@@@@@@@@@@@@@@@@@@@@
@@@@@@@@@@@@@@@@@@@@@@@@@@@@@@@@
@@@@@@@@@@@@@@@@@@@@@@@@@@@@@@@@
@@@@''''''''''!!!!!!!!!!!!!!!!!!!!~~~~~~~~~~~######??????

"IS THIS YOUR NEW BABY?"

"NO."

OLD PEOPLE LAUGH AT NOTHING.

NO CONDOMS IN DISABLED TOILETS...

Quiz – Do You Remember 1996-97? – Page 20

1 2-2, Carey and Hughes for Wrexham/ Johnson and Yorke for Villa, **2** Andrei Kanchelskis,**3** Jason Soloman, **4** Bruce Grobbelaar, **5** Huddersfield Town, **6** Waynne Phillips **7** Craig Skinner, Steve Watkin, **8** Jon Sheffield, **9** Andy Marriott, Waynne Phillips, **10** Dave Brammer, Waynne Phillips, Martyn Chalk, **11** Barry Jones, 1-1, **12** No one – they received a bye, **13** Deryn Brace, **14** Colwyn Bay,**15** Bryan Hughes, **16** 39 seconds, **17** Mark Sertori, **18** Hereford United, **19** 7-0, **20** Paul Roberts, **21** Sligo Rovers, **22** Steve Watkin, **23** Tony Humes, **24** Neil Roberts, **25** Stockport County, **26** Kevin Russell, **27** Crewe Alexandra (Wrexham lost 1-0), **28** Bryan Hughes, **29** Martyn Chalk, **30** Burnley, 0-0, **31** Kevin Phillips, **32** Karl Connolly, 14, **33** 4,112

Divorce
Community Legal Advice Reference Number: 801305
Allington Hughes – 01978 291000
Gwilmn Hughes – 01978 291456
Appointment with Allington Hughes – Thursday 21 May at 12.

8.9	Difficulty in using household facilities, e.g. appliances and heating	X	Dependent on others for all extended domestic activities of daily living
8.1	Needs help with moving and handling	X	Unable to independently transfer, moving and handling issues
8.11	History of falls	X	Fell once getting into Car – had to call 999 – Other falls have been previously been dealt with by wife.
8.12	Difficulty with mobility inside the home	X	Uses wheelchair to manoeuvre.
8.13	Difficulty with mobility outside home / external access	X	Ditto
8.14	Difficulty with personal care e.g. on/off toilet, dressing, bathing	X	Dependent on others for all personal care

Mr Chaplin – Wrexham Central Estate Manager
Housing Services,
Ruthin Road
Wrexham
LL13 7TU

Direct Number: 01978 29-x-x-x-0
Housing Services General Line: 01978 31@!%300

Motability customer services number: 0845 456 <&^#
www.motability.co.uk

08448///00 – grants department

Aspect Conversions

01704)**(+00 – Steve

Wheelchair measurements

Width (widest point)   64cm
Length (including footrest)   104cm
Height (ground to top of head) 133cm
Height (ground to eye line)   121cm

There is a wide range of delicious home cooked meals and the spacious rooms and suites are designed to the highest possible standards. The tranquil setting and landscaped gardens are surrounded by open countryside, yet are close to Wrexham town centre and all its amenities. Other therapies including music are also available in addition to a whole host of activities and outings.

☺〰️♈〰️♈☯+&♌er〰️☯+&er♎〰️+♎⧓◆〰️+☯●♎⧓◆〰️+♎
〰️〰️●⧓◆⚜︎☜〰️☜+♆☜〰️☜+♰☜♆+☜♆☜♆☜♆☜♆♆☜♆⊡☜🌑⚜︎♟✠♆✠♆
⊡♟🌑⚜︎⊡♟☺☜☜☺☺♆☜☺♆☜☺♆☜☺♆☜☺♆♆☺
♆☺♆☺☜☜☺☺☺☺☺☺☺☜☺☺♆+☯♆✠♟☆▭☺☺♟🎴☺
🖐☆💧♆🖐❂✝︎☆❂➔🖐♆✝︎♆☆🖐🖐✝︎♆♆❂➔✝︎♆☠

EVERY SILVER LINING HAS A CLOUD Nathan Lee Davies

I was so bored and directionless that I would also spend desperate minutes spinning round and round my room in ever decreasing circles until I was sick and my wheelchair battery had died. Looking back at this pointless and desperate exercise it can be seen as an artistic expression of how my life had spiralled out of control.

MD2: 8350e5a3e24c153df2275c9f80692773
MD4: 31d6cfe0d16ae931b73c59d7e0c089c0
MD5: d41d8cd98f00b204e9800998ecf8427e
CRC 8, ccitt, 16, 32 :

CRYPT (form: $ MD5? $ SALT $ CRYPT):
1SpK4zSro$ZWbxCm8LrF1OLwXBUHYi30
(form: SALT[2] CRYPT[11]):
psVCB8A3RH3lI

SHA1: da39a3ee5e6b4b0d3255bfef95601890afd80709
RIPEMD-160:
9c1185a5c5e9fc54612808977ee8f548b2258d31

There is a wide range of delicious home cooked meals and the spacious rooms and suite

10110101010101010101010101010101010101010101010101010
10101010101010101010101011010101010101010101010101010
10101010101010101010101010101010101010101010110101010
10101010101010101010101010101010101010101010101010101
01010101011010101010101010101010101010101010101010101
01010101010101010101010101010110101010101010101010101
01010101010101010101010101010101010101010101010101101
01010101010101010101010101010101010101010101010101010
10101010101010110101010101010101010101010101010101010
10101010101010101010101010101010101101010101010101010
10101010101010101010101010101010101010101010101010

An example of a binary search tree

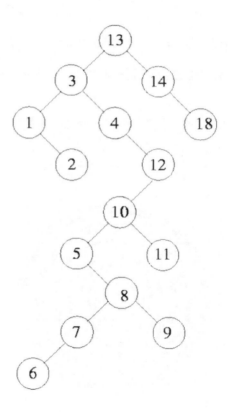

EVERY SILVER LINING HAS A CLOUD Nathan Lee Davies

In between dodgy meals and daytime television, there was nothing but the deafening sound of silence as I served a sentence for a crime I didn't commit in my own self-constructed prison. I should've joined the rest of the residents for games of bingo, art classes or daytrips to Llangollen, but I couldn't face being bracketed with these type of people. The only thing I had in common with the rest of the group was my disability and the fact that we were all patronised and treated like second class citizens by the rest of society. I wasn't ready to throw in the towel just yet as I still had ambitions and dreams burning inside me that I was yet to fulfil, coupled with a stubborn determination not to let the bastards grind me down.

Simon and Garfunkel Louise Wener Sleeper Space

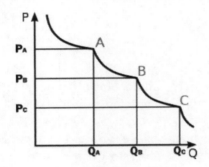

I wanna feel for you
I wanna steal for you
Everybody needs a home
Well, are you strange enough
Are you deranged enough
Every fucker needs a home

[Ends]

Llanelli 0 The New Saints 1

Corbett Sports Welsh Premier League
Saturday, 3 September 2011
15:45

Stebonheath Park / Parc Stebonheath
Attendance: 163

> I jumped in the car for the journey home and it really hit me. I'm not ashamed to say I had tears running down my face. That short trip home was the toughest journey of my life. I looked at the baby seat in the car and it struck me I might never see my daughter [Alicia] grow up.
>
> *Alive and Kicking*
> Andy Legg
> Accent Press

I'm not in the habit of recommending other people's books, but once you've finished reading my bitter and twisted tales, I suggest you pick up a copy of *Alive and Kicking* by Andy Legg. Of course, it doesn't compare to the masterpiece you are currently reading, but nevertheless it is the absorbing story of the current Llanelli manager's battle against cancer.

Legg's career with a host of Football League clubs – including Swansea City and Cardiff City – is briefly alluded to, but the main focus of this mini-autobiography – part of the Quick Reads series of books, specifically written for emergent readers and adult learners – is on "the hardest battle of the lot".

It is impossible to read Legg's emotional accounts of his treatment and whole outlook on life without being impressed and inspired by a thoroughly decent bloke, who refreshingly makes no attempts to inflate his own importance. Instead, he writes about his experiences to help others who might be going through similar circumstances, and to thank the football fraternity for their support during his darkest days.

After absorbing the recollections of a super-fit individual, who was struck down after finding a cancerous lump on his neck and continues to live with the fear that the disease could return with a vengeance, I was forced to reflect on my own negative, self-indulgent moans that are evident in the previous pages.

What right do I have to moan when there are millions of other people worse off than me? I'm surrounded by friends and family, while enjoying a debt-free, single lifestyle without chains, so I recognise that I have no real defence.

It's all relative though. The fact that I haven't been dealt the worst cards in the pack is all well and good, but this doesn't disqualify me from whinging and complaining. Indeed, it's within these clouds of misery and depression that I've found the creativity and self-deprecating humour that you've been enjoying so far. I just wanted to reassure my readers that I'm thankful for much in my life and realise that, in the grand scheme of things, I'm really rather lucky.

It was with this positive spirit that I left the Premier Inn, Llanelli and made the short journey to Stebonheath Park where the local side were hosting The New Saints in a match that was to be screened live on S4C. I was growing increasingly attached to the south Wales Reds after witnessing their sensational Europa League victory at Parc y Scarlets and being humbled by their inspirational manager. A win today against the rabble from Shropshire would surely cement their position as my Welsh Premier team of choice. What could possibly go wrong?

I was about to find out.

***

Ever get the feeling you've been cheated?

Johnny Rotten
Winterland, San Franscisco
14 January 1978

The remnants of Hurricane Irene echoed around a near-empty Stebonheath Park as I grappled with my umbrella and struggled to keep my dignity in front of thousands of armchair fans who'd wisely chosen to watch this game from the comfort of their homes. I must have cut a lonely, frustrated and depressed figure to the televised audience as thunderous downpours and strong winds threatened to sweep me away.

The majority of spectators at the ground were huddled together underneath an inaccessible shelter, while I perched at the side of the pitch directly opposite television cameras that captured my miserable image and beamed it nationwide for others to enjoy and ridicule. I imagined comedic co-commentators highlighting my plight with a "hilarious" quip about my mental state or, if I was lucky, a more sympathetic tribute to my undying dedication to the Welsh Premier League. This was a real possibility as there was precious little happening on the pitch...

Speaking to the *Llanelli Star* ahead of the game, Legg said:

"We always look forward to our battles with TNS. We have a special relationship with them and the games between us are usually entertaining."

The players seemed unaware of this as they served up an unspeakably turgid encounter on a desperately bleak afternoon. The two sides are regarded as being among the elite in the league, but both looked like relegation fodder on this evidence. The ball was aimlessly pumped back and forth, which led to few goalmouth incidents. The highlight of the first half came when a close range header from Craig Moses was somehow kept out by Saints keeper Paul Harrison, but as the rain continued to hammer down it appeared likely that I was about to experience my first goalless draw of the tour.

I looked around the deserted and damp stadium through deflated eyes. The Robbie James Stand – named after the former Llanelli player-manager who tragically passed away at Stebonheath Park, whilst playing in a Welsh League match against Porthcawl Town on 18 February 1998 – was a cosy haven for fans who could scale the flight of stairs that lead to 700 seats in a raised seating area underneath an angular roof and central gable. The changing rooms, club offices and, joy of joys, a disabled toilet are situated below. To the left of this structure is a café selling refreshments while the Jock Stein Bar to the right is reserved for posh patrons and visiting officials. Both buildings mimic the main stand and are topped with semi-circular gables making for a uniform and stylish pitch side.

At Farrar Road and the Gnoll, I was provided with shelter but no toilet facilities to relieve myself. The opposite was true at Stebonheath Park, where I could carry on at my convenience but was forced to brave the unforgiving elements without protection. I was sitting in front of the main stand near a small wooden hut that was being used as a club shop. On top of this structure was an advertising hording promoting "Sheds n Chalets – Quality with Strength to last".

A club official ran past me towards the inviting shelter of the stand. Without breaking his stride, he shouted:

"Sorry. You'll get wet. Nothing I can do about the rain."

While it's true that he had no control over the swathes of low pressure blanketing Britain, he could've teamed up with his colleagues to provide a covered area from which disabled supporters could watch matches. I turned towards the sensibly attired official with a steely glare, pointed defiantly at the three-foot sign that offered a future solution and hoped he would take the hint by visiting www.shedsnchalets.co.uk on Monday morning.

Opposite the unfriendly main stand is a bank of uncovered seating that runs along one-half of the pitch and is named after former player and manager Gilbert Lloyd. The social club sits behind these 300 seats that flank a large TV gantry, positioned on the halfway line. This seems a well-appointed structure, but on this blustery occasion, S4C needed plenty of extra tarpaulin to safely broadcast the match. Every effort seemed to have been made to ensure the extra cameras and equipment stayed dry, while I was left to fend for myself under dark clouds. Not even a friendly wave from the sodden Llanelli mascot, Reddy Bear, could cheer me up.

Behind both goals there was little to interest. The pitch is surrounded by an odd athletics track, which is mostly only two lanes wide, with only the TV gantry side being separated from the pitch by a four-lane sprint straight. The area to my left seemed to be unused, while the larger space to my right featured a full half-circle athletic track and training area leading to a steep grass bank on which a portacabin teetered.[1]

Back on the field of play, TNS defender Steve Evans hit a speculative long range effort before he was involved in a midfield scuffle with Ashley Evans of Llanelli and TNS teammate Aaron Edwards. This led to all three players being shown a yellow card as the referee double-checked his watch. Before the whistle even left his lips, I was inside the greasy-spoon gazing at the decorative pennants and scarves that were on display, bemoaning my selection of denim jeans over waterproof trousers and hugging the nearest radiator. I composed myself with a milky cup of tea and an average pie before

---

[1] Llanelli moved to Stebonheath Park in 1922. FA Cup holders Tottenham Hotspur were invited to mark the occasion by playing a friendly against the Reds. Remarkably, Llanelli won the match 2-1 as they began building a reputation as one of the leading non-league clubs in Britain.

relaxing with the match day programme as hailstones threatened to shatter the windows of this glass-fronted tea hut.

I'd enjoyed the Llanelli programme I'd read at Parc y Scarlets back in July, so I was hoping that editor Neil Dymock and his team of contributors had maintained their high standards. I'm happy to report that they'd excelled themselves once again with a bumper 60-page issue that was bursting with well-researched and entertainingly written articles. I flicked through the pages, not knowing where to start.

Maybe I'd read about the League encounter between the same sides back in 2000 that ended in a 3-3 draw? Would a focus on the achievements of Ryan Batley and Craig Moses at the World Student Games in China prove engaging? Perhaps I should take this opportunity to be introduced to the match officials? Decisions, decisions, decisions...

In the end, I concentrated on a heartwarming story about the club's five guests from Bijela Children's Home in Montenegro. Valentina Salihi, Bojan Soskic and Danilo Korac, were accompanied by their carers Miketic Darko and Slavika Ilic, on a trip financed and organised by Gol — the Welsh supporters' official charity to support underprivileged children wherever Wales play. Travelling fans visited the home in Bijela after the 1-0 defeat to Montenegro in September 2010, which proved to be John Toshack's last match in charge of the national side. Fast forward twelve months, and the poor blighters from Eastern Europe had been flown over to a foreign land to watch their countrymen loose to Gary Speed's rejuvenated national team at the Cardiff City Stadium. To make matters worse, they were now watching headless chickens stagger about in a south Wales storm. It wasn't much of an advert for Welsh domestic football, and what was billed as a charitable trip now must've seemed more like torture.

I jest of course. This was an unbelievable opportunity for these children who will have benefitted greatly from the experience. Credit must be given to the selfless group of fans behind this charity, whom I salute and applaud. For more information on Gol visit www.golcymru.org.

Before the second period got underway, I was also able to pour over a double-page interview with former TNS winger Craig Williams to find out that he has an NVQ in cooking, supports Manchester United and enjoys a game of golf when not starring for the Reds.

By the time I ventured back outdoors the worst of the storm had passed and the visitors celebrated this rainfall respite by taking the lead on 50 minutes. Llanelli failed to deal with a corner kick, allowing Greg Draper to rifle the loose ball into the top corner. The New Zealand international had struck his first goal in the WPL, but unfortunately this was not a signal to spark the game into life and the home side continued to mimic a bunch of Sunday League substitutes after a Saturday night on the sauce.

To be fair, the mute crowd of 163 did little to inspire them. It must be disheartening to be part of a consistently successful team – Llanelli have not finished outside of the top three in the last five seasons, and were crowned champions in 2008 – but still draw in such paltry attendances. Indeed, I'd only just finished reading the views of Craig Williams, who admitted that the European experience against Dinamo Tblisi wasn't exactly what he'd been dreaming of:

"I was really disappointed with the turn out for the home leg after the boys had done so well in bringing the Welsh Cup to Llanelli for the first time in their history. I thought there would have been a lot of support for us in such a big game."

This poor turn-out was further evidence of a deep-seated problem, which threatens the very future of the club. According to an article by the *Llanelli Star*, club chiefs believe that the success of Swansea City had severely hit their crowds.

EVERY SILVER LINING HAS A CLOUD Nathan Lee Davies

"Three years ago, our average home crowd was around the 400 mark. Since then it's steadily declined," said Llanelli general manager Nigel Richards.

"There are a lot of factors behind that, but the Swans have had a big effect. During that period, Swansea became a successful Championship side and then got promoted to the Premier League. A lot of our regular fans have bought season tickets down the Liberty and some of them travel away.

"We can't compete with a club in the Premier League, but if things carry on like this I don't know what we'll do."

The Reds' gates have almost halved in the last three years and they're now bottom of the WPL attendance table.

The club has launched several promotions in an attempt to lure people to Stebonheath Park, but ultimately, Richards favours a switch to summer football. In his opinion, such a transition would help to improve crowds and give Welsh Premier clubs an advantage in their European campaigns, which begin in July. However, there is opposition to the move from a number of other WPL clubs, so the chances of shifting the season appear slim.

"In summer there would be much less competition for spectators and for media coverage," he said.

"And look at the success Irish clubs have had in the Europa League.

"They have a summer season and Shamrock Rovers have reached the group stages of the Europa League where they will play Tottenham. The New Saints beat Bohemians, so I don't think their teams are much better than ours. But they are more suited to doing well in Europe. Can you imagine what it would be like if we made it into the Europa League group stage?"

EVERY SILVER LINING HAS A CLOUD Nathan Lee Davies

Manager Legg also insists his players deserve to be playing in front of bigger crowds.

"We're one of the best sides in the division in terms of the football we play," he said.

"We've got one of the best pitches and some of the best facilities, but still people don't want to watch us.

"I feel sorry for the players, but we just say to them now to make their own atmosphere because we know there won't be any at Stebonheath.

"I also feel sorry for the chairman because he keeps sticking his money in and all he seems to get is a slap in the face."

I don't have a magic solution, but even a 2011 friendly against a strong Swansea side only attracted around 200, so something clearly needs to be done. Despite playing poorly on this occasion, I can confirm that, based on the performances at Bangor in April, against Dinamo Tblisi at Parc y Scarlets, and highlights I've watched on *Sgorio*, Llanelli play the most attractive style of football in the WPL by a country mile. This makes the lack of appetite for the game in these parts even more bemusing.

Llanelli made ten unsuccessful attempts to join the Football League between 1922 and 1951 from the Southern League, a highly regarded division of the English pyramid. Maybe if one of these bids had been successful things would've been different, but it seems as if local glory-hunters grew tired of constant rejection, abandoned the grassroots game and turned their attentions solely towards a more thuggish sport.

On this occasion though, those supporters who'd braved the storm were left wondering why they'd bothered as their disjointed side never really threatened to get back in the game. Their best chance of securing at least a point fell to Craig Moses, who lost his footing with only Harrison to beat after a good through ball from Chris Venables. This just about summed up the Reds overall performance as they'd allowed an ordinary TNS – who finished with 10-men, following the late dismissal of Matty Williams for a second caution – to pick up three points without having to break sweat. Andy Legg was not amused:

"It's possibly the last game we can afford to lose for a while," Legg said.

"We need to go on a run now and win four or five games in a row, if we don't we are going to be in trouble and we're not going to be competitive and, if I'm at the club, I want to compete.

"So there will either be changes made to myself or the players.

"At the end of the day we've lost two games already in four games so I'm not very happy about it.

"It's the same again as last week, missed chances," he added.

"I thought we were the better team today actually but, if you don't score goals, you don't win games and that's proved the point today.

"At the moment we are struggling to defend set-plays, which is really frustrating – two goals from two corners in the last two games."

***

Back at the Premier Inn, I was thoroughly miserable as I attempted to dry my saturated denim with a hairdryer from reception while flicking through dreadful Saturday night television, headed by the amateurish pantomime antics of the nauseating *X-Factor* and backed up by *Total Wipeout* and *Dr Who* on the other side. I'm not a cultural dullard, so I threw the remote control out of the window and resumed reading *Alive and Kicking.*

Legg was struggling to cope with his radiotherapy treatment, but recalled how his turning point came when he saw a little girl in hospital, who was also undergoing therapy:

> She could have been no more than six or seven years old. She had lost all her hair. Yet she was smiling and looking happy. Compared to the life I had enjoyed, that little girl had had nothing, yet was smiling as she went through hell. I stopped feeling sorry for myself the minute I saw her. I've always been sure the nurses had something to do with me being there while she was there.

I was shamed into my first smile of the day and was reminded that, for ten minutes at least, I should look on the bright side of life.

***

I chose the wrong week to visit Stebonheath.

Just eight days later, Llanelli responded well to their manager's resignation threats by demolishing Newtown 9-2 at the same venue.

Former Newtown striker Craig Moses scored a hat-trick, while goal-machine Rhys Griffiths also hit a treble. Midfielder Chris Venables grabbed a brace with Craig Williams also scoring.

Nick Rushton and Jamie Price replied, the latter also being sent off to add to Newtown's woe.

Robins boss Bernard McNally said: "It was the worst day in footballing terms for me personally as a coach or manager, we completely lost our way."

EVERY SILVER LINING HAS A CLOUD Nathan Lee Davies

I watched the goals on S4C with a heavy heart. I felt particularly aggrieved as the sun seemed to be shining brightly.

Llanelli
Stebonnheath Park

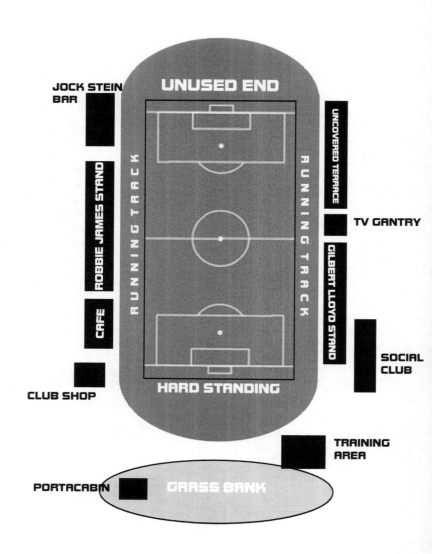

13
What a Carry On!!

EVERY SILVER LINING HAS A CLOUD Nathan Lee Davies

Sunny days
Where have you gone?
I get the strangest feeling you belong
Why does it always rain on me?
Is it because I lied when I was seventeen?

Travis
Why Does It Always Rain On Me?
1999

I was sweating and shivering amidst a chaotic collection of cardboard boxes and bulging bin bags stuffed with oversized clothes. As I juggled with fragile crockery wrapped in crumpled copies of the *Highland News*, I could feel my heart beating rapidly, but it wasn't until I coughed up thick blood-stained mucus that alarm bells started to sound in my head. This was followed by a frantic fight to catch my breath and an insistence from my carers that they take me to casualty. I smashed an old Wrexham AFC mug against the kitchen wall in frustration and reluctantly agreed. I'd been in my new home for less than 72 hours.

***

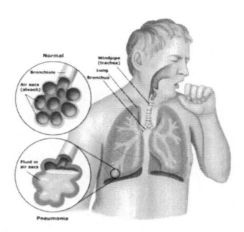

http://hospitalacquiredpneumonia.net/causes-of-pneumonia.html

EVERY SILVER LINING HAS A CLOUD Nathan Lee Davies

The doctor was throwing allsorts of new words at me that confused and befuddled my tiny mind. I didn't understand anything I was being told and just wanted him to cut to the chase while I made a mental note never to compete against a member of the medical profession in a game of Scrabble. The damage they could inflict with a triple-word square is frightening.

Apparently, I'd developed pneumonia, which is an inflammatory condition of the lung, especially affecting the microscopic air sacs or alveoli. It is associated with fever, chest symptoms, and a lack of air space (consolidation) on a chest X-ray. Pneumonia is typically caused by an infection, but there are a number of other causes. Infectious agents include: bacteria, viruses, fungi, and parasites, according to Wikipedia.

I was weaker than I'd ever been before and absolutely exhausted as I fought for breath in the High Dependency Unit at Wrexham Maelor Hospital underneath an oxygen mask with an intravenous drip lodged in my jugular. Despite the seriousness of the situation, my overriding emotion was one of frustration. I was less than a mile away from my new bachelor pad after 13 months of lonely isolation in a care home, but would have to wait before I could decorate, unpack, arrange and organise my house – or bungalow if you're being pedantic – into a home.

Worse still, my girlfriend was due to visit from London in less than 24 hours and I'd planned to take her to the MEN Arena in Manchester to see Travis in concert with my sister and brother-in-law. The tickets were bought and paid for, but they'd remain unused unless I could contact lead singer Fran Healy and persuade him to relocate the gig to the more clinical climes of an Emergency Room in north Wales. This seemed highly unlikely.

***

EVERY SILVER LINING HAS A CLOUD Nathan Lee Davies

I'd first met Ana, a beautiful ray of Spanish sunshine from Madrid, during the dark days that followed the end of my marriage. There is no doubt that I owe her a lot as she helped me through difficult times with regular phone calls, texts and webcam chats. Our first communication was through a popular social network site and after she relocated to London, we met on several occasions, one thing led to another and with a certain air of inevitability we became lovers.

Ana was everything my frumpy ex-wife wasn't – intelligent, sexy, funny, thoughtful and generous. I was definitely punching above my weight, but was determined to enjoy the relationship while I could, as even when I was at my lowest ebb she made me feel like the luckiest man alive and gave me the strength to carry on.

The sex was great too.

My Madrilena was in town for a week before returning to her hectic life in London, which consisted of a full-time job with a corporate giant and having to cope with being the sole carer for her mentally troubled brother. By spending her precious free-time with a wheelchair-bound bloke, some would say she was a glutton for punishment, but she was one of those rare people, who can see beyond physical imperfections to the beauty that lies beyond – even in me apparently.

It soon became clear that I'd be confined to my hospital bed for the duration of Ana's visit, so she made plans to extend her stay and I searched for enough energy to convince doctors that they could send me home. It wouldn't be easy as I was still struggling to breath without assistance and barely had enough energy to hold my head up. I'd been in hospital for eight long days, but had made little progress. Even attempts to improve my medical chart at the foot of my bed with red biro and a tub of Tipp-Ex were foiled by a nosy nurse who more closely resembled Hattie Jacques than Barbara Windsor. It was just my luck.

EVERY SILVER LINING HAS A CLOUD Nathan Lee Davies

My main motivation to recover was sex. Ana was a busy girl with many commitments, so opportunities to spend time away from her adopted home were rare. I knew I had to make a quick recovery if I wanted to see her modelling the sexy Santa costume and matching lingerie I'd bought for her the previous Christmas from www.lovehoney.co.uk. This was all the incentive I needed.

[Please insert a Sid James style lecherous yak or an incredulous frown at this point, depending on your moral barometer]

With six days of Ana's visit remaining and against all medical advice, I returned to the cluttered disorganisation of my bungalow, which was quickly transformed into our very own love shack. The action wasn't all confined to the bedroom though as Ana also proved her worth in the kitchen by cooking some delicious meals. I also proved I'm more than just a filthy pervert as I'd lovingly prepared 32 gifts for my girlfriend – one for every year we'd spent apart. They weren't all from www.lovehoney.co.uk either.

***

I enjoy people watching at busy railway stations as you can usually guarantee a fair amount of drama amidst the routine procession of corporate commuters and retired day-trippers. The reunited couple hold each other in a tight embrace that won't be broken until the next time the husband decides he needs the comforting bosom of his young lover, frolicking teenagers race against departing trains until they run out of platform, and disgruntled tax payers bemoan the privatisation of the railways to beleaguered staff. They're all here. I'd thoroughly recommend buying a Boots Meal Deal (Chicken & Stuffing sandwich + Roast Beef Monster Munch + 500ml of Diet Coke) and spending an afternoon at your local station, where you'll be entertained and engrossed by all manner of people. It's all good fun, unless you're one of the central characters bidding farewell to the girl you love.

EVERY SILVER LINING HAS A CLOUD Nathan Lee Davies

As the train disappeared into the distance I broke down in tears. I was obviously going to miss the company, support and sex provided by Ana, but my emotional response to her departure ran deeper than this. It was true that I still had a building full of valueless cardboard boxes to sort through, and Pneumonia still lingered in my left lung, but if I'm truthful with myself, I was upset at the end of a beautiful friendship that was leading nowhere.

Ana just didn't have enough time to commit to me as a family-centred workaholic, who'd never discuss the future or share stories from her past. I knew little about her of any real substance and whenever I talked about commitment I was silenced by her favourite word, "maybe", which only succeeded in giving me false hope and frustration. I was kept hanging on by the idea of how great our relationship could be one day.

Sadly, that day would never come...

***

Tears were still rolling down my face as I clambered into my lonely double-bed that evening. I couldn't rest without anyone to cuddle or keep awake with my snoring, so I reached for my laptop computer and decided that decisive action was needed to save myself from my only remaining bedfellows – loneliness and depression.

I visited www.lovehoney.co.uk and ordered myself an inflatable sex doll.

PHWOAR!

Carmarthen Town 1 Bangor City 2

Corbett Sports Welsh Premier League
Saturday, 17 September 2011
14:30

Richmond Park / Parc Waun Dew
Attendance: 337

It was time for another wet weekend in south Wales, starting with a visit to Richmond Park to watch Carmarthen Town host defending WPL champions Bangor City. I opened my umbrella and entered the ground with all the enthusiasm of a dyslexic in a library. After all, I'd seen Bangor lose twice the previous season and also witnessed Carmarthen get trounced at Bala in April. The omens for a classic weren't good, especially as Town had started 2011-12 with only three points from six games to find themselves second from bottom. The Old Gold, as the club is affectionately known, was beginning to tarnish under the leadership of Tomi Morgan.

I paid my entrance fee and, after progressing through a turnstile gate, I immediately found myself underneath untidy steel scaffolding that supports a television gantry and sits level with the halfway line. A row of drab and uninspiring buildings that did little to brighten the grey afternoon run along this touchline, with room for hard standing between them and the pitch. The single-storey units comprise of a study centre and club shop, while a larger two-floor clubhouse runs along the other half of the pitch. This building has a metal stairway leading to the first floor social club, which wasn't a promising sight, but I didn't have time to dwell on this as I searched for shelter.

Depressingly, Richmond Park can only offer uncovered, flat standing areas behind both goals, but I was heading towards the impressive Clay Shaw Butler Stand, which holds 1,000 black and yellow plastic seats – they couldn't afford gold – under a cantilever roof. This provides unrestricted views and protection from the elements for the majority of fans, but the wheelchair spaces at the front of the stand are not fully covered by the overhanging roof. This meant I was forced to unveil my waterproof trousers and matching anorak that I'd purchased from Primark to save myself from another soaking.

After arriving late at the ground, thanks to a combination of heavy goods vehicles, tractors and a bickering pair of aging drivers, who insist they don't need satellite navigation telling them which way to go when they've got an AA road map from 1989 to argue over, I barely had enough time to inform my friends on Facebook and Twitter of my whereabouts before both teams took to the field.

Prior to kick-off, there was an impeccably observed minute's silence in memory of the four miners so tragically lost days earlier – some 30 miles away at the Gleision Colliery. I like to use such silent periods to reflect on what has happened and offer my respects to all those involved. On this occasion, I was also relieved not to be notified of a comment on my status or a retweet, which would've triggered the Nokia jingle and ruined a well-observed tribute.[1]

As the match got underway, I wondered if I'd finally see Bangor at their best. I wasn't holding my breath. Nev Powell's men had made a slow start to the season, had just suffered a 0-3 home defeat against TNS, and were nestled unspectacularly in mid-table ahead of kick-off. I was certainly impressed by their travelling support though, which may have only numbered about 50, but other away teams get absolutely no support; anyone who has ever endured the arduous journey from north to south Wales will realise how impressive this

---

[1] The four men who tragically died at Gleision Colliery – Charles Breslin, 62, David Powell, 50, Garry Jenkins, 39, and Phillip Hill, 45, all from the Swansea Valley area – had been working 295ft into the drift mine when the retaining wall gave way.

Hopes that the men might have found an air pocket and survived were dashed as the bodies were found one by one. All died close together in an area near to where they had been blasting.

modest figure is. After sitting in the back of a Fiat Doblo as it weaved and wobbled along windy roads for almost four hours while nursing a heavy hangover from the night before, I could certainly sympathise with these weary travellers from Bangor. Not to mention the players.

As seen previously, clubs at this level just don't have the budget to pay for overnight accommodation ahead of away games. Subsequently, semi-professional athletes are expected to jump off a cramped coach after a two, three, or four hour journey and then do battle on the football pitch for 90 minutes, with the return journey still to look forward to. It's expecting too much. Nevertheless, the hosts were just as bad as the sluggish visitors during a dire first half.

Aimless shots cleared the crossbar, or sailed hopelessly wide, before the Citizens actually bundled the ball into the net. However, celebrations were muted as the referee was quick to notice that Chris Jones used his hand to propel the ball over the line and booked the wide-man for his troubles. Maradona he is not. There was quite a lot going on, but it was all of such poor quality that it came as little surprise when Town's Jack Christopher found himself through on goal with just Idzl to beat, only to fluff his lines. Carmarthen were in the ascendency at this stage though, and it was left to Nick Harrhy to capitalise on some embarrassing defending and break the deadlock on 41 minutes to extend my record of not attending a goalless game at this level.

I now had to decide how to spend the 15 minutes of half-time. I could either perform an investigative lap of the stadium, visit the club shop, look for a disabled toilet and find out if I could access the seemingly inaccessible social club – all while getting wet – or stay exactly where I was and read the match day programme, under a bumbershoot, while my dad dashed to buy me a pie...

Priced at £1.50, this 52-page programme satisfied my statistical needs and included one or two decent articles amongst the adverts, but what marked this issue out from the others I've read on the tour is the predominant use of the Welsh language. I suppose I shouldn't have been surprised as I was in the Welsh heartlands, where 83,802 can speak Welsh according to the 2001 census.

The local council is rightly proud that the Welsh language is widely used in Carmarthenshire and is increasing in many areas – with more young and older people learning and using the language. The language is encouraged and promoted in this county to a far greater degree than I'm used to in Wrexham. This is highlighted through the programme editor's decision to print articles in Welsh first and English second, sometimes using italics for English to emphasise that you're reading a foreign language and are failing as a Welshman. *I was made to feel a right thick twat.*

I began this tour full of hope. I was excited about discovering my true cultural identity, but nine months on, as I attempted to decode untranslatable text and listened to teenagers displaying impressive bilingual skills, I felt more isolated and ignorant than ever...

My dad returned from the tea bar with some much-needed sustenance. I'd been looking forward to this meaty treat since reading the following paragraph on the Welsh Premier's official website during the summer:

> Despite averaging the fourth most expensive match day deal, Carmarthen Town hope to entice locals into Richmond Park with Welsh food produce, such as their excellent home-made pies from a local butcher. Priced at a competitive £1.20 they are below the average price of a pie and certainly worth tasting.

I can only assume the local butcher had died because this disappointing pie was the worst I'd ever tasted at a football ground. The pastry was thick and crunchy, and held watery mincemeat that was barely edible. It turned my stomach, but now I had to sit through an equally unappetising 45 minutes.

EVERY SILVER LINING HAS A CLOUD Nathan Lee Davies

Neville Powell had clearly given his players a right good rollicking in the dressing room, as they began to show the forceful creativity and determination that I'd been told was their trademark. The home side had finished the first half with a glut of corner kicks, but now it was City's turn to pile on the pressure with three corners in quick succession before levelling matters on 56 minutes. Chris Garside was the man who powered home a bullet header from Alan Bull's cross. It now seemed that there'd be only one winner as Bangor piled on the pressure, but they didn't have it all their own way. Carmarthen's Tim Hicks unleashed a piledriver from 30-yards that agonizingly hit the crossbar, rebounded off Idzi's back and was trickling over the line, until the highly-rated goalkeeper turned around, pounced on the ball and averted disaster. The visitors seemed to have luck on their side and kept plugging away, until Neil Thomas volleyed home from 15 yards with just seven minutes remaining.

Football is a game of opinions. Maybe my recollections of the game were overly critical due to my tiredness and innate negativity. For whatever reason, it's clear that Bangor boss Neville Powell saw the game through more positive eyes than me.

"Garside and Thomas controlled the midfield – everything came through them," said the City chief.

"It was fitting that they both scored as they were the game's most dominant players.

"We showed great character and deserved the three points," he added.

"We dominated the first half, only to concede just before half-time, but in the second half we were well on top and managed to convert two of the chances we created.

"It was a very important three points for us today."

EVERY SILVER LINING HAS A CLOUD Nathan Lee Davies

Tomi Morgan shared his views on S4C in fluent Welsh...

He sounded pissed off.

***

I left Richmond Park without investigating the outwardly unfriendly social club, sent my dad to the club shop to pick up a pin badge and never found out if this rather bland ground provides toilet facilities for disabled supporters. I just wasn't in the right frame of mind to explore deeper. All that travelling had sucked away my energy and enthusiasm and had left me in much the same state as the Bangor players during the first half.

The unpredictable showers made way for weak sunshine as I watched elderly gentlemen in action on the bowling green that sits behind the main stand. It was just as engrossing as the football match I'd been watching. I looked to the heavens for help determining my next move. Storm clouds were gathering, but I was conscious that the original intention of this tour was to see more of Wales, chat with fellow countrymen and attempt to paint a clearer picture of my own identity.

This was an ideal opportunity for me to fulfil such objectives as Carmarthen's historic town centre was less than five minutes' walk away, while St Peter's Church – the largest Parish Church in Wales – was just across the road. I also wanted to see Picton's monument, which was erected in memory of the gallant Sir Thomas Picton, who died in the Battle of Waterloo. In addition, this was my chance to visit Nott Square where a statue of General Nott was erected in 1851. This was also the location for the execution of Bishop Robert Ferrar of St Davids in March 1555, during the Marian persecutions.

There was a loud clap of thunder. Smartly attired sportsmen sighed with hands on hips before rushing around the lawn to retrieve their plastic bowls. I bundled myself into the back of my Fiat Doblo and headed to the Premier Inn, Llanelli. After my Stebonheath soaking, I wasn't getting wet for anyone, even Sir Thomas Picton.

I'd had enough of being rained upon...

Carmarthen Town
Richmond Park

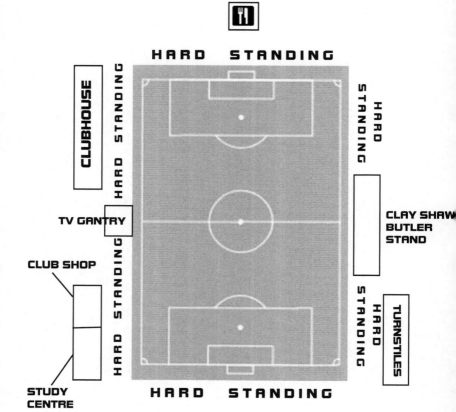

15
#justsaying

Nathan Lee Davies

@nathanleedavies

Writing book on the Welsh Premier League while in search of inspiration, love and Elvis.

Tweets

Nathan Lee Davies @nathanleedavies: Wank. Lucozade Sport. Bed.

5 June 10

Nathan Lee Davies @nathanleedavies: can't sleep all tucked in. #seinfeld #thetrip @IJasonAlexander

3 June 10

Nathan Lee Davies @nathanleedavies: is watching Seinfeld, Season 4, Episode 1, The Trip - Part One.

3 June 10

Nathan Lee Davies @nathanleedavies: Reading When Saturday Comes at Exact Editions
http://exacteditions.com/browse/378/407/31975/3/10/ ...

2 June 10

Nathan Lee Davies @nathanleedavies: won't need much rocking tonight. #imturningintomydad

31 May 10

Nathan Lee Davies @nathanleedavies: has been released on bail.

31 May 10

Nathan Lee Davies @nathanleedavies: has had his catheter removed. Young nurse had an eyeful. #Kissitbetter

31 May 10

EVERY SILVER LINING HAS A CLOUD Nathan Lee Davies

Nathan Lee Davies @nathanleedavies: is packing.

31 May 10

Nathan Lee Davies @nathanleedavies: is singing Please Release Me by Engelbert Humperdinck.

31 May 10

Nathan Lee Davies @nathanleedavies: Maybe tomorrow, I'll find my way home. #stereophonics

30 May 10

Nathan Lee Davies @nathanleedavies: has read racist, homophobic report celebrating role of Royal family. Blood pressure through the roof.

29 May 10

Nathan Lee Davies @nathanleedavies: is trying to raise his blood pressure by reading the Daily Mail.

29 May 10

Nathan Lee Davies @nathanleedavies: hopes the medical staff have a great weekend while I remain stuck here. I mean that most sincerely.

29 May 10

Nathan Lee Davies @nathanleedavies: doctor to review me on Monday before deciding if I can go home. Another weekend stuck here :(

29 May 10

Nathan Lee Davies @nathanleedavies: needs to get out of this place but his blood pressure remains low.

29 May 10

Nathan Lee Davies @nathanleedavies: thinks its not their fault they are engulfed in red tape.

27 May 10

EVERY SILVER LINING HAS A CLOUD Nathan Lee Davies

Nathan Lee Davies @nathanleedavies: still has low blood pressure.

26 May 10

Nathan Lee Davies @nathanleedavies: would rather expire in a gush of warm sympathy in a small hospital than be kept alive in the efficient if cold altruism of a large one.

25 May 10

Nathan Lee Davies @nathanleedavies: might as well just grin and bear it, 'cos its not worth the trouble of an argument. #blur #badhead

25 May 10

Nathan Lee Davies @nathanleedavies: is being made to feel a nuisance by stressed out nurses.

25 May 10

Nathan Lee Davies @nathanleedavies: thinks modern nursing is all about paperwork to the detriment of care. #Wishiwasathome

25 May 10

Nathan Lee Davies @nathanleedavies: thinks that poor bloke is in some distress and pushed his bell about 10 minutes ago.

25 May 10

Nathan Lee Davies @nathanleedavies: No reply oh can't you see, No reply it's ruining me, Even if I ask the reason why, I get no reply no reply. #buzzcocks #noreply

25 May 10

Nathan Lee Davies @nathanleedavies: Although the lights were switched off 45 mins ago, I am awake as someone is snoring his way through Beethoven's 5th symphony in C minor.

24 May 10

EVERY SILVER LINING HAS A CLOUD Nathan Lee Davies

Nathan Lee Davies @nathanleedavies: wonders if Lucy Meacock has a brother called Suck?   24 May 10

Nathan Lee Davies @nathanleedavies: Same could be said of events in Fishguard or Merthyr Tydfil I suppose. #Regionaltvfornorthwales
24 May 10

Nathan Lee Davies @nathanleedavies: tuned in to see local news. Dont care about unemployment on the Wirral or the number of potholes in Blackburn, Lancashire.

24 May 10

Nathan Lee Davies @nathanleedavies: lives half a mile away. At home I enjoy BBC Wales and ITV1 Wales on 32 inch. Here we have BBC North West and Granada on 18 inch.

24 May 10

Nathan Lee Davies @nathanleedavies: I'm not here, This isn't happening, I'm not here, I'm not here. #radiohead #howtodisappearcompletely

22 May 10

Nathan Lee Davies @nathanleedavies: is sitting by an open window...
22 May 10

Nathan Lee Davies @nathanleedavies: "Welcome to the O2 messaging service, the person you are calling is unable to take your call. Please leave your message after the tone."

22 May 10

Nathan Lee Davies @nathanleedavies: is a model you know what I mean, And I do my little turn on the catwalk #rightsaidfred
22 May 10

Nathan Lee Davies @nathanleedavies: can't work out why these gowns are stamped with 'Property of Wrexham Maelor' in coloured letters. #Undesirable

22 May 10

Nathan Lee Davies @nathanleedavies: is not going to pull while wearing this hospital gown and carrying a bag of his own discoloured piss.

22 May 10

Nathan Lee Davies @nathanleedavies: is too sexy for my love, too sexy for my love, Love's going to leave me #rightsaidfred

22 May 10

Nathan Lee Davies @nathanleedavies: thinks incompetent nurses are doing their best to raise his blood pressure.

22 May 10

Nathan Lee Davies @nathanleedavies: wonders if any of these nurses have been given moving and handling training.

22 May 10

Nathan Lee Davies @nathanleedavies: is sitting on his balls after being aggressively shifted from bed to wheelchair by naggy nurses.

22 May 10

Nathan Lee Davies @nathanleedavies: needs to get out of bed before he develops bed sores.

22 May 10

Nathan Lee Davies @nathanleedavies: thinks a friend in need is a pain in the arse.

22 May 10

Nathan Lee Davies @nathanleedavies: is counting the ceiling tiles.

21 May 10

EVERY SILVER LINING HAS A CLOUD Nathan Lee Davies

Nathan Lee Davies @nathanleedavies: will run out of blood at this rate – another blood sample.

21 May 2010

Nathan Lee Davies @nathanleedavies: has low blood pressure.

21 May 10

Nathan Lee Davies @nathanleedavies: "OK mate. We all get the idea."

21 May 10

Nathan Lee Davies @nathanleedavies: has "silent stones" that he doesn't even notice.

21 May 10

Nathan Lee Davies @nathanleedavies: feels like a fraud. Bloke next to me in agony as stone leaves kidney and squeezes down ureter.

21 May 10

Nathan Lee Davies @nathanleedavies: is starving.

19 May 10

Nathan Lee Davies @nathanleedavies: is given a cheese sandwich followed by jelly and ice cream. #Thatsyourlotuntilmorning

19 May 10

Nathan Lee Davies @nathanleedavies: could eat a horse, which reminds me to renew my subscription to www.oldmcdonald.net

19 May 10

Nathan Lee Davies @nathanleedavies: remains full of shit. #Backinbed

19 May 10

Nathan Lee Davies @nathanleedavies: thinks the chattering of pensioners is not conducive to a satisfying dump.

19 May 10

EVERY SILVER LINING HAS A CLOUD Nathan Lee Davies

Nathan Lee Davies @nathanleedavies: unqualified nurses roughly hoisted me out of bed and onto commode chair. A thin curtain separates me from the rest of the ward.

19 May 10

Nathan Lee Davies @nathanleedavies: needs to read up about his human rights when he gets home.

19 May 10

Nathan Lee Davies @nathanleedavies: Just argued with nurse as she wants me to use bed pan while I want her to use a hoist to help me use the loo.

19 May 10

Nathan Lee Davies @nathanleedavies: wants to get his arse over a toilet but thinks it'll be easier said than done.

19 May 10

Nathan Lee Davies @nathanleedavies: needs a shit.

19 May 10

Nathan Lee Davies @nathanleedavies: usually enjoys a light lunch but has been given toad in the hole with mountains of veg and jam sponge and luke warm custard for desert.

19 May 10

Nathan Lee Davies @nathanleedavies: is giving another blood sample.

19 May 10

Nathan Lee Davies @nathanleedavies: is snoring in his weetabix.

18 May 10

Nathan Lee Davies @nathanleedavies: was sleeping well until they opened the curtains. #Inconsideratebastards

18 May 10

Nathan Lee Davies @nathanleedavies: is wearing a urinary catheter. #Sexy

16 May 10

Nathan Lee Davies @nathanleedavies: P Anandaram is a nice bloke and the first professional to show sympathy, warmth and promise decisive action.

16 May 10

Nathan Lee Davies @nathanleedavies: has his first operation in 4 weeks time but in the meantime he has to drink like a fish. #Nonalcoholic

16 May 10

Nathan Lee Davies @nathanleedavies: has never been under anaesthetic. #Worriedtofuck

16 May 10

Nathan Lee Davies @nathanleedavies: P Anandaram wants to perform at least 3 keyhole operation to stop the buggers causing urine infections.

16 May 10

Nathan Lee Davies @nathanleedavies: X-rays show hundreds of thousands of kidney stones. I'm like a pepperpot.

16 May 10

Nathan Lee Davies @nathanleedavies: is going for an x-ray #ohtheexcitement

15 May 10

Nathan Lee Davies @nathanleedavies: is giving a blood sample.

15 May 10

Nathan Lee Davies @nathanleedavies: is having his blood pressure taken.   15 May 10

Nathan Lee Davies @nathanleedavies: is under the care of P Anandaram according to the wipe clean board above his bed.

15 May 10

Nathan Lee Davies @nathanleedavies: When I phone you night and day, I get no reply no reply, #buzzcocks #noreply

15 May 10

Nathan Lee Davies @nathanleedavies: has freedom of speech within strict parameters.

14 May 10

Nathan Lee Davies @nathanleedavies: Unattractive nurse demands I remove my card from view. Someone needs a good fuck.

14 May 10

Nathan Lee Davies @nathanleedavies: has two Get Well Soon cards, one of which proclaims 'Get Well Soon You Fuckin' Fuck'. Cheers @paddockpete #sentimentalbastard

14 May 10

Nathan Lee Davies @nathanleedavies: Many concerned faces around my hospital bed but no sign of the one I want to see.

14 May 10

Nathan Lee Davies @nathanleedavies: Fever fading but preferred busy streets of Manhattan to hospitalisation in North Wales.

14 May 10

Nathan Lee Davies @nathanleedavies: apologises for non-sensical tweets. Been dressed down by nurses. Was wandering the wards, bellowing excerpts from Sinatra's back catalogue.

14 May 10

Nathan Lee Davies @nathanleedavies: I thought this was supposed to be the city that never sleeps.   14 May 10

Nathan Lee Davies @nathanleedavies: is wandering around Times Square naked #bollocksout

13 May 10

Nathan Lee Davies @nathanleedavies: They're coming to take me away, ha ha, they're coming to take me away, ho ho, hee hee, ha ha
13 May 10

Nathan Lee Davies @nathanleedavies: is waiting for an ambulance.
13 May 10

Nathan Lee Davies @nathanleedavies: has a burning fever but is freezing cold.

13 May 10

Nathan Lee Davies @nathanleedavies: is in agony with a urine infection.

13 May 10

Nathan Lee Davies @nathanleedavies: is pissing blood.
13 May 10

Nathan Lee Davies @nathanleedavies: is happy to receive a new TV remote control after vomiting on the old one. What did we do before ebay?

12 May 10

Nathan Lee Davies @nathanleedavies: is glad to see table's turning - it's her turn to cry -- Rolling Stones - It's All Over Now http://www.youtube.com/watch?v=m3YnRQOXLWo via @youtube
20 Apr 10

Nathan Lee Davies @nathanleedavies:
http://www.americansweets.co.uk/hostess-twinkies-cakes-box-of-10-cakes-cakes-dated-090311-5504-p.asp

19 Apr 10

Nathan Lee Davies @nathanleedavies: Louise Hopwood and I want some Twinkies. Expensive here. Would it be cheaper for a US friend to send a box in return for black pudding?

19 Apr 10

Nathan Lee Davies @nathanleedavies: just spent £238.80 on a 3.5ft soft whip ice cream, plus flake.

13 Apr 10

Nathan Lee Davies @nathanleedavies: is like a one man band clapping in the pissing rain #paulweller

11 Apr 10

Nathan Lee Davies @nathanleedavies: thought we were cool-de-la? #thecarpoollane #curbyourenthusiasm

5 Apr 10

Nathan Lee Davies @nathanleedavies: #GoalsIWillAlwaysRemember @therealMickeyT – Wrexham v Arsenal, FA Cup Third Round, 1992

3 Apr 10

Nathan Lee Davies @nathanleedavies: hopes he never sees another cardboard box as long as he lives, which won't be long if this pneumonia doesn't shift soon.

1 Apr 10

Nathan Lee Davies @nathanleedavies: misses you like the deserts miss the rain... @zabagaz

30 March 10

Nathan Lee Davies @nathanleedavies: is rebuilding his strength after a particularly nasty bout of pneumonia.

25 March 10

EVERY SILVER LINING HAS A CLOUD Nathan Lee Davies

<u>Nathan Lee Davies @nathanleedavies</u>: Free from hospital and care home. Must be time to create another self-constructed prison.

23 March 10

<u>Nathan Lee Davies @nathanleedavies</u>: is depressed to be joining Twitter like everybody else...

13 Nov 09

Port Talbot Town 0 Prestatyn Town 0

Corbett Sports Welsh Premier League
Sunday, 18 September 2011
14:30

GenQuip Stadium / Stadiwm GenQuip
Attendance: 245

I've always been a keen groundhopper. Since watching Wales crush Spain at the Racecourse in 1985, I've been to about 70 different Football League grounds. Many have since lost arguments with bulldozers and been replaced with retail units, while clubs relocate to heartless homes that have all too often traded unique architecture and traditional charm for staid functionality and boring blandness.

While I was living in Scotland, I probably visited an extra 30 arenas from the likes of Tynecastle and Easter Road in the Scottish Premier League, to Station Park and Mosset Park in the semi-professional Highland League. During 2005-06, I attended as many football grounds as possible, in a bid to raise money and awareness for Ataxia UK. This took me all over Britain and I succeeded in raising over £1,500 for my chosen charity by auctioning memorabilia, taking bucket collections and attracting sponsors. It is therefore fair to say, despite some glaring omissions from my list of grounds visited, that I'm reasonably well-travelled as a football fan.

As soon as the dependable Doblo rolled through the entrance gates of the GenQuip Stadium and came to rest at the top of a grass bank that affords a great view of the pitch that sits in a dip below, I was reminded of a similar set-up at Wick Academy's isolated Harmsworth Park – home of Scotland's most northerly senior football club. There is a quaint attraction in being able to drive into a stadium and enjoy a match from the cosy confines of your car, while rain beats against your windscreen and Five Live keeps you bang up to date with all the afternoon's latest scores. Despite similarities in the lay of the land,

EVERY SILVER LINING HAS A CLOUD Nathan Lee Davies

I'm happy to report that once I left my vehicle I was welcomed by soft south Wales accents and not growled at indecipherably by po-faced Highlanders.

The first person to greet us on an afternoon of blustery showers was a charming middle-aged gent, who pulled up in the parking space next to us. He began chatting to my dad as if he was an old friend as they recognised each other from the previous days game at Richmond Park. As they chatted away about Carmarthen's poor form and the likelihood of a better game this afternoon, I wandered off to buy a programme and try to work out why the character making small talk with my old man was wearing a sweatshirt emblazoned with the initials MJ.

I turned to page three of the attractive 36-page programme and found MJ gurning back at me. It turns out that the sociable bloke in conversation with my dad was none other than Mark Jones, manager of Port Talbot Town. I wasn't exactly overwhelmed to be in the vicinity of the former Maesteg Park legend, but while I, and thousands like me, fretted over fantasy league selections, it was reasonably exciting to meet a man whose team selections and tactical nous counted for more than bragging rights around a water cooler. It should also be remembered that Nigel Adkins had cut his managerial teeth at Bangor City and went on to enjoy success in the Football League with Scunthorpe United and Southampton, so who knows what the future holds for Jones? Wherever he ends up, I hope he remains an amiable man of the people.

I joined in the conversation and was asked my opinions on yesterday's game, but before I could impress him with my achievements in charge of Nottingham Forest via play-by-mail during the early nineties, it began to rain and we dashed for shelter in opposite directions. I found cover in the rather sparse club shop, which is tucked between a control tower and a low seated stand, which accommodates 300.

EVERY SILVER LINING HAS A CLOUD Nathan Lee Davies

Tatty boxes of old football programmes from assorted clubs were decomposing beneath plastic pennants and a limp rail held tired and discoloured t-shirts. It felt as if I was in a teenage boy's garage sale. Beside the cash register randomly stood a 4-shelf pie warmer, which had all manner of pastry encrusted meat treats on offer. It was a million miles away from the carpeted luxury of a merchandise megastore that you might expect of a club playing in the top league of their country, but nevertheless I was in heaven.

"How much are the badges?" I asked the attractive young lady on duty.

"50p" she sang back in her sweet south Walian tones.

I was flabbergasted as I usually fork out between £2.50 and £3 for a club crest. My eyes were out on stalks as I processed this bargain price but the sexy shopkeeper obviously mistook my excitement for disgust.

"I know, it's a rip off isn't it? I tell you what you can have this one on me but don't go telling anyone."

I snatched the badge off the counter and quickly left the store before she could change her mind and deprive me of a freebie. As promised, I averted a stampede by keeping my exclusive deal under wraps and haven't told a single soul, until now, so mum's the word.

Prestatyn player-manager Neil Gibson was being interviewed by the local press in the aforementioned seated stand as I trundled past. It's a cosy structure that houses the dressing rooms, but only modestly straddles the halfway line. When sitting in this stand the control box and club shop is on your left, along with portable toilets for all and hard standing, while the right hand side is dominated by a funky PTTFC wall mural painted on an exterior wall behind a flat standing area. Unattractive plastic dugouts can also be found along this touchline.

EVERY SILVER LINING HAS A CLOUD Nathan Lee Davies

I then rolled along the concrete path that runs behind the Burns End goal, in the shadow of an imposing 15ft high fence that stops stray balls going into the houses of Burns Road.

This brought me to the Lake Road side of the ground and the new main stand, which was erected in 2007 and named after Port Talbot legend Gerald McCreesh. The single-deck cantilever stand has around 700 blue plastic seats on a single tier, a compact TV gantry on the roof and this cover is also pierced by two modern, but dull, floodlight pylons. However, my favourite aspect of this stand is undoubtedly the disabled section at the rear. There were plenty of wheelchair spaces next to plastic seats for able-bodied companions, which were accessible from the back of the stand. Being able to watch the action from the back row, while intermingling with hardcore fans, made such a refreshing and exhilarating change from being isolated at pitch level without adequate cover.[1]

Either side of the stand, the ground retains its flat standing areas and grass banking. There is a wide expanse of land at the rear of the stand, which forms the entrance to the club car park.

My dad and his missus had left me reading the programme while they returned to the club shop to try to get a heavily discounted pie. I was reading about the likelihood of an increase in payments to WPL clubs playing in European competitions, when I was interrupted by more friendliness. After experiencing warm hospitality at nearby Marston's Stadium a few weeks earlier, I'd come to the conclusion that there must be something in the water in these parts. Maybe they should bottle it as this reserved misery guts for one would certainly benefit from such an elixir. I'd never dream of sidling up to

---

[1] The self-explanatory wheelchair spaces were marked with the International Wheelchair Symbol, just in case any retard wondered why there was a lack of seats in the back row. Some imaginative scamps armed with a marker pen had scrawled a stick penis on the wheelchair symbol and added an extra character sitting on the cock in question while stating "I like it up the bum" in a speech bubble. It made me smile.

a stranger and opening a conversation from scratch as the stadium announcer, notebook in hand, was doing with me now.

Kick-off was approaching. I munched my way through an ordinary pie that clearly came from the same supplier as the one I'd sampled in Aberavon a few weeks earlier. It was nothing to shout about and not as appetising as it had looked while on display in the shop, under the deceptive glow of the pie warmer. My appetite was not helped by having to listen to Jessie J, Wiz Khalifa and Enrique Iglesias, featuring Ludacris & DJ Frank E, over the public address system as part of the dreadful *Now 78* compilation. Let me assure you that this is most certainly NOT what I call music, though I forgave the disc jockey when, following our conversation, he stopped the noise to welcome me to the GenQuip, plug my forthcoming book, and wish me all the best for the future.

As the game got underway I had a lovely warm feeling in the pit of my stomach that I recognised from my time supporting Wrexham as a teenager. It was made up of appreciation, acceptance, recognition and friendship. Little things make a big difference and after such hospitality, a chat with the manager, a free badge and an excellent view from a thoughtfully designed stand, I'd certainly be cheering on the home side this afternoon.

It was a confident start for the Blues as they had shots blocked, a penalty appeal rejected, and threatened from distance. The Steelmen – Port Talbot Steelworks underpins the local economy – also looked solid and composed in defence with goalkeeper Kristian Rogers saving well from Steve Rogers, who had Prestatyn's only real chance of note.

While it wasn't the best match I'd seen on the tour, the main stand was certainly home to the best atmosphere I'd sampled thanks to a small group of vocal and extremely passionate fans, who, according to Wikipedia, are widely regarded as some of the best in the league. Unless supporters of Aberystwyth or Newtown prove me wrong, I'd say this faction of self-proclaimed Ultras are unrivaled for noise generated within the WPL – though I should note that lively pockets of fans can also be found at Bangor and Bala. This enthusiastic collection of Steelmen use trumpets, humour, and bang loudly on the back of the stand to conjure a carnival atmosphere.

You may pour scorn on the notion that a generous handful of south Walian scallies can add much excitement to a mid-table encounter in an anonymous league, but after attending games in this league at which it is possible to hear a pin drop, the efforts of those who often congregate behind the Burns Road goal were much appreciated.

Unfortunately, these fanatics spent much of the first period dishing out abuse and moans towards referee Huw Jones and Prestatyn playmaker Neil Gibson, although it must be noted that much of their vitriol was laden with humour and, more often than not, fully justified.

Why anyone would want to be a football referee is beyond me? These officials are routinely vilified, verbally abused and have their decisions and fitness levels scrutinised by millions at the highest level. This isn't the highest level, so replace the word "millions" with "hundreds" to get a more accurate picture. When Huw Jones kept awarding free kicks to the visitors for "soft" challenges on Gibson, who struggled to stay on his feet all match, both individuals were the victims of abusive catcalls and chanting.

However, the main incident occurred in the 41st minute, when Jones awarded the home side a penalty after Cortez Belle was brought down in the box by Paul O'Neill. The Prestatyn defence complained bitterly to the referee's assistant that the challenge was fair and outside the area, so Jones ran across to consult linesman M. Davies. After a brief discussion, Jones changed his decision to a free-kick on the edge of the area. As you can imagine, the fans went berserk and some of them went over the top in their verbal criticism. Although it's disappointing that some people don't know where to draw the line, it feels wrong to overly criticise this vocal minority as much worse behaviour has been known at football grounds. The frustration I was witnessing was a result of deep-seated passion and desire to see their team succeed, which is something I haven't seen a lot of in the WPL.

Things calmed down at half-time as the Ultras moved to the other end of the stand in preparation for the second period, which continued in much the same vein as the first half with Port Talbot looking the likeliest side to break the deadlock. Chris Hartland, Martin Rose and Cortez Belle all went close but had left their shooting boots at home.

I found myself losing interest in the match and gazing at the colourful characters sitting around me, from the group of attractive WAGS whom I mentally undressed, to the drunken wastrel who, thanks to one too many swigs from his hip flask, thought he was at Mexico '86 and tried to trigger a Mexican wave.

I resolved to buy a hip flask.

A typical father and son were sitting a few rows in front of me. The youngster was ignoring the game that his dad had paid good money for and was running back and forth to the burger van, instead of being inspired by the action in front of him. The adult looked disappointed that the planned bonding experience was not working out in the romantic way he imagined. In reality it was never going to happen. A greasy cheeseburger with lashings of tomato sauce will always be more appealing to a youngster than the pedestrian meanderings of part-time wannabes. It was an unremarkable scene that is repeated regularly, wherever overenthusiastic father figures attempt to impregnate their offspring with second-hand passion. The only reason that I mention these familiar occurrences is because the characters in this particular episode were black.

EVERY SILVER LINING HAS A CLOUD Nathan Lee Davies

Sadly, this is the first time I have seen non-white supporters at any game in the WPL and, although I haven't been witness to any overt racism in the competition, it is noticeable that the teams are made up of predominantly white players and nurtured by Caucasian coaching staff. This is unrepresentative of modern, multicultural Wales and something that clearly needs addressing if the sport hopes to grow and flourish throughout the country.

Thankfully the FAW, often criticised for being out of touch and stagnant, have displayed commendable social awareness and positive forward thinking by throwing their weight behind the Show Racism the Red Card (SRtRC) campaign. At every ground I have visited there have been prominent billboards, loudspeaker announcements, or pages in programmes to help educate ignorant retards, and remind them that racist outbursts are highly offensive and won't be tolerated.

Wales manager Gary Speed highlighted the FAW's stance against racism and said: "I'm very supportive of SRtRC, I think football is a place where racism does happen and hopefully with the help of SRtRC it can be eradicated as football is a great tool to help break down the barriers and to stop prejudices."

The message was being constantly reinforced in the run-up to a Fortnight of Action. This period of concerted action encourages participation from all sections of society to celebrate diversity and tackle racism.

"This season will see more clubs than ever unite across Wales. All clubs are to host an event for school children, which will see WPL players talking to pupils about their experiences. This is a big step towards stopping racism in the playground and in the community," said Jason Webber, SRtRC Wales campaign worker.

SRtRC's work is funded by the FAW. A spokesperson for the governing body underlined its importance:

EVERY SILVER LINING HAS A CLOUD Nathan Lee Davies

"The Fortnight of Action, which Show Racism the Red Card coordinates in Wales, is a hugely important event in the football calendar. The Football Association of Wales believes that the support from its clubs during this campaign will help to educate and re-educate football fans of all ages in order to stamp out the threat of racism in the terraces and on the football pitches in Wales."

I truly hope that the Fortnight of Action proves a groundbreaking success and encourages more over-enthusiastic fathers to introduce disinterested children to football and cheeseburgers in Wales, regardless of their racial or ethnic background.

Back on the pitch there was more controversy as the home side were reduced to ten men. Chris Hartland was issued a straight red card for his challenge on the much-maligned Neil Gibson after 67 minutes. The referee was not afraid of putting himself in the limelight and, after watching the incident countless times on *Sgorio*, his decision does seem rather harsh. There is no denying that the challenge was poorly timed, but it wasn't two-footed and despite the theatrical reaction of Gibson there seemed to be minimal, if any, connection between the players. This is my opinion anyway. The Talbot fans made their feelings clear. Gibson's every touch was thereafter met by a chorus of boos.

I only had two grounds left to visit after this one and was proud of my record of not seeing a goalless encounter throughout the tour. I looked at my watch anxiously. There were 20 minutes left.

Despite being a man down, Port Talbot remained in control and would've proved worthy winners had Brookes, Rose and Walters taken their chances. It seemed as if it was going to be one of those days. With time running out, the home side began to tire and Prestatyn threatened to snatch an undeserved victory, but Jon Fisher-Cooke and Steve Rogers both saw poor efforts sail hopelessly high of the crossbar.

EVERY SILVER LINING HAS A CLOUD Nathan Lee Davies

So that was it. I'd previously seen 32 goals in just nine WPL games, but on this occasion a mixture of competent defending, controversial refereeing and woeful finishing spoilt my record. Mark Jones summed the game up well:

"It's rare for a referee to overturn a penalty he had awarded. He told me his assistant overruled him, but the ref had a better view of the situation.

"Prestatyn are masters of scrapping for a point and they set out to spoil and got their reward.

"Our keeper did not have a save to make all afternoon and we were clearly the better side and should have won.

"But we lacked that little bit of composure in the box and we have to be incisive when we are on top."

Neil Gibson was unavailable for comment as he was busy plotting his next mischievous deed with the wicked witch, Dastardly Whiplash and the rest of the pantomime villains.

***

I was looking forward to leaving south Wales for the final time, but before I did there was time to join players, staff and supporters for a few bottles of cheap European lager, while watching Manchester United demolish Chelsea on a widescreen TV in the Port Talbot social club. As Chris Smalling, Nani and Wayne Rooney put United in an unassailable half-time lead, I wished the Port Talbot players has shown similar killer instincts in front of goal. Still, at least these semi-professionals could pick up tips from these prima donnas in time for their next match at Llanelli's Stebonheath Park.

I looked across the crowded bar area at the players I'd been willing to score just minutes earlier. As the goals flew in at Old Trafford, the exhausted amateurs were huddled together with their backs to the scintillating action, grazing over a mouth-watering buffet. They were concentrating so intently on replenishing the energy they had just expended that they even missed Fernando Torres notch his first goal of a barren season. It wasn't until the goals had dried up that the part-time athletes stopped scoffing and gave their full attention to the game. They were just in time to watch Torres skip around United goalkeeper David de Gea before catastrophically shooting wide with the open goal at his mercy.

It therefore wasn't much of a surprise to learn that Port Talbot lost 2-0 at Llanelli and looked particularly toothless in front of goal.

Port Talbot Town
GenQuip Stadium

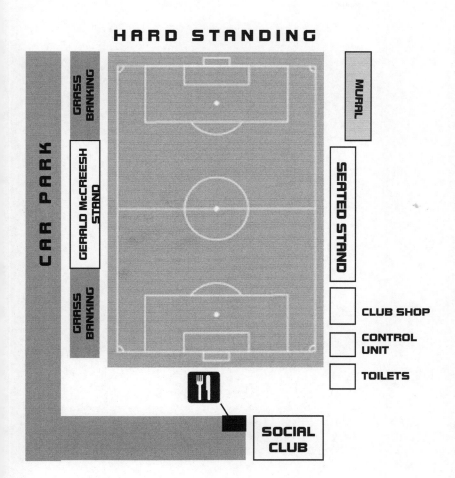

HARD STANDING

CAR PARK

GRASS BANKING

GERALD McCREESH STAND

GRASS BANKING

MURAL

SEATED STAND

CLUB SHOP

CONTROL UNIT

TOILETS

SOCIAL CLUB

THE NEW SAINTS

Temporary seating in front of the leisure centre
PHOTOGRAPH BY ROB HOPWOOD

The new 500-seat cantilever stand, opened July 2012
PHOTOGRAPH BY ROB HOPWOOD

RIGHT
Looking towards the Burma
Road end
PHOTOGRAPH BY PAUL DAVIES

RIGHT Dugouts, TV gantry and police control unit PHOTOGRAPH BY PAUL DAVIES

BELOW The Martin Walsh Stand
PHOTOGRAPH BY MARK JONES - Prestatyn Town

PRESTATYN TOWN

Disabled Enclosure - PHOTOGRA
MARK JONES - Prestatyn Town

BANGOR CITY

rtacabin on stilts
PHOTOGRAPH BY PAUL DAVIES

Phoenix Metals & Demolition Ltd.

Bangor City v Llanelli AFC

Seated stands and covered terracing (below) at the dilapidated Farrar Road
PHOTOGRAPHS BY PAUL DAVIES

Dugouts and TV gantry
PHOTOGRAPH BY PAUL DAVIES

BALA TOWN

LEFT A warm welcome at Maes Tegid

PHOTOGRAPHS BY PAUL DAVIES

Croeso i'r
BALA
welcomes you

AIRBUS UK BROUGHTON

Retractable floodlights at rest

LEFT Seated stand and TV gantry

PHOTOGRAPHS BY PAUL DAVIES

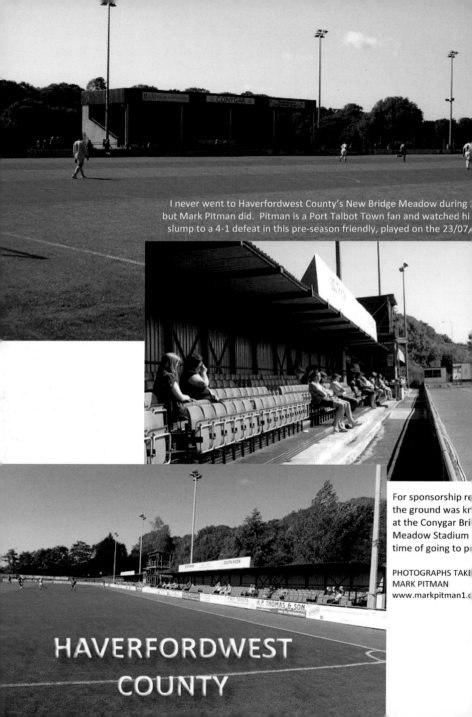

I never went to Haverfordwest County's New Bridge Meadow during
but Mark Pitman did. Pitman is a Port Talbot Town fan and watched hi
slump to a 4-1 defeat in this pre-season friendly, played on the 23/07,

For sponsorship re
the ground was kr
at the Conygar Bri
Meadow Stadium
time of going to p

PHOTOGRAPHS TAKE
MARK PITMAN
www.markpitman1.c

HAVERFORDWEST
COUNTY

PARC Y SCARLETS

Parc y Scarlets - heart and soul rugby country
Hywel Wiliams and licensed for reuse under a Creative Commons Licence

Statue of Ray Gravell
graph taken from www.walesonline.co.uk by an uncredited photographer

West Stand
PHOTOGRAPH BY PAUL DAVIES

ABOVE Home team dugout
BELOW Dugouts, seated stand and TV gantry at the
Marston's Stadium
PHOTOGRAPHS BY PAUL DAVIES

AFAN LIDO FOOTBALL CLUB

STADIWM MARSTON'S STADIUM

**AFAN
LIDO**

Main sta
PHOTOGRAPH BY PAUL DAV

Uncovered and covered
terracing at Neath
PHOTOGRAPHS BY PAUL DAVIES

NEATH

Uncovered terrace, TV gantry and Gilbert Lloyd Stand
PHOTOGRAPH BY PAUL DAVIES

LLANELLI

The Robbie James Stand
PHOTOGRAPH BY PAUL DAVIES

Stebonheath Park in 2006
© David Luther Thomas and licensed for reuse under a Creative
Commons Licence.

CARMARTHEN TOWN

ABOVE Clay Shaw Butler Stand

RIGHT Club shop

BELOW Clubhouse

PHOTOGRAPHS BY PAUL DAVIES

PORT TALBOT TOWN

The Gerald McCreesh Stand
PHOTOGRAPH BY PAUL DAVIES

THE STEELMEN
TALBOT TOWN FC
v Prestatyn Town

Mural at the GenQuip Stadium
PHOTOGRAPH BY PAUL DAVIES

The Dias Stand
PHOTOGRAPH BY PAUL DAVIES

RIGHT
The lofty and narrow main stand
PHOTOGRAPH BY PAUL DAVIES

BELOW
Executive boxes, TV gantry and media unit
PHOTOGRAPH BY PAUL DAVIES

ABERYSTWYTH TOWN

Dogs are not welcome at Park Avenue
PHOTOGRAPH BY PAUL DAVIES

The new main stand at Latham Park
PHOTOGRAPH BY PAUL DAVIES

Uncovered bank of s
where away suppor
usually congreg
PHOTOGRAPH BY PAUL DA

Sgorio   S4/C

DISABLED
SEATING
AERA

Shocking spelling
PHOTOGRAPH BY PAUL DAVIES

ANGOR CITY

Seated stands and TV gantry
PHOTOGRAPH BY PAUL DAVIES

e plush main stand at Bangor City's new home at Nantporth
OTOGRAPH BY PAUL DAVIES

Mold Road Stand
PHOTOGRAPH BY ROB HOPWOOD

WREXHAM

Wrexham Football Club
Welcome to the Racecourse

Croeso i'r Cae Ras

LEFT The Turf
PHOTOGRAPH BY
ROB HOPWOOD

BELOW Home
© Roger Cornfoot and
licensed for reuse under a
Creative Commons Licence

16
Sunday Bloody Sunday

EVERY SILVER LINING HAS A CLOUD Nathan Lee Davies

> Every woman on the face of the earth has complete
> control of my life, and yet I want them all. Is that irony?
>
> George Costanza
> *Seinfeld* – "The Baby Shower"

I can't stand Sundays.

Most men my age – or at least the fictional majority that live in my mind and taunt me endlessly with their perfect lives that I can only dream of – cherish this peaceful day and fill it with all sorts of activities, ranging from reading newspapers over a pint or three in an idyllic country pub, discovering a rare piece of football memorabilia at a car boot sale, or watching their youngest son in action for the local under-10 football team down the park, while looking forward to a roast dinner with the in-laws.

I can understand the attraction of savouring the last day of rest before the resumption of the working week, but when you're single and unemployed, all that's left is crap TV, no mail, the inconvenience of shops closing at 4pm and the build-up of jealous frustration as no-one answers telephone calls, texts or emails. They're too busy having fun with friends and family at the local multiplex, while I prepare to go to hell for wanking over the female vicar featured on *Songs of Praise*.

It's no fun being single. There are certain advantages, such as not changing your socks for a month and not having to ignore inane chatter while trying to concentrate on *Match of the Day*, but these small benefits are completely outweighed by the lack of regular sex and having to learn how to use a microwave.

With such an enlightened attitude it's a wonder that I'm still on the market.

I definitely need to fix myself up though. Not only am I living in a world that is geared to providing entertainment and opportunities for couples and families, but the aforementioned female vicar was well past her prime and sported a five o'clock shadow.

Subsequently, I'm forced to prostitute myself via various dating websites, social networks and escort agencies. In particularly desperate moments, I've even offered substantial amounts of money in return for "company" to women selling used underwear on eBay. How low can a human being go? It doesn't help that I've always been confused about the differences between love and sex. I want both, but it took me too long and many regretted unions to realise that sex is a cheap and nasty business without the softening sheen of love.

With this in mind, I'm forced to remain patient in the unrealistic hope that my online adverts will result in a flood of replies. I won't hold my breath...

***

NATHANLEE01: Genuine Bloke

Age	**34**
Height	**5'10"**
Build	**Average**
Eyes	**Brown**
Location	**Wrexham, North Wales**
Occupation	**Writer**
Religion	**Non-Religious**
Starsign	**Aquarius**
Smoker	**No**
Pets	**No**
Marital Status	**Divorced**
Longest Relationship	**7 Years**

EVERY SILVER LINING HAS A CLOUD Nathan Lee Davies

Do you....?

SMOKE?	NO
HAVE CHILDREN?	NO
WANT CHILDREN?	UNDECIDED
TAKE DRUGS?	NO
DRINK?	SOCIALLY
HAVE A CAR?	YES

INTERESTS: Comedy, Cinema, Architecture, Football, Writing, Reading, Music, Concerts, Modern Art

ABOUT ME

Thanks for taking the time to read this. I am a genuine, honest and loyal bloke with a big heart that happens to suffer from a progressive, genetic disease of the nervous system known as Friedreich's Ataxia. This has confined me to a wheelchair but not slowed me down as I still cram as much as possible into life. In the past, I've performed a parachute jump, spent six months as a student in the USA and travelled from Southampton to New York on the QE2.

I am currently writing my first book, to be published later this year. My music taste is rich and varied and includes: Stereophonics, Radiohead, Oasis, Stone Roses, Buzzcocks, Sex Pistols, Charlatans, Frank Sinatra, Beethoven and Elvis.

EVERY SILVER LINING HAS A CLOUD Nathan Lee Davies

I enjoy watching live music and comedy.

Any questions just message me :)

***

YOU HAVE JUST RECEIVED A NEW MESSAGE FROM Pinky78

A heady mixture of hope and excitement hangs in the air. The email is from a 33-year-old from Liverpool with photographs attached. They're just downloading.

While I wait patiently for pictures of Pinky78 to magically appear before my eyes, I began to reflect on the barren, affectionless years since my divorce. I turn my face towards the mirror. It didn't crack. You may think I'm biased and deluded, but while I recognise that I don't compete with film and television stars in terms of looks, neither do I think I have a face for radio that turns people off their dinner. So why is there such a lack of interest?

We both know the answer but you won't admit it, especially if you're a woman, for fear of being labelled as shallow and heartless. It's therefore up to me to point out that I'll always struggle to get laid due to my disability. There is nothing sexy or appealing about having a genetic disease eating away at your brain, or having to have your bollocks washed by a third party. Never mind the fact that I'm a caring soul with a heart of gold and good sense of humour, who boasts a good track record in the bedroom that never fails to satisfy. What really seems to matter is the fact that I can't kill spiders, shake my booty on the dance floor, or go for romantic walks along the beach.

I'm disillusioned with the whole dating scene. It's a superficial and image-conscious world in which I clearly don't belong. I don't know what the answer is, but unless my new Scouse friend fulfils the potential suggested on her profile page, I foresee a lonely future with only a box of man-sized tissues to keep me company.

DOWNLOAD COMPLETE

Oh, dear God.

Just because I use a wheelchair, doesn't mean I'd sink that low. I'd rather date the female vicar from *Songs of Praise* – five o' clock shadow and all. It's a vicious circle of my own contradictory making, but I'm only treating others as they treat me.

With a deep breath, the search continues...

***

I don't normally hang about on BBC Three once *Family Guy* has finished, but the other week I found myself watching *Cherry Healy: How to Get a Life.* Any advice is welcomed so I gave it five minutes. This particular episode was entitled "How Prejudiced Are We?" Cherry spends an hour on a quest to find out how prejudiced we are in today's politically-correct world. She asks if we are as open-minded as we like to think and examines if intolerance and bigotry are still rife in the UK? To help her get a snapshot of modern Britain she meets a female firefighter, a black ballet dancer, a wheelchair user and a victim of discrimination in the workplace.

It wasn't the greatest piece of investigative journalism I've ever seen, but I was intrigued by her discussions with Leah Caprice, a wheelchair user from Caerphilly, who worked as a lap dancer and porn star until an accident left her in a wheelchair and threatened her career. Quite rightly, but much to Cherry's disbelief, she continued working in "adult" circles and merely changed her target audience to those with a fetish for women in wheelchairs. For more information visit Leah's personal website at www.paraprincess.com – you won't be disappointed.

Anyway, I digress. What I found really interesting were the statistics that Cherry shared during her interviews. Apparently, 70% of "us" –

she must be addressing "normal" people – wouldn't consider having sex with someone who has a physical disability. Further still, only 4% of people admit to having a disabled sexual partner. If I can admit to wasting eight years on my overweight ex then why can't others admit to sleeping with those with disabilities? After all, every hole's a goal.

Seriously though, if such statistics are credible, it seems I'm fighting a losing battle and am destined to be alone. I can only hope the 30% of people who would sleep with a spastic are not all gormless munters.

Aberystwyth Town 1 Prestatyn Town 3

Corbett Sports Welsh Premier League
Sunday, 25 September 2011
14:30

Park Avenue / Coedlan Y Parc
Attendance: 314

There were 23 minutes on the clock when Neil Gibson latched on to a Chris Davies through ball and steered a firm shot beyond Steve Cann in the Aberystwyth goal. The goalscoring midfielder celebrated his strike with a full-length Klinsmann dive in front of a jubilant handful of Prestatyn fans, who appreciated the ironic gesture after the referee's performance at Port Talbot the week previously.

This was the fourth time I'd seen Prestatyn during this tour. This wasn't intentional, but turned out to be a happy coincidence as player-manager Gibson had assembled a squad that played an attractive, passing game that was a pleasure to watch when all was going to plan – as it was now.

In the time remaining before the interval, the Black and Greens had opportunities to equalise through James McCarten and the ever-dangerous Geoff Kellaway, but it was Prestatyn who could've doubled their tally before the break. Gibson and Steve Rogers combined effectively to set up Ross Stephens, who was unlucky to see his shot sail wide of the upright.

At least the home side completed the opening 45 minutes with all 11 men on the pitch. I'd watched Aberystwyth's first game of the season at Neath when defender Sion James picked up two yellow cards and was sent for an early bath after only 18 minutes. This dismissal began a worrying trend as Aber had collected five red cards and 15 yellows in six games ahead of this game.

"We obviously need to address our disciplinary record, and we have had our quota of red cards for the season, but the number of cards that are being issued is something that needs to be looked into," said Town manager Alan Morgan.

"It is not that we are making bad tackles all of a sudden, and we are not a dirty side, anyone who has played us has said that, but at this rate players will be afraid to get involved in tackles at all."

The former Tranmere midfielder was recognising that his side had a discipline problem that needed addressing, but that didn't stop Wyn Thomas from picking up a second yellow card on 58 minutes for a clumsy challenge on Prestatyn's Paul O'Neil.

Yet again, Aberystwyth were forced to regroup and reorganise with only ten men at their disposal, but it was apparent that they were becoming adept at this. Just two minutes later, Andy Parkinson's cross was cleared and Lewis Codling equalised with a shot into the top corner. This new found sense of attacking purpose didn't last for long though, as barely a minute later, the visitors regained the lead – Gibson's shot rebounded to Mike Parker, who drilled home from fifteen yards.

Despite their best efforts, Aber were on their way to a third consecutive home defeat and would end the day struggling in tenth position, which was a crying shame for a club of such size and tradition, who play at one of the most impressive grounds in the WPL.

Although Aberystwyth Town FC were officially formed in 1884, the club probably existed in the 1870s in an earlier incarnation. It seems that this town team played at Vicarage Field, Smithfield Road and Barracks Field but moved back to Vicarage Field in 1893. They remained here until 1906 when Aberystwyth University bought the ground and evicted Town, forcing them to return to Smithfield Road, which was renamed Park Avenue in October 1934. The site was first recorded as being used for football as far back as 1881. You'd never guess it as it's been developed and well-maintained ever since, resulting in a venue that is often used by the FAW when searching for a neutral venue to hold cup finals and other showpiece games. The splendid facilities on offer are made all the more attractive by its mid-Wales location and good transport links.[1]

According to the *Corbett Sports Welsh Premier League Guide 2011-12*, Park Avenue has a capacity of 2,502 of which 1,002 is seated. I enjoyed the game from a raised wooden platform in the corner of the Town End that was positioned next to hard standing and a block of uncovered, temporary seating along a chaotic and eclectic mishmash of a touchline, which also includes a turnstile and toilet block, a TV gantry on top of a two-storey set of executive boxes, grass banking and a media unit, where the match programmes and team-sheets are printed. The club website is also updated from here.

On the opposite side of the pitch stands a tall but narrow main stand, which straddles the halfway line. This structure houses the changing rooms below a raised seating area of 250 seats, which is covered by a sloping roof that has been painted with ABER FC in standout letters, to avoid any confusion as to your whereabouts. When positioned amongst the lofty seats it's possible to peer down through glazed side panels onto a 5-a-side court to the right hand side, and a vast array of buildings to the left, including a club shop, social club and tea bar.

Behind the goal to the left is an undeveloped grass embankment while the Dias Stand – a modern cantilever structure complete with 322 seats in seven rows – runs the width of the penalty area behind the Town End goal to the right. This stand is named after club legend

---

[1] On 7 July 1956, Park Avenue held a number of boxing bouts, including a contest between Newport-born Dick Richardson and Gunther Nurnberg of Germany, for the European Heavyweight Championship. Richardson, who had held his training sessions at the Royal Pier on Aberystwyth seafront, won the fight with a third round knock-out.

David "Dias" Williams, who holds the club scoring record of 476 goals in only 433 games, between 1966 and 1983.

Alan Morgan would certainly benefit from being able to call on such a prolific goalscorer on this occasion as despite the valiant efforts of the ten men, they couldn't find a way past a resolute Prestatyn defence. Aber's misery was compounded in the last minute when Steve Rogers crowned a hardworking display by the visitors with a goal from a classic counter attack.

An over-salted cheeseburger at half-time meant my need for liquid refreshment was pressing, so before leaving the ground I visited the John Charles Lounge to quench my thirst. This is a spacious bar with the usual array of memorabilia, flat-screen televisions, hideous carpeting and attractive barmaids. Clubs certainly take pride in their watering holes throughout the WPL, but the regulars at Park Avenue have more reason than most to cherish their impressive facility, which was completely overhauled and modernised following a devastating fire on 20 November 2004.

Aberystwyth had travelled to near-neighbours Newtown for a WPL clash earlier that afternoon. It was an absorbing contest that finished 2-3 to the visitors, whose fans returned to Park Avenue to celebrate the victory in familiar surroundings. The doomed venue was hosting an obscure comedian, who wasn't exactly going down a storm, when the unamused occupants of the bar were suddenly evacuated due to a small fire. The lack of laughter lasted long into the night as the flames caught hold, quickly spread and set about destroying this popular social spot.

A spokesman for Dyfed-Powys Police said: "The fire was discovered by a member of staff in an area of the clubhouse that was unoccupied at the time. Enquiries conducted jointly by Dyfed-Powys Police and fire service investigators have revealed that there is nothing to indicate that the origin of the fire is suspicious."

EVERY SILVER LINING HAS A CLOUD Nathan Lee Davies

Aberystwyth club secretary Rhun Owens said it was impossible to put a price on the memorabilia that was lost. "About six amateur international caps have been destroyed, trophies from the old Welsh League have melted down and photographs of some of the club's top players have been destroyed. Some of the items stretch back decades to the 1950s. The lounge area was destroyed and the boardroom suffered smoke damage."

Thankfully, there were no casualties or injuries. In the end, Aberystwyth received a healthy insurance settlement of £151,000, which they put to good use judging by the well-appointed phoenix that has been raised from the ashes. The local community has certainly helped rejuvenate the building by donating masses of old photographs and assorted pieces of memorabilia from Aberystwyth's past. These items were probably discarded and forgotten about at the back of wardrobes until the fire resulted in an appeal to locals to help breathe new life into their social club – it certainly seems as if they've stepped forward.

After quenching my thirst, a trip to the little boy's room was in order. I was happy to be directed to accessible toilet facilities situated down a carpeted corridor, which was decorated with some random but impressively priceless collectors' items. Framed and signed portraits of the Arsenal Invincibles of 2003-04, Ally McCoist of Rangers and Jimmy Johnstone of Celtic featured alongside photographs of George Best with Denis Law in their United heyday, plus a shot of Ricky Villa notching the winner in the 1981 FA Cup final, next to a signed replica of his jersey. This treasure trove even included a signed England replica shirt from the 40th anniversary of their 1966 World Cup success and photographs of Geoff Hurst's third goal in the final, along with imagery from the 1970 World Cup, when Gordon Banks pulled off that miraculous save from Pele. Just what all this was doing at Park Avenue I'm not sure, but nevertheless it was an impressive collection that captured my attention before and after I relieved myself.

EVERY SILVER LINING HAS A CLOUD Nathan Lee Davies

On the way back up to north Wales, I browsed the 28-page programme for two minutes but soon gave up as I can't translate Welsh and had little interest in reading Prestatyn pen pictures for the third time this season. Before closing the magazine, it did amuse me to discover that, according to his manager's notes, Alan Morgan was planning to attend a meeting on the laws of the game where he would be asking for greater consistency from referees. I would argue that six red cards in seven games is a consistent indictment of Morgan's team, who would clearly benefit from their manager drilling home the lessons he learnt from the laws of the game conference, sooner rather than later, if they want to avoid a relegation battle.

The tour was almost over. Just one more ground to go. I'd like to report that I spent the remainder of the journey deep in reflective thought about the success of the tour, considering what I'd learnt about Welsh football and my own identity, but instead, I stared aimlessly out of the window and thought about sex.

Aberystwyth Town
Park Avenue

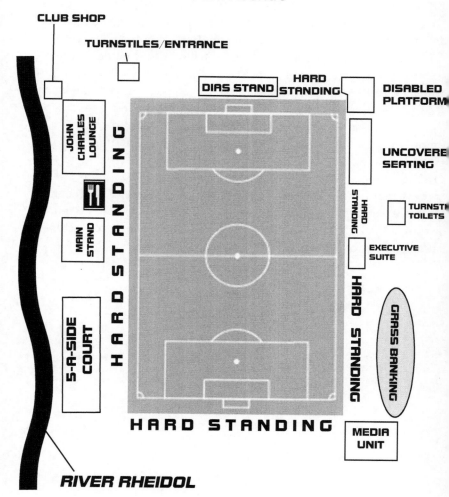

17
Are you Sitting Comfortably?

Mr. Cynic

by Nathan Lee Davies

[Illustrator's instructions: A portrait of Mr Cynic should appear on the front cover. This character is made up of a large red face – complete with straggly beard and glasses – with long arms and wheels instead of legs. He should always wear a frown and frustrated facial expression]

It was a cold, dark night.

Mr Cynic sat alone in his bungalow watching *Coronation Street*. He enjoyed watching the miserable lives of fictional characters as it made him feel better about his own pathetic life.

You didn't know there was such thing as a cynic, did you?

Well, there is.

Cynics believe all people are motivated by selfishness and have a habitually negative outlook on life.

[*Illustrator's instructions: Show Mr Cynic watching TV. Include a window through which it is possible to see the night sky, illuminated by a white half moon and a sprinkling of yellow stars*]

Mr Cynic was the most cynical person you've ever met in your entire life.

He was cynical in everything he did. To make matters worse, he combined this negative attitude with unhealthy amounts of pessimism, and always predicted that the worst possible scenario was about to unfold.

Deep down, Mr Cynic was a nice person, but he'd suffered appalling misfortunes that meant he could no longer look on the bright side of life.

DIVORCE

HOMELESSNESS

ILLNESS

[*Illustrator's instructions: This picture page should simply be printed entirely in black to portray the dark and depressing days that resulted in such negativity*]

Mr Cynic did not think he was a cynic, but a realist with life experiences.

[*Illustrator's instructions: Draw three glasses half full of yellow liquid. The three glasses should stand above descriptive text. Glass one is labelled Optimistic, Glass B is Pessimistic and Glass C is Realistic. Above each glass should be the following phrases – Glass A: "I'm half full", Glass B: "I'm half empty", Glass C: "This yellow liquid is an old man's piss" Thanks to www.sodahead.com for the inspiration*]

Coronation Street finished and was followed by the *Pride of Britain Awards*, which celebrates the achievements of truly remarkable people, who make our world a better place.

Mr Cynic felt nauseous and switched off the television in disgust.

What to do now?

[*Illustrator's instructions: A TV remote being thrown across the room towards a television featuring a heart of gold*]

Mr Cynic decided to put on his raincoat and venture outside into the gloomy darkness.

Before leaving his bungalow, Mr Cynic, being Mr Cynic, put a padlock around his fridge, hid his valuables and dead bolted the front door again and again and again, to keep his home safe from burglars, who were bound to strike his quiet neighbourhood one day.

Mr Cynic trusted no one.

[*Illustrator's instructions: A fridge- freezer with a padlock around it while a disgruntled mouse looks on in frustration*]

Mr Cynic went to visit his friend Mr Bitter, who lived on the other side of a moonlit wood.

It was a particularly large wood, with lots and lots and lots of trees, which were home to all manner of creepy crawlies. Mr Cynic didn't really mind because he was in a reckless mood that evening.

So he rolled and rolled and rolled between the trees until he came to the other side.

[*Illustrator's instructions: Mr Cynic surrounded by trees in a moonlit wood*]

Mr Cynic was grumbling and groaning as he dusted cobwebs from the wood out of his hair.

All of a sudden, he saw a figure out of the corner of his eye.

It was Mr Liar – the right-wing loon who was standing in the forthcoming local elections.

[*Illustrator's instructions: A head and upper torso portrait of Mr Liar, who is wearing a blue suit, blue tie and blue rosette, which says Vote Liar on it. The clean-shaven Mr Liar is also wearing a black top hat, decorated with blue ribbon*]

"Can I count on your support at the forthcoming local elections?" asked Mr Liar.

"Don't talk to me about voting or politics. I'm not interested. All politicians are self-serving and corrupt. My vote won't change a thing," said our negative friend before pushing past a crestfallen Mr Liar.

Mr Cynic continued on his way to visit Mr Bitter.

[*Illustrator's instructions: Mr Cynic rolling towards a village set in distance. The houses are picked out by street lights*]

Eventually, Mr Cynic reached Mr Bitter's house, but the curtains were closed and the lights were switched off.

Mr Cynic knocked, banged and thumped on Mr Bitter's door but to no avail.

No one was home.

"The bastard is probably having fun with others, without inviting me," moaned Mr Cynic.

[*Illustrator's instructions: Mr Cynic's red fist thumping against Mr Bitter's green front door*]

While he was on this side of the wood, Mr Cynic decided to pay a surprise visit to Little Miss Twisted.

Don't tell anyone but Mr Cynic had a secret crush on Little Miss Twisted as not only did she have big boobs, but she was the only person who could make him smile.

Optimism and hope were not familiar feelings to our miserable mate, but whenever he was with Little Miss Twisted he had a sunnier disposition.

[*Illustrator's instructions: Facial portrait of Mr Cynic, who is deep in thought with a thought cloud showing that he is thinking about Little Miss Twisted – a leggy blonde dressed in black lingerie, stockings and suspenders*]

On his way, Mr Cynic bumped into Mr Holy, the local vicar.

"Good evening," said Mr Holy. "Can we expect you at Church on Sunday? You'd be very welcome."

"I don't have time for your sanctimonious shit. Religions are all alike – founded upon fables and mythologies," growled Mr Cynic.

"But..."

It was too late. Mr Cynic had stormed off in the direction of Little Miss Twisted's house.

[*Illustrator's instructions: A full body drawing of Mr Holy. He should have a black shirt and white dog collar combination. He is an elderly, wrinkly man with a comb-over. He should be clutching a Bible in one hand and a walking stick in the other*]

Eventually, he reached Little Miss Twisted's house, but the curtains were closed and the lights were switched off.

Mr Cynic knocked, banged and thumped on Little Miss Twisted's door but to no avail.

No one was home.

"The bitch is probably having fun with others, without inviting me," moaned Mr Cynic.

[*Illustrator's instructions: Mr Cynic's red fist thumping against Little Miss Twisted's yellow front door*]

Mr Cynic was out of options, so he decided to visit the local pub for a pint before heading home.

On the way, he was accosted by Mr Camelot who implored him to play the National Lottery.

"£1 for a combination of six numbers and you can have as many different combinations as you wish. You can now play on Wednesday and Saturday. It could be you."

"Bah. Do I look like an idiot? I won't pay a working class tax for middle class causes," protested Mr Cynic as he stormed off towards the pub.

[*Illustrator's instructions: A full body drawing of Mr Camelot, who is wearing a white suit, embroidered with green pound signs and golden coins. He is holding a bottle of champagne and has wads of money spilling out of his pockets*]

Eventually, Mr Cynic reached the pub and found two doors side by side. One was marked with the letter A, while the other door was marked with the letter B.

Mr Cynic didn't know which door to open. Door A or Door B?

Can you help him decide?

Turn to page 30 if you think Mr Cynic should open Door A

Turn to page 32 if you think Mr Cynic should open Door B [Warning: Parental Guidance Advised]

[*Illustrator's instructions: Two black doors marked with big silver lettering. The left hand door should be marked A, while the right hand door is marked B. The wall surrounding the doors should be coloured bright orange*]

DOOR A

Mr Cynic opened Door A.

"Surprise!".

Mr Cynic was lost for words. He had forgotten all about his birthday, but fortunately his family and friends hadn't.

They were all here – even Mr Bitter and Little Miss Twisted, who gave him a big kiss on the lips.

My Cynic rolled around the dance floor, ate mountains of sausage rolls and unwrapped hundreds of presents from well-wishers. He had a great time.

From that night onwards, Mr Cynic stopped being so cynical. He learnt to be more optimistic and started to give people the benefit of the doubt.

Mr Cynic began going to church and even tried his luck with a lottery ticket, but he drew the line at voting for Mr Liar and his Tory chums...

... that'd just be stupid.

[*Illustrator's instructions: Party scene – Balloons and streamers float around a banner that reads 'Happy Birthday Mr Cynic'. The room is full of Mr Cynic's family and friends – including Mr Bitter and Little Miss Twisted – who are smiling with their hands in the air. Running down the centre of the room is a table piled high with presents and party food*]

DOOR B

Mr Cynic opened Door B and soon wished he hadn't.

He had ventured into a spit and sawdust pub, with smashed windows, broken stools and topless barmaids.

In the centre of the room a group of cheering, leering men were gathered around a young couple performing oral sex on each other in the 69 position – it was Mr Bitter and Little Miss Twisted.

Mr Cynic vomited all over the floor. He had been stabbed in the back by his two best friends.

"Fucking bastards" said Mr Cynic and went home alone for a lonely wank.

No wonder Mr Cynic is so cynical...

[*Illustrator's instructions: The pub scene as described above*]

[*Note to editor: Door B needs to be included as a realistic ending that offsets the sickly sweet and contrived events through Door A. It teaches youngsters that the real world is full of hatred and disappointment. I do not wish to publish a patronising fairytale*]

Newtown 2 Afan Lido 1

Corbett Sports Welsh Premier League
Saturday, 01 October 2011
14:30

Latham Park / Parc Latham
Attendance: 205

The British media – and by extension the general populace of these isles – have an annoying and overenthusiastic tendency to harp on about the weather above any other subject. Whenever we get a light sprinkling of snow, or experience scorching sunshine, it is deemed important enough to knock stories of genuine political interest off the front pages. Who cares about nuclear weapons being built in the Middle-East when the sun is shining? Why worry about children starving in Africa when we can get down to Saundersfoot and eat ice cream? If Mother Nature decides to offload a portion of snow on our bewildered souls then the hysterical masses can't seriously be expected to show concern or compassion for victims of a mass murderer in the United States. They're much too busy moaning to a local journalist about the council's shortage of grit and the fact that they've run out of tea bags.

It was unseasonably hot as I arrived at Latham Park for the final stop of the tour of my homeland, but, instead of forming a guard of honour to applaud and pay tribute to my achievement, locals could only marvel at the 26-28C temperature, while discussing the possibility of a Wales v Ireland encounter at the Rugby World Cup in New Zealand – if the boyos could beat Fiji convincingly the next day. Uninterested in such small talk, I focussed on my surroundings.

This venue – home to Newtown since 1951 – was named after local sporting hero Captain George Latham, who played for Liverpool, Stoke City, and Cardiff City at the start of the century, winning 12 caps for Wales in the process. After entering the ground through

EVERY SILVER LINING HAS A CLOUD Nathan Lee Davies

entrance gates in the corner, I wondered where to start my exploration. I don't want to be critical of Latham Park as it is home to some excellent facilities, but the planning clearly hasn't been overseen by a single visionary. Instead, it is home to a number of different stands and structures that lack co-ordination and symmetry, but make up an eclectic mix to fascinate a ground enthusiast such as myself.

I found myself rolling along a flat standing area between the near goal and a line of trees that run along a steep slope to provide a natural border that encloses the ground from the car park beyond. This dusty slope includes a few slivers of terracing, randomly positioned crush barriers and some quaint wooden benches that provide a perfect view of the Dolfor Hills, which rise above the goal opposite and dwarf the block of uncovered seating for 322 bums that sit at this end.

I settled on watching the match from the busiest side of the ground and positioned myself in front of the modern main stand. This impressive structure has a capacity of 408 and houses the home and away changing rooms at the rear of the stand, meaning players have to scuttle past supporters before, during and after a match. The same applies to the referee and his assistants who would be wise not to make any controversial decisions judging by the number of tattooed bruisers sitting in the stand.

The first row of seats on the right hand side of the stand had been removed in an attempt to fashion some spaces for disabled patrons. This was all well and good, but the area cleared wasn't wide enough for my wheelchair to squeeze into, thanks to a needless foot-high fence that bordered the stand. As a result, I wasn't covered by the oversized roof. Thank heavens it wasn't raining. My hackles were raised further when I noticed that the signage attached to the fence proclaimed this spot as the "DISABLED AERA". It's one thing to accidently make a typographical error, but quite another to ignore it and put it on display to the paying public in the hope they won't notice. Unbelievable.

Moving on, there is then a small gap before the next collection of 326 blue and red seats, though the low roof on this stand only covers the rear rows of seating. A refreshment kiosk is then set back behind the ugly Perspex dug-outs and this side is completed with dark brick buildings that include a two-storey executive suite and a social club that was rebuilt to a high standard after a major fire in September 1989.

Opposite this hive of activity is the Police Station Side, which features more hard standing with luscious green views as well as a two-tiered, narrow stand with 120 seats below a TV gantry on the upper level. This structure straddles the halfway line and neighbours a beautiful old turnstile block that remains in working order, and a low, narrow modern cantilever stand that holds 182 seats on a single tier.

I was exhausted after my ground investigations so settled down with the match day magazine before kick-off. There is not a lot I can say about the 48-page programme that I haven't said on numerous occasions throughout these pages. The standard of match day magazines is fairly average at this level – with one or two notable exceptions. Unfortunately, this edition falls into the familiar "well-produced advertising brochure category", which leaves little of interest to the casual groundhopper. Having said that, if I'm ever in need of greasy sustenance while visiting mid-Wales, I now know that I can call on the friendly folk at Jarman's – the home of great fish and chips – based on Newtown High Street. Not only does this establishment boast a restaurant and takeaway facility, but they also welcome telephone orders on 01686 625505 and were named Welsh Food Hygiene Award Winners in 2005, 2007 and 2009.

My junk food dreams were shattered by the clip-clop sound of studs on concrete as players and officials emerged from the changing rooms and made their way down the steps of the stand and onto the pitch, amidst polite ripples of applause. I couldn't help feeling Newtown have missed a trick here. If it was up to me, I'd employ a minor celebrity to call out each players name before inviting them to "Come on down" through clouds of dry ice. This would get the crowd and players really pumped up and create an explosive and unique atmosphere before a ball has even been kicked. It's just an idea, but maybe it explains why my application to become commercial manager at Latham Park was returned without thanks.

As it was, it took only nine minutes for the deadlock to be broken. Newtown striker Nick Rushden – on loan from Wrexham – picked up the ball 30 yards from goal and went on an unchallenged run before steering a low drive past the despairing dive of Chris Curtis in the Lido goal. Things seemed to be going right – for once – for the struggling home side and their beleaguered boss, Bernard McNally

The Robins dominated the first-half but failed to extend their slender advantage, which was wiped out in the 72nd minute when the resurgent visitors were awarded a soft penalty for something and nothing. It was converted confidently by Andrew Hill.

With the game now finely balanced, both goalkeepers made some stunning saves, but it was Lido who pressed hardest and looked the more likely side to pinch the points. The Aberavon seasiders were being roared on by their vocal travelling support – one burly bald bloke, who I won't describe further in case he hunts me down and rips my lungs out – but with nine minutes left, Newtown's Shane Sutton unleashed an unstoppable 25-yarder and the home support burst into life, drums and all.

It was a class strike worthy of winning any game at any level and undoubtedly the best goal I'd seen on the tour. However, my sympathies were with the lone Lido fan, who'd probably be driving home to south Wales in tears while his Mini Metro reverberated to "The Winner Takes It All" by Abba on a constant loop. Maybe he'd stop his car in a lonely spot on top of the Brecon Beacons and allow his distressed mind to dwell on the lonely and pointless journey he'd made to cheer on a bunch of amateurs. I could picture him opening the car boot and searching for the hose pipe he'd borrowed from his ex-wife to water the window box that adds a pathetic splash of colour to his bland and dreary high-rise flat.

Before my mind could race any further, I realised that this is the WPL, a set-up based around communities and enjoyment rather than finances and pressure. The lone supporter would just as likely be travelling home on the team bus and sharing jokes and laughter with the players he'd just been encouraging. Football isn't more important than life or death to most Welshmen. That honour inexplicably belongs to rugby.

***

So that's it. The end of the road and mission completed. I celebrated by visiting Jarman's for a battered cod, a portion of chips and a side order of mushy peas. I demolished my dinner in the High Street sunshine while browsing www.welsh-premier.com on my iPhone to catch up with all the day's results and league standings.

Newtown's crucial victory had lifted them off the bottom of the table, where they were replaced by Airbus UK Broughton, who'd slumped to a 3-1 defeat at tenth-placed Carmarthen. Meanwhile, The New Saints had regained top spot with a 3-2 victory over Aberystwyth Town at Park Hall, after Neath had briefly claimed pole position with a 1-2 win at Port Talbot on the Friday evening. Elsewhere, Prestatyn failed to capitalise on home advantage with a 0-2 reverse against Llanelli, while Bala were due to entertain Bangor in the Sunday game.

I checked my emails, while scooping dollops of mushy peas from a polystyrene carton with chunky chips. All of a sudden I lost my appetite as I digested the email I'd just received from Matt Smith, my publisher at Blackline Press. He began by congratulating me on visiting 13 stadiums throughout Wales during 2011 and asked me if

EVERY SILVER LINING HAS A CLOUD Nathan Lee Davies

I was enjoying the weather, before alerting me to an article he'd happened upon on the Bangor City website. What he was doing on this site is anyone's guess, but I suppose I should be grateful as he'd uncovered news that I should've picked up on months ago. The article in question quoted Bangor City chairman, Dilwyn Jones, welcoming the start of construction at the Citizens' new Nantporth ground.

"After so many years of uncertainty, it's good news that work is progressing well, and we expect it to be completed in January 2012," said Mr Jones

"We will be moving into the new ground as soon as this work is finished, so this means changing stadiums in the middle of the season. Obviously this is not ideal, but we really have little option given the ongoing deterioration in the fabric of Farrar Road, and the ongoing cost of maintaining the old stadium."

Matt felt that it'd be appropriate to visit this ground, in addition to the 12 I'd just visited, as a neat and comprehensive conclusion to the book. I felt he'd just pissed on my celebratory chips, so I dumped them in a litter bin and began looking for directions to Nantporth.

The tour was far from over...

Newtown
Latham Park

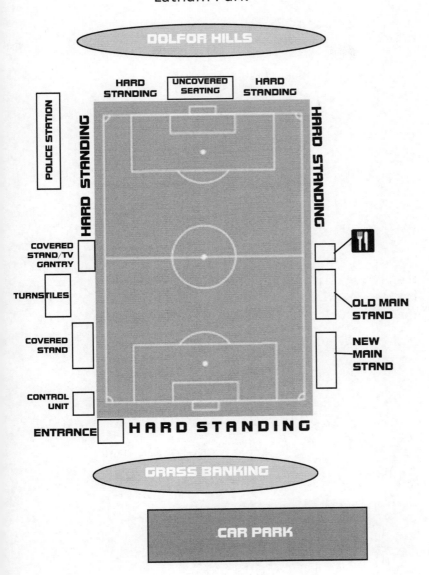

After my entertaining, exhausting and enlightening escapades around Wales, I was left with notebooks full of witty observations and a hard drive loaded with photographs of near deserted football grounds. I'd hoped to compile each chapter before venturing to the next new ground, but this was almost impossible for someone with the attention span of a circus flea who needs inspiration and motivation before opening Microsoft Word. I soon had a backlog of stories to recount and now was the time to knuckle down and play catch-up.

It was going to be a long few months.

Of course, while I was busy organising my random thoughts into an entertaining and readable structure, the WPL continued to entertain, confuse, intrigue and amaze. Subsequently, the following pages provide a monthly round up of the headline news from the rest of the season, excerpts from my own personal diary to provide some light relief and a bonus chapter on the final leg of my journey to Nantporth, Bangor.

Did I ever come to any meaningful conclusion about my own Welsh identity? Would Bangor City be able to regain the title? Is it likely that I'll ever have sex again? Could the WPL continue to provide me with material worthy of inclusion in this book? For the answer to these questions – and a few more – you'll just have to read on…

[*Many of the news items that appear on the following pages have been reproduced and revised from the excellent work of a small band of journalists and reporters who focus on Welsh domestic football. Name checks and further details can be found in the Acknowledgments section*]

18
October 2011

Sunday, 09 October 2011

I'm happy to be really busy at the moment. I'm still continuing with my book and am currently writing chapter seven. As I progress I'm sending each chapter to my publisher, Matt Smith at Blackline Press, and receiving extremely positive feedback. After reading the chapter on Bala Town he wrote:

> Once again I found it fantastic. I laughed out loud three times. My wife is reading them too and equally enjoying the story even though she has little interest in football. The great news is that I found myself repeating some of your stories at a recent social event ... that has to be good!

I am grateful to Matt for the praise and subsequent confidence boost. It particularly heartens me that his wife is enjoying the book as I'm trying to fashion a volume that will appeal to all types of people and not just those football fans in anoraks who celebrate their 40th birthday with a slice of Victoria Sponge that mum bought from Iceland.

***

Last Monday, I received an email from Andy Lyons, editor of When Saturday Comes magazine:

> We often put up short previews of forthcoming matches for the Daily Comment section of the WSC website. We thought it would be good to do something on the Hayes & Yeading v Wrexham game this coming Sunday as a way of reflecting on Dean Saunders' departure from Wrexham and fans' expectations for the season etc. Would you have time to write a short piece? It need only be 400 words or so. But we'd need it by Friday afternoon if possible.

EVERY SILVER LINING HAS A CLOUD Nathan Lee Davies

I was delighted to be given such an opportunity and rattled off an article. It was especially pleasing to get asked to write for *When Saturday Comes* as I once had an article rejected by them; they thought I focussed too much on myself and not enough on football. Does that sound like me?

The short piece I wrote, in return for a 12-month digital subscription to the magazine, follows.

www.wsc.co.uk

HOME | WSC DAILY | October 2011 | Wrexham fans enjoy some long-awaited good news

Wrexham fans enjoy some long-awaited good news

On Sunday, Wrexham will travel to face Hayes and Yeading United but I won't be programming the Church Road postcode into my satellite navigation system as I've done on our previous two visits to face the giants of Middlesex.

After selling the 4,500-capacity site to housing developers, United are currently groundsharing at Kingfield Stadium, home of Woking, while their new stadium is built on the site of Yeading's old ground, the Warren. This seems fair enough until you consider that loyal supporters will be expected to make a 40-mile round trip to Surrey for "home" games and that club finances will be strained by paying rent and losing peripheral sources of income until they transfer to Yeading.

Work on the Beaconsfield Road stadium is due to be completed before the end of the season but, following years of being tricked and deceived, Wrexham fans are ideally placed to advise United fans to take nothing for granted.

EVERY SILVER LINING HAS A CLOUD Nathan Lee Davies

Such a suspicious outlook is the by-product of years of financial uncertainty, protests over the club's owners and doubts about the future of the Racecourse. The clouds of depressing gloom that have dogged the club for years have recently started to clear though and – whisper it – there are even reports of sunshine on the horizon.

In August, Glyndwr University signed an agreement to buy Wrexham's Racecourse stadium and Collier's Park training ground while last month, after protracted negotiations, Wrexham Supporters Trust were given the green light to buy the club from shameless asset strippers. At the time of writing, the Trust are running the club under a license agreement until the football authorities sign off their full ownership, expected to happen within the next two to three weeks.

Amid all this political progress there have also been some impressive performances on the field of play, with the team amongst the early pacesetters at the top of the Blue Square Bet Premier. League clubs were alerted to this modest success and when Doncaster Rovers sacked Sean O' Driscoll they lured Dean Saunders away from the Racecourse as his replacement. Reaction to this news was mixed but the more considered supporter saw his departure in a positive light due to his high wage demands, fractious relationship with the Trust and his assembly of a budget-stretching playing squad.

There is no shortage of applicants for the vacant managers job but caretaker manager Andy Morrell has won three of his four games in charge to lead the Dragons back to the top of the table and earn himself an extended period at the helm. While Morrell maintains the momentum stumbled upon by Saunders, he will enjoy the backing of the fans who, for the time being, are free from boardroom squabbles and concentrating on the beautiful game, whichever county they're visiting.

News Round-Up

The manager of the month for August/September is Carl Darlington of The New Saints, while Llanelli's Rhys Griffiths scooped the player of the month award.

After a shaky start in August, TNS picked up form and won the next six matches up to the end of September, including an impressive 0-3 win at reigning champions Bangor City. They also beat fellow full-time outfit Neath and proved victorious against Llanelli, which meant that in the space of three weeks they beat their three main contenders for the title.

Having won the WPL Golden Boot award for the last SIX seasons, marksman Rhys Griffiths has started the season as he means to go on, with ten goals from six starts. Nine of the goals came in September and included two consecutive hat-tricks, against Newtown and Bala.

***

Terry Boyle's Wales semi-professional team secured their first ever win in the International Challenge Trophy, at the seventh time of asking.

Wales have competed in the three-match campaigns on two previous occasions, without a win, so their 1-2 victory over Estonia in Tallinn was one to celebrate, particularly as Wales started the match with nine WPL players.

Kai Edwards of Neath captained his country. Unfortunately, they fell behind to a tenth minute Artjom Dmitriev goal at the Le Coq Arena but equalised through Neath's top scorer Luke Bowen just two minutes later.

EVERY SILVER LINING HAS A CLOUD Nathan Lee Davies

It was another of Boyle's club players at Neath who got the winner. Chris Jones scored on 64 minutes with an excellent strike from outside the box. Llanelli's Craig Moses, who had three goals in five caps going into the game, squandered additional chances to put the game out of sight.

A delighted Boyle said: "It should have been more convincing as we played very, very well and we could have scored four or five, but I'm really happy with the win.

"Despite going behind, we had enough in our team for me to know we would be okay and we responded straight away with a great team goal, which Luke Bowen finished.

"We were very solid at the back throughout and Chris Jones did very well and deserved to get the winner.

"We'll now look forward to the Norwegian game at the end of the season with confidence, and hope to build on the foundations that we built today."

***

Neath moved to reassure fans about the club's future, despite having problems paying players' wages this month and the sudden departure of goalkeeper Lee Kendall.

The Eagles admit there have been "issues", which meant delayed and partial payments for the squad – but say the long-term financial situation is sound.

Fans have become increasingly worried after chairman Geraint Hawkes's import business, FG Hawkes, entered administration.

EVERY SILVER LINING HAS A CLOUD Nathan Lee Davies

Kendall has walked away from the club amid the financial troubles, while there have been rumours suggesting star striker Lee Trundle could also be on his way out.

A club spokesman said: "Long-term the club is on a sound financial footing with good sponsors and good partners who are fully behind the club.

"There have been some issues this month which have resulted in payments coming into the club late and that has delayed the payment of salaries – not totally but partially.

"These issues are being addressed this week, and by the end of the week it will be business as usual and everything will be up to date.

"The club is looking forward to the challenges up to Christmas and in the Super 12."

The spokesman also confirmed Kendall's exit.

"Lee Kendall has left the club – all the players were given the option of leaving or having the delayed payment, and Lee is the only one who chose to go."

***

League legend Gary Lloyd was the recipient of the inaugural WPL Clubman Award, which was presented at the FAW's annual dinner at Cardiff Museum. The current coach of Welsh Cup holders Llanelli, left-back Lloyd made 481 starts in the League, as well as 28 appearances from the bench, in a playing career that spanned from the opening 1992-93 season until 2008-09 when he hung up his boots. In addition, he made 29 European appearances.

After retiring, Lloyd immediately took up a coaching role at Stebonheath Park, meaning his one season with Newport County in

EVERY SILVER LINING HAS A CLOUD Nathan Lee Davies

2003-04 was the only campaign in which the 39-year-old has not been involved with the national competition.

The defender will best be remembered for his eight seasons as a full-time professional with Barry Town, where he won seven Championship medals.

"I had great times at Barry and what made it special was the experience of playing in Europe.

"I played in some fabulous ties, the best of which was probably against Aberdeen in the UEFA Cup. We played them away first and Dean Windass gave them an early lead, but Richard Jones soon equalised with a great shot from 25 yards.

"We eventually lost 3-1 but Dave O'Gorman scored after five minutes of the return game and it was "game on" again. Even after Billy Dodds hit two for Aberdeen, we still made a game of it with a penalty from Darren Ryan and a goal from Tony Bird to make it 5-4 on aggregate, but they scored a last minute goal to draw 3-3 on the night."

Lloyd also played in the Barry team that beat Portuguese giants FC Porto 1-0 at Jenner Park – sadly the result in Portugal had already put the tie beyond them – and he played in successful ties against Latvians FC Dinaberg and Budapest of Hungary.

After the financial problems at Barry in 2003, Lloyd found himself at Newport County, then operating in the Dr Martens League, but rejoined the fray with Carmarthen Town in 2004. During his spell with the Old Gold, he played in Europe as well as making an additional 48 domestic appearances. In 2005-06 he moved back to Llanelli, where he claimed his final League trophy.

Lloyd is also a former Wales 'B' international who was called up by Bobby Gould for the full-international squad during his time with Barry Town.

EVERY SILVER LINING HAS A CLOUD Nathan Lee Davies

"There was a rumour that a League of Wales player was in line for international recognition but I had no idea what was going on when Gary Barnett, who was then Barry manager, called me into his office and asked me to speak to Bobby Gould on the phone.

"He said he was pleased to tell me I was in his squad to travel to Belgium and though I did not play it was a great experience."

Lloyd also captained the Wales semi-pro side.

It is clear that Lloyd has always been a tremendous supporter of the national league and can be relied upon to give back to the community. He has given up his time when on European duty with the Reds to visit orphanages and also frequently visits schools in the Llanelli area to coach football.

This award really was a fitting token of appreciation for a dedicated defender...

The Awards night also celebrated Bangor City's Welsh Premier League title, Llanelli's Welsh Cup win, TNS's League Cup win and Neath's play-off success.

[With acknowledgement to Mel Ap Ior Thomas and Andrew Lincoln as per usual as well as Ray Jones of ww.newport-county.co.uk]

***

Soccerfile Wales have been analysing match attendances for the opening weeks of the 2011-12 WPL programme, but the figures don't make for good reading.

Overall the average attendance for all games shows a drop of 11.96% on the final averages for 2010-11.

EVERY SILVER LINING HAS A CLOUD Nathan Lee Davies

Whilst Bala Town have seen a massive 34% rise in attendance, probably due to their excellent start, all other clubs, bar Newtown, have seen a fall varying from a 0.4% drop for Prestatyn Town to a near 35% drop for reigning champions Bangor City.

Shockingly, second-placed Llanelli are the worst supported club in the League – barely topping 200 per match on average.

Even Friday night fixtures, popular in the past, have seen a dip at most clubs, but increases of 20% at TNS and 18% at Aberystwyth Town prevent the average loss of 14% from being even worse.

Saturday, traditionally the worst day for support, with so many local leagues in operation, shows less of a fall than Friday evenings but even so Bala, Bangor and Aberystwyth recorded massive falls and only Prestatyn achieved an increase.

Six clubs have chosen to use Sundays as match-days so far this season. But even here we have a significant drop on last season. Bala's 68% upsurge is offset by downturns at Neath and Port Talbot.

WPL table as of 30/10/11

Pos	Team	P	W	D	L	F	A	GD	Pts
1	TNS	13	10	2	1	30	11	+19	32
2	Bangor City	13	9	1	3	28	17	+11	28
3	Llanelli	13	8	3	2	32	12	+20	27
4	Neath	13	8	2	3	26	12	+14	26
5	Bala Town	13	7	3	3	21	15	+6	24
6	Prestatyn Town	13	5	2	6	20	18	+2	17
7	Port Talbot Town	13	5	2	6	16	18	-2	17
8	Airbus UK B'ton	13	2	6	5	16	23	-7	12
9	Aberystwyth Town	13	2	4	7	14	25	-11	10
10	Afan Lido	13	2	4	7	7	19	-12	10
11	Newtown	13	3	1	9	17	38	-21	10
12	Carmarthen Town	13	2	0	11	9	28	-19	6

Top six/bottom six split after 22 games

19
November 2011

Wednesday, 12 November 2011

I've never been so excited to be a Welsh football fan and truly believe the national team could be on the verge of a genuinely golden era under the tactically sophisticated management of Gary Speed.

I must admit to being highly doubtful when the FAW first made the appointment as Speed had been struggling in his first managerial role at Sheffield United. After only a few months in charge at Bramall Lane, surely Speed didn't have the experience needed to succeed at international level?

Initial results or performances did little to reassure me and back in August, our national pride was wounded when Wales were ranked 117th in world football by FIFA; an all-time low, beneath the likes of Azerbaijan, Guatemala, Guyana, Korea DPR and Haiti. This was a humiliation too far that served to reinvigorate Speed's previously hapless charges, who looked inspired and organised as they proved their doubters wrong and began climbing the world rankings.

A 2–1 home win against Montenegro was followed by an unfortunate 0-1 reverse at the hands of England at Wembley, a 2–0 home win against Switzerland and a 0-1 win against Bulgaria in Sofia. Consequently, in October 2011, Wales were ranked 45th in the world by FIFA. It's been quite a turnaround in fortunes and the good form continued this evening with a sublime demolition of Norway at the Cardiff City Stadium.

Wales won the game 4-1, courtesy of goals from Gareth Bale and Craig Bellamy, plus a Sam Vokes brace. It's the first time since 2008 that Wales have won three consecutive matches, and after tonight's dazzling display it is difficult not to conclude that the future looks bright...

***

How quickly and cruelly things change.

November saw the passing of the founder of the League of Wales and the national team manager in the space of a few devastating weeks. Instead of discussing their deaths amongst football-related news and tittle-tattle, I will show my respects in a separate chapter that can be found in the final few pages of this book.

In the meantime, the seemingly relentless juggernaut of football news continued to trudge onwards...

News Round-Up

Carl Darlington of The New Saints has been named as manager of the month for October, while Bangor City goalkeeper Lee Idzi lifted the player of the month prize.

The Pro Licence coach has now claimed back-to-back awards as the Saints sit proudly at the top of the WPL. Darlington was quick to praise the contribution of director of football Mike Davies following the announcement.

Meanwhile, Idzi has been in outstanding form as the last line of defence for the current champions, who climbed up to second during the month with four wins from five matches.

The former Haverfordwest County and Neath stopper was named man of the match by three opposing managers in those games, including the 2-0 win over Aberystwyth Town, when the Merthyr-born semi-professional international made a fantastic double-save from a penalty.

***

The Football Association of Wales have appointed Gwyn Derfel to the role of Welsh Premier League secretary. Derfel has a very strong media background and has been involved with sports broadcasting and management for over twenty years. The 43-year-old will start his employment with the FAW in January and will succeed the long-serving John Deakin in June.

"First and foremost our gratitude and thanks must go to John Deakin for his loyal and dedicated service to Welsh football," said Jonathan Ford, chief executive of the FAW.

EVERY SILVER LINING HAS A CLOUD Nathan Lee Davies

"John has been instrumental in taking the League from its inception through to the most recent re-structuring changes of last season. He will be a hard act to follow for sure, but in our appointing Gwyn, we are confident that we have found somebody to take on this opportunity and deliver against the modern media and administrative needs of the League."

Derfel said: "I am delighted to be appointed the League secretary and very much look forward to taking up the position. The League and Welsh football in general is a key passion for which I will be determined to do my utmost to ensure that it continues to go from strength to strength.

"I'm overjoyed to have the opportunity to work for the Welsh Premier League. Having worked with them for three years when BBC Wales produced *Y Clwb Pêldroed*. I have professional experience of how the League works.

"I have also followed the League as a spectator and can see a successful future ahead for the WPL – but the FAW, the clubs and the fans need to work together to move it forward.

"My aim is to improve the product we have . We need to improve facilities, playing surfaces and increase attendances. It is not going to happen overnight but if all parties co-operate we can attain this goal.

"Low attendances are a concern but I firmly believe that clubs should build a strong link with their communities. Once a club becomes the centre-point of its individual community then youth players will create a basis for the future, young fans will bond with their club and their families and other followers will come through the gate.

"It may sound simple but that, I believe, is the foundation to a solid plan, which we need to implement to see the League develop. The current two-phase format is the most positive development for years providing competition from start to season finish and we can build on this."

John Deakin, a former Football League referee, became the inaugural secretary of the League of Wales when it was formed in 1992 and has carried out the role ever since.

***

Neath have parted company with management team Terry Boyle and Peter Nicholas after only five months and named midfielder Kristian O'Leary as caretaker boss.

A club statement read: "Despite making the transition to full-time, the board felt that results and performances this season were not reflective of this.

"Kristian O'Leary has kindly agreed to assume control of first team affairs in a caretaker capacity, until such time as a decision is made on the future management structure of the club.

"On another note and contrary to rumours that are currently circulating, the club can confirm that all players have been paid up to date."

The rumours referred to above were based on the financial "issues" suffered at the end of last month.

***

Mike Davies has sensationally resigned as director of football after just 18-months in charge at The New Saints.

Since replacing Andy Cale in April 2010, Davies has led TNS to triumph in the Loosemores League Cup and a second place finish in last season's WPL. They also recorded their first victories in the

EVERY SILVER LINING HAS A CLOUD Nathan Lee Davies

Champions League and Europa League under his tutorship.

In April 2011, Davies was appointed director of football with Carl Darlington becoming first team manager to meet the requirements of the European licence.

Davies insists his decision is not due to recent results. The former leaders have dropped to third in the league after winning just one point from nine.

"I think I can go with my head held high," said the 32-year-old. TNS have suffered back-to-back defeats against Bangor and Afan Lido in November, but trail leaders Bangor by just two points.

Interviewed by BBC Radio Shropshire, Davies said: "I'd like to make the point that there's no problems with me and the club. Me and Mike [Harris] have been good friends for a long time and will continue to be good friends.

"The decision hasn't come lightly but I've made that choice and it's one I've got to live with.

"A lot of people were shocked, but the reaction has been good from my point of view – a lot of people sending positive messages. For me it's about what lies beyond and what direction I'm going to go in next.

"I'm very proud of what's been achieved, you look back and there's some fantastic memories, the success that we've had in Europe in particular, and I think that the group of lads I've been working with over the last few seasons have been a credit to work with and I'll miss every single one of them.

"I will miss it, but it's time to move on and I'm excited about the future and what it holds.

"I'm going to switch the phone off for a week, have a holiday with the family down in Cornwall and come back and see what awaits.

"I haven't thought about anything else but having some family time and that's what I'm going to focus on now. We'll just see what happens when I get back," Davies added.

Carl Darlington will remain in control of first team affairs.

WPL table as of 29/11/11

Pos	Team	P	W	D	L	F	A	GD	Pts
1	Llanelli	18	12	3	3	42	17	+25	39
2	TNS	18	12	3	3	42	22	+20	39
3	Bangor City	18	12	2	4	39	23	+16	38
4	Neath	18	9	6	3	36	17	+19	33
5	Bala Town	18	8	6	4	28	21	+7	30
6	Prestatyn Town	18	8	3	7	27	23	+4	27
7	Airbus UK B'ton	18	4	7	7	25	32	-7	19
8	Afan Lido	18	4	6	8	17	26	-9	18
9	Port Talbot Town	18	5	3	10	19	29	-10	18
10	Newtown	18	5	1	12	22	48	-26	16
11	Aberystwyth Town	18	3	5	10	20	32	-12	14
12	Carmarthen Town	18	3	1	14	15	42	-27	10

Top six/bottom six split after 22 games

20
December 2011

Sunday, 04 December 2011

I found my unedited December 2007 diary entry on an old memory stick and decided to share it with you below as it saved me from shedding the blood, sweat and tears required to create something fresh and original. In addition, it also meant that I could make use of the *Match of My Life: Billy Ashcroft* article that I wrote before things went pear-shaped. It is a decent interview with a hero of mine that deserves an audience.

So, without further ado...

Thursday, 15 December 2007

Earlier this year, I was asked by Know the Score Books (www.knowthescorebooks.com) to edit a book on Wrexham FC as part of their Match of My Life series. Basically, these volumes are made up of interviews with sixteen of the club's icons about the most memorable game they played for the club. I've just finished writing up the Billy Ashcroft chapter and have recorded interviews with Dixie McNeil, Joey Jones, Graham Whittle, Dave Smallman, Arfon Griffiths, Steve Buxton and Neil Roberts. Things are ticking along nicely.

It isn't easy writing a book on a north Wales football club from a base in the Scottish Highlands, but all the effort, travel expenses and hotel bills will be worth it once I'm a published author. Credit must also go to my wife who is actively encouraging me to spend time away from home and pursue my goals. She is very understanding.

You would've thought I'd be happy as I'm making the creative progress that I've been threatening for years, am finally settling in Inverness – frequent trips away are helping – and am even discussing the possibility of creating a new life with my wife. Everything is slotting into place nicely, but smiles of satisfaction and contentment are still struggling to make an appearance through nagging clouds of anxiety and self-doubt.

How can I possibly relax when things are running smoothly? Deep down, I know that things can only get worse. Prolonged periods of happiness can only end in tears.

As my granddad used to say – every silver lining has a cloud...

Billy Ashcroft

Centre Forward 1970-1977

Born: 1 October 1952, Garston, Liverpool
Signed: 1 October 1970
Wrexham career: 246 games +26 as sub, 96 goals
Honours: Welsh Cup Winner 1972 and 1975, Northern Floodlit League Cup Winner 1970, Alves Cup Winner 1970, PFA Third Division XI 1977, North Wales Coast XI 1972
Left: Transferred to Middlesbrough, 1 September 1977, £120,000

You wouldn't think it to look at me now, but I used to be a bit of an athlete when I was younger. I was a City champion for the triple jump and was the best swimmer in Lancashire at one stage. I think this athletic background served me well during my football career as it helped me develop my two major attributes – strength and aerial ability.

Despite being good at other sports and spending all my spare time at the swimming baths around the corner from our house in Garston, I always wanted to be a footballer. I'd been watching Everton from the age of six, but I don't know how I had the audacity to think I was going to make it as a footballer without even trying. Believe it or not, it wasn't until I was 14 years of age that I actually started playing football. I had a part-time job delivering groceries, which paid about 50p a week, so I spent 25p on my first football and within nine months I was with Blackpool – my first professional club. It was weird. It really was weird.

At that stage, I still didn't fully understand and appreciate the intricacies of the game. I just followed the ball around the pitch and waited to see what happened. Football really wasn't my game. After about six months with Blackpool, I had to quit because the journey from Liverpool to Blackpool was killing me – this was in the days of the horse and cart of course. My parents didn't want me to use the train on my own, so I had to rely on relatives to get me to Bloomfield Road. In the end we decided to look for a club closer to home.

It was then that I started playing in the Liverpool Sunday League. I was still only 15 and actually too young to play in the competition, so I began playing under a variety of assumed names. Meanwhile, a lad called David "Yozzer" Hughes – who actually made one appearance for the Robins – told the Wrexham scout for the Liverpool area to come and watch me. His name was Jack Daniels, like the whiskey, so that suited me down to the ground.

I was playing centre-half on a Sunday, but when I got a trial for Wrexham things changed. Jack Daniels saw my size – I was 6'2" and 14 stone even as a teenager – and played me up front. I started scoring a few goals and that was the mould I was set in, but I never took myself seriously as a player and never believed I had a talent – if you've seen me play you'll know what I mean.

I signed for Wrexham straight from school and immediately settled. It was a real family club with some real characters from the groundsman, Aly McGowan, who'd let us get away with murder, down to Mrs Dexter the tea lady. As groundstaff boys, we had to cut the grass, mark the pitch, clean the stands and fix the kit for the other guys. My first job was cutting the grass and putting the white lines on the pitch.

I'd spend all week in Wrexham but go home to Liverpool on weekends. This was fine until Monday morning came around. I had to report at the Racecourse for 9am so that meant leaving home at 4:30am. It was tough going, but I didn't dare complain. Aly was a top man. When he found out what I was doing he put me on kit duty and told me to have a kip in the drying room as long as I kept my mouth shut and tried not to snore. Mind you, he would make me do twice as much work the next day.

After serving my apprenticeship, I signed professional forms on my 18th birthday and made my debut for the Wrexham first-team in a goalless draw at Reading, just two days later. John Neal told me he was going to play me a few weeks before, but I had to wait as I broke my nose in a reserve match and was sidelined for three weeks. I got back to fitness in time to play at Elm Park and then went on to score my first goal the following week in a 1-2 win at Bury. Brian Tinnion set me up for a simple side-foot into the net, but it felt brilliant to make my mark in the Football League.

The team we had in them days was just phenomenal. It was a balance of the older generation such as Mel Sutton and Arfon Griffiths – who was a genius – and the youth and fervour of the groundstaff boys, such as Graham Whittle, Dave Fogg, Alan Dwyer, Dave Smallman, Mickey Thomas and Joey Jones. It was a pleasure to play in such a good football team. We had a really solid defence and a powerful midfield that kept the ball going. Instead of just knocking the ball forward as far as they could, they'd go and pick the ball up off the back four and play through midfield. That's how we shocked a lot of the bigger teams as they didn't expect us to do that against them.

I was fortunate enough to play in some unforgettable games for Wrexham. In 1976 we beat Spurs 2-3 at White Hart Lane, in the third round of the League Cup. They were struggling near the foot of the

EVERY SILVER LINING HAS A CLOUD Nathan Lee Davies

First Division at the time, but they were still a top team, with the likes of Pat Jennings, Steve Perryman and Glen Hoddle playing for them. I think they thought that it was a foregone conclusion that their class would tell, but we surprised them by the standard of football we played. A brace from Mickey Thomas actually gave us a two-goal lead at half-time. It could've been more, but for a couple of wonderful saves from Jennings and only a goal line clearance stopped Mickey from getting his hat-trick. In the second half we carried on where we'd left off and I scored another on 50 minutes to really rub salt in their wounds. They got back into it with goals from Glen Hoddle on 55 minutes and Ian Moores on 63 minutes. We were tiring, but we held on for a win after a performance that never seems to get the recognition it deserves.

Later that same season we played Sunderland at Roker Park in the third round of the FA Cup. We drew 2-2 and I scored one of the goals, but what I really remember about that day was my battle with their massive centre-half big Jim Holton. He was a colossus – standing at about 6'2" and weighing 18 stone – and stood all over me. I was covered from head to toe in bruises. It was so bad that John Neal had to take me off with about ten minutes remaining because Holton had been giving me a right pasting. We'd already used our sub so we had to finish the game with 10-men, but we hung on. Straight after the game, Big Jim bought me a pint and we had a chat about the game. I had cuts and bruises all over me, but there was no malice between us. He was a great bloke. I think he felt sorry for me because he didn't touch me in the replay at the Racecourse. I went on to score the only goal of the game and we claimed another First Division scalp.

Another of my favourite games was when we beat Chesterfield at their place 0-6 – again during the 1976-77 season – and I scored four as I bagged my only career hat-trick. I didn't get many days like that but every shot I had seemed to end up in the back of the net. What you've got to remember though is that Bobby Shinton and Graham Whittle were playing for us. The movement and pace they brought to the side suited my game. I managed to score four but anyone could have got them. If Dixie McNeil had been playing for us that season then he'd have got seven or eight.

When I look back at my time with Wrexham though, the European nights stand out. We beat Cardiff over two legs in the 1972 Welsh Cup final to qualify for the European games, but I still couldn't believe we'd made it to the Cup Winners' Cup for real. I thought it must have been some competition they'd come up with in Wales. It was only when John Neal started sending scouts to far flung places to do their homework that I realised that it must have been the real thing. It was just hard to believe that we were in the same competition as the likes of AC Milan, Atletico Madrid, Sporting Lisbon and Schalke 04.

Our first match was at FC Zurich of Switzerland. We drew 1-1, which was a good result. They'd taken the lead but just two minutes later, Albert Kinsey scored the club's first-ever goal in Europe to equalise. We won the second-leg 2-1 at the Racecourse after coming from behind. I scored our equaliser and Mel Sutton grabbed the winner in front of a massive crowd. There were over 18,000 in the ground that night and that was the start of the really big Racecourse nights of the Seventies.

After beating Zurich, we met Hadjik Split in the next round and gave them a football lesson at the Racecourse. We hammered them 3-1 but got absolutely murdered in the away leg, lost 0-2 and were eliminated on away goals. We'd learnt a lot from these games and had got the appetite for playing in Europe. We were confident that we could progress even further as we'd proved to ourselves that we could give anyone a game – wherever they came from.

In 1975 we beat Cardiff again to lift the Welsh Cup and qualify for another bite of the European cherry. As a Scouser, the Welsh Cup didn't mean a great deal, but the possibility of qualifying for Europe again meant that we were all up for it. We won 2--1 on the Racecourse, which set us up nicely for the second leg at Ninian Park. I scored twice down there as we demolished them 5-2 on aggregate.

EVERY SILVER LINING HAS A CLOUD Nathan Lee Davies

It was a really good day. We'd beaten our Welsh rivals, won some silverware, qualified for Europe and hoped we'd be going somewhere hot. Unfortunately, everywhere we went was bloody freezing.

Our aim at the beginning of the 1975-76 season, and every season come to that, was promotion. Our rivals for promotion to Division Two were all good football sides, such as Hereford, Brighton and Crystal Palace and there weren't any sides trying to kick themselves out of the division. There was a little mini-league of the best football teams in that division and we always thought we were top of that league, but we never quite got that push for promotion.

If you're not going to get promotion then the only bonus you're going to get is playing in a team of such great players. It really was a buzz. Going to training wasn't a chore. You wanted to be involved as they were a great group of lads. On a Saturday we'd be really confident of beating whichever mob we were playing. We thought we could beat anyone whether they were Third Division, Second Division or First Division.

We got off to an inconsistent start to the season – winning six matches at home but losing seven on the road. Despite this unpredictable form, we still fancied our chances in Europe – our mentality was that we were in the Cup Winners' Cup because we deserved to be. We knew we had it in us to beat anyone over two legs and there was no doubt that we were in it to win it.

I don't remember too much about playing Djurgardens at home in the first round, although I believe we won 2-1, but I do remember the away leg as they had a massive château behind one of the goals and a running track around the pitch. Graham Whittle scored in a 1-1 draw, which meant we won 3-2 on aggregate. After the game we all went out to get drunk, but you can't get drunk in Sweden because the beer is that bloody expensive.

EVERY SILVER LINING HAS A CLOUD Nathan Lee Davies

We were hoping to be drawn somewhere cheaper in the next round. Spain would've been nice for a bit of San Miguel and sunshine, but instead we had to go behind the Iron Curtain to play Stal Rzeszow in Poland. We beat them 2-0 on the Racecourse, thanks to a brace from yours truly, but then we had to go to their place. It was a small, industrial little town. It was like going back to bloody Merseyside. I remember it was a very dour place where no one smiled. At the airport, there was loads of military with guns and we were absolutely terrified, but with a two-goal lead we were confident we could do the business on the pitch. John Neal told us to keep it tight, so we shut up shop to earn a 1-1 draw on the night. This meant we were the first Third Division side to reach the quarter-finals of a major European competition.

Ahead of the Anderlecht game, we were confident we could score in Brussels. I was scoring goals, Stuart Lee could score goals and Graham Whittle could hit them from the halfway line, so we had no fear. Anderlecht were the biggest team we'd played in Europe, and they had some big international players, such as Arie Haan, Robbie Rensenbrink, Fancois Van der Elst and Ludo Coeck. They were a class act, but we weren't scared of anybody and felt we had a great chance.

The people in Belgium were fantastic with us because they thought we were going to get slaughtered. They felt sorry for us and made sure we enjoyed their hospitality and the beautiful city of Brussels. It's such a historic place, but that was lost on some of us. On the little walkabout we had on the day of the game, the younger players, myself included, were looking for the pubs that we'd go to after the match because we knew we were going to be celebrating.

As the game got closer the lads began to get more nervous – everyone except Graham Whittle that is. He could fall asleep on the coach on the way to the ground and we'd have to wake him up when we arrived. He could sleep anywhere and he'd eat like a horse, getting it down his neck as quickly as possible in case someone nicked it. His bottom lip would barely move more than an inch from his plate and he could shovel food in without breathing. We used to stand well back to avoid the sparks that came from his knife and fork – hence his nickname of Nosher. Then on the coach on the way to the ground, when we were all hyped up, we'd look to the back of the bus and Graham would be flat out asleep. No nerves at all. It was great for the rest of the lads because it'd calm our nerves as well.

The Parc Astrid Stadium was a tight little stadium – like an English ground – and the atmosphere was brilliant. They've totally rebuilt and renamed it now. In the dressing room before the match, you could see a lot of the faces were drawn because it was a nerve-wracking atmosphere. When the whistle blew for us to leave our quarters, we were all roaring, screaming and shouting. The Anderlecht players must have heard us, so they were in no doubt that we were up for it.

We usually played 4-3-3 with me, Stuart Lee and Brian Tinnion upfront, but John Neal was a shrewd tactician and decided to play with two strikers, while using the extra man in midfield to counter their international class engine room. Brian Tinnion was the forward who was sacrificed while the midfield comprised of Mel Sutton, Arfon Griffiths, Mickey Thomas – the three fittest players at the club who could run all day and weighed in with a few goals – and Graham Whittle, who could score from anywhere on the pitch and, in my opinion, was the best player ever to play for Wrexham.

We had about 2,000 of our fans in Brussels that night and they definitely helped us. They're a vociferous lot that never go quiet on you, so you always know that they're there supporting you. Those present could see that we were on the verge of achieving a special result and made more and more noise as the game went on. Those 2,000 fans sounded more like 10,000...

For the opening fifteen minutes, Anderlecht gave us a bit of a run around. They scored through Gilbert Van Binst after 11 minutes, but we seemed to get stronger from that point. Our defence – Brian Lloyd in goal with Mickey Evans, Dave Fogg, Eddie May and Gareth Davies in front of him – had to stand-up and be counted and they did that, which allowed the rest of us to start making chances.

I was having fun against their goalkeeper, Jan Ruiter, who was about 6'2" in stocking feet. However, when he jumped into the air he was about 5'8". The lads exploited this with a series of high crosses. Ruiter was looking for me before he even jumped for the ball. I was loving this and managing to win all of our aerial battles. One of these headers dropped to the unmarked Stuart Lee, but he shot wide. Then, just before half-time, Ruiter had to make a fine save from Stuart's 20-yard drive.

We continued to pile on the pressure in the second-half. Mel Sutton forced a good save from Ruiter, and I had a couple of headers that went just over the bar. Anderlecht were shocked and shaken, you could see it in their eyes, and on another night, with a little bit more luck, we would've got a result.

When we came off the pitch we were all congratulating each other. Our chests were out and we really felt as if we'd achieved something. The Anderlecht coach Hans Croon admitted we were favourites for the second leg – they weren't good travellers and had lost their previous two European away games while we'd won both of our home legs. Their fans were also surprised at how well we had played and seemed downcast about their chances at the Racecourse.

The headline in one of the newspapers the next day was "The Bear of Brussels". I was wondering what the hell the story was about and then realised it was all about me. I didn't even think I'd had a good game. I knew the defence and midfield played well, but we missed a couple of chances upfront. I took the plaudits anyway because when people started slagging me off I had to take that as well. I must've done something right that night as within a few weeks Anderlecht had tried to sign me. I believe they offered a few bob for me, but John Neal wouldn't let me go as he said I was too young. They signed Duncan McKenzie instead.

We were expecting 25,000 for the return leg at the Racecourse. We had a little walkabout before the match to see what the pitch was like, but the ground wasn't that full. Everyone was in the Turf, or in the pubs down the road, so when it was time for us to walkout we didn't know what to expect. When we eventually emerged for the game this wall of noise came up. It was deafening. We were all a bit surprised at first, but then we quickly began smiling because we knew these fans were all on our side. Anderlecht were on our turf now.

The pitch was in an awful state. It always was back then. It wasn't exactly conducive to our style of play, but we learnt to adapt our game. We had to keep the ball off the ground and spread it to the wings as the pitch would sometimes be six inches deep in mud. Nevertheless, we put up a good performance that night.

We knew that we wouldn't score early. We set out to probe and keep it tight and we were confident the goal would come. We knew that there were goals in our team. It wasn't often that we got a full house, so we were floating on air throughout the game. It was only a matter of time before we scored.

We were shooting towards the Kop in the first half. We had plenty of possession in and around their penalty box but didn't manage a clear shot on target. Despite our overall superiority, they were always dangerous on the break. Indeed, we had Brian Lloyd to thank for a fine save, just before the break, to deny Van Binst. That was a really important save that kept us in the game at half-time.

After 61 minutes, Mel Sutton crossed the ball in for Stuart Lee to knock-in at the far post. The crowd exploded and a wall of noise hit us. At that stage we still had half an hour to go and we all believed we had another goal in us, especially with the crowd behind us. We pushed forward in search of the winner, but despite bombarding their box with crosses we were restricted to half-chances.

Ruiter remained their weakest link. The Dutch shot-stopper came charging out of his goal to punch the ball clear, but he got tangled up with me and one of his own defenders. Subsequently, he didn't get a clean contact on the ball, which landed at the feet of Stuart Lee on the edge of the area. Unfortunately, his shot went over the bar. Had that gone in, I think their heads would've gone completely. They would've been absolutely destroyed, but I think that miss gave them the impetus they needed. They knew they had got away with it and that motivated them to give it a little extra push.

They started to create a few chances of their own as we committed men forward and left gaps at the back. On 77 minutes, the bottom fell out of our market as they showed their class by putting together a nice passing move that started in their own area and finished with Coeck sliding the ball through for Rensenbrink to shoot past Lloyd from 15 yards. After that, the game petered out a bit and, although Graham Whittle hit a bullet from the edge of the area that Ruiter did well to save, we never really looked like getting the two goals we then needed.

I think if it'd gone to extra-time then we'd have lost it because they didn't put a great deal of effort into it. It was the same in the first leg. They had the skilful players while we had the lads who were really grafting, so the extra half-hour would have tired us out and allowed them to take the ascendancy. You get a sort of nervous energy in big games like that, but once the 90 minutes are up, you just end up completely drained. We'd put so much effort in that we had nothing left to give.

Anderlecht then went on to beat BSG Sachsenring Zwickau of East Germany in the semi-final to set up a final against West Ham United, which they won 4-2. I actually watched that game on TV and remember thinking that it could've been us. We would've given a better performance than the Hammers. I know it's an awful thing to say but I'm really glad Anderlecht won as it meant that we'd lost to the eventual winners.

Our involvement in the Cup Winners' Cup most definitely affected our league form. We were in that competition to win it, so when Anderlecht beat us it knocked the stuffing out of us. For the rest of the season we were too inconsistent and let other teams walk all over us, dropping vital home points to the likes of Preston, Walsall and Southend and finishing sixth in the table. Instead of losing momentum, we should've looked at how much we'd achieved, how well we'd played and shown teams how we'd just given Anderlecht a spanking. Unfortunately, we didn't and our heads went down, which was disappointing.

The following season was doubly agonising. We dumped Leicester City and Tottenham Hotspur out of the League Cup and beat Sunderland in the FA Cup – all First Division sides at the time – while I netted 20 league goals and was picked for the PFA Division Three XI along with Arfon. Somehow though, we still missed out on promotion.

With two games of the season left, a point against Crystal Palace at home was all we need to go up. We found ourselves two down but goals from Graham Whittle and John Lyons put us on the brink of promotion. At ten past nine we were up but by quarter past they'd won 2-4, with a couple of late goals. We were devastated and there were tears in the dressing room, but a win against Mansfield Town at the Racecourse on the last day would still have sent us up. We lost 0-1.

I didn't want to leave Wrexham. I really didn't. If we'd won promotion that season I wouldn't have gone anywhere. I don't think John Neal would've either. It was always my ambition to play in the top flight, but I always thought that I could do it with Wrexham and that we could be the Welsh team to make it to the English First Division.

EVERY SILVER LINING HAS A CLOUD Nathan Lee Davies

I was so disappointed after the Mansfield game. We all went out and got drunk after the game, but my hangover lasted for months. I just never really got over it and then John Neal moved to Middlesbrough. It seemed like things were falling apart. At the start of the 1977-78 season, I wasn't in great form and managed only one goal in the opening three games as we made a poor start to the season. I knew that John wanted to take me to Ayresome Park as the newspapers were full of speculation, so I asked Arfon, who was now player-manager, if I could go.

I'd played at Chesterfield and I'd played at Port Vale and I'd played against Chester, but I'm an Evertonian and I wanted to play at Goodison Park, beat Liverpool at Anfield and score the winner against Manchester United at Old Trafford. John gave me that opportunity. The money was great, don't get me wrong, but it wasn't about that. I wanted to better myself.

Looking back, I wish I'd stayed one more season as we eventually won promotion in 1977-78, but my leaving was probably the best thing that ever happened to Wrexham. They signed Dixie McNeil to replace me and that was the signing that finally got them the promotion they deserved.

News Round-Up

Andy Dyer was named WPL manager of the month for November after guiding Afan Lido to a three-match unbeaten run. This run included a goalless draw against Bangor City at the Marston's Stadium, a shock 3-1 demolition of TNS at the same venue and a 2-5 hammering of Carmarthen Town at Richmond Park, which was their first away win of the season.

The player of the month was Llanelli central defender and captain Stuart Jones, who helped his side keep three clean sheets in November. Jones also proved his worth at the other end of the pitch with goals against Newtown and Port Talbot Town.

***

Newtown had three points deducted by the WPL after being found guilty of fielding players who had not received international clearance in the games at Carmarthen Town and Aberystwyth Town on August 13 and 19 respectively.

***

The managerial merry-go-round continued apace into the last month of 2011. Carmarthen Town manager Tomi Morgan was sacked after his side progressed to the fourth round of the Welsh Cup with a 2-1 victory over Bridgend Town at Richmond Park.

"That's the problem with winning, you get sacked," said Morgan.

"I did see it coming to be honest because when you're in a room and all the doors shut on you, there's only the fire escape left.

"You hear whispers and the signs are there to see, but I feel I can go away with my head held high.

EVERY SILVER LINING HAS A CLOUD Nathan Lee Davies

"We have had little to spend on players, so I have had to get by with youngsters and I have to say they have been fantastic and a pleasure to work with."

He added: "It has been a difficult campaign and we have blown hot and cold, but that's what happens with a young set of lads."

It is the second time that Morgan has been shelved by the board at Richmond Park, following a previous six-year spell that ended in 2003.

He had been in his second spell for just 18 months, but his side were languishing at the foot of the table after just three wins all season.

"We are grateful to Tomi for his contribution to the club over the past eighteen months," commented club chairman Gareth Jones.

"It was his skills and experience that kept us in the Welsh Premier League last season when we faced a difficult period after the resignation of Deryn Brace.

"Unfortunately this season has not seen the club move forward on the field and it was decided that a fresh face needed to be brought in to improve performances."

Neil Smothers was installed as player-manager at Richmond Park after being poached from Welsh League side Bridgend Town – the outfit that the Old Gold had just fortunately eliminated from the Welsh Cup.

"Neil is a former player, he knows the club inside out," said Jones.

"He was delighted when we approached him to ask him to return to Carmarthen Town to become player-manager."

***

EVERY SILVER LINING HAS A CLOUD Nathan Lee Davies

Neath have said they are looking forward to the rest of the season – despite facing a winding-up order in the High Court.

Fans of the WPL side have become increasingly worried about its future in recent months after players' wages were delayed, legal action was started against the company which runs it, and chairman Geraint Hawkes's import business, FG Hawkes, entered administration.

But now the club has reassured fans than the Eagles are still in business – and are aiming high.

Spokesman Chris Jones said: "We are trying to achieve something with Neath.

"The current situation is not ideal but we will work through it.

"I am confident the matters can be resolved through negotiations, and everyone is looking forward to the rest of the season.

"We are currently fourth in the Welsh Premier League and very much looking forward to future success.

"Everyone is backing us and is positive about the future. The club is good for the area."

A petition for the winding-up of Neath Football Club Ltd has been lodged at the High Court of Justice (Chancery Division) in London by Her Majesty's Revenue and Customs.

The matter is due to come to court on 16 January 2012.

The club faced similar proceedings by the taxman in June – but that case was thrown out after the club paid-off what it owed.

Mr Jones said the current legal action was "very similar" to what had happened over the summer.

***

Prestatyn Town have announced that player-manager Neil Gibson has signed an extended deal that will tie him to the club until 2014. Gibson said he was only too happy to pledge his future to the Prestatyn cause.

"I am delighted to be signing a new contract and extending my stay as player-manager at Prestatyn, my hometown club and one that means a great deal to me.

"I have enjoyed my four-and-a-half years in charge and am very pleased with the progress that we have made, developing from a mid-table Cymru Alliance team to one that can compete with the best teams in the Welsh Premier League. This has been based on togetherness from a strong, hard-working playing staff, coaching staff, board and our incredible band of loyal supporters, which makes Prestatyn the close knit community club it is.

"Hopefully extending my stay can help to keep the continuity and allow our progress to continue. Seeing the progress made by so many local players gives me great confidence for the clubs future.

"Having spoken with Phil Merrick and board members, who share my ambitions for taking the club forward, it was an easy decision to commit myself to the club for the next two-and-a-half years. I would like to thank everyone who has helped and supported me so far, and I hope we can repay our loyal supporters with more progress in years to come."

Chairman Phil Merrick added: "Gibbo is very important to us; he is one of the best young managers around and is still an excellent player who is in great form this season.

EVERY SILVER LINING HAS A CLOUD Nathan Lee Davies

"We can now start working together to build the team that will challenge the very best of the Welsh Premier League. These are exciting times for the club and we will be looking to offer new contracts to some of our other players very soon.

"Neil is a former professional with Tranmere Rovers and Sheffield Wednesday and has been at the Town since 2005-06, taking over as player-manager in 2007-08.

"He has been the target of a number of other clubs this season and has a great career ahead of him in football management when he decides to hang up his boots.

"In the short term, however, Neil has his ambitions firmly set on helping his hometown club achieve success in the Welsh Premier League."

***

Aberystwyth Town have welcomed back ex-Wales international Christian Edwards to Park Avenue as director of football.

Edwards joined Aberystwyth Town as a centre back in January 2007. He played 89 games for the club, including the Welsh Cup final of 2009. The former defender later became caretaker manager (Oct 2009) and assistant manager (Nov 2009-Feb 2011).

He resigned from this position ten months ago, but now returns to work alongside manager Alan Morgan as the club bids to improve its Welsh Premier League standing.

"I'm absolutely delighted to have Christian back on board. It'll be great to have him back. We've been friends for years and enjoy challenging each other's ideas on the team. It's our best signing of the season," said Morgan.

EVERY SILVER LINING HAS A CLOUD Nathan Lee Davies

Chairman Tony Bates said: "We are delighted to have Christian back within the fold. We were disappointed when he had to leave last season, and his return gives us great confidence looking forward to the second half of our season in 2012."

Edwards has been working with Welsh League side UWIC and masterminded the students' run to the Welsh Cup quarter-final in 2010-11.

***

On the eve of 2012, Airbus UK Broughton boss Craig Harrison left the Airfield to become the new director of football at TNS, succeeding Mike Davies who resigned in November.

A former Middlesbrough, Crystal Palace and Preston North End defender, Harrison was appointed manager of the Wingmakers at the beginning of July 2008, following the shock departure of Gareth Owen.

"Full-time football is a massive lure for me, I've been a professional footballer for six or seven years previously, so to get back into full-time football in a club like this is brilliant," said Harrison.

"It was the main attraction. You are in a privileged position to be a professional footballer and earn a living from it and it's something that's in my blood.

"Obviously I finished my career early and I've got a burning desire to go and finish what I probably should have as a player.

"This will only be a stepping stone to greater things if I do a very good job, if I'm not doing a good job I'm not going to go any higher.

"If I am doing a good job then it's a two-win situation. If the club are doing well and I'm doing well, then we'll see what happens from

311

there.

"Another massive attraction is that TNS play very attractive football, which is something I tried to imitate when I was at Airbus. TNS were almost the model of where we wanted to be in the standard of football, and they have also got very good players."

Looking to the second half of the season, Harrison outlined his targets.

"For a club of this size, we'll be going into every single game trying to win the league. Full stop. That's the aim for the players and staff from top to bottom."

Harrison will work with current first-team manager, Carl Darlington, who was also his assistant at the Airfield for a spell.

WPL table as of 27/12/11

Pos	Team	P	W	D	L	F	A	GD	Pts
1	Bangor City	21	15	2	4	48	28	+20	47
2	TNS	21	14	4	3	47	24	+23	46
3	Llanelli	21	14	3	4	47	21	+26	45
4	Neath	19	10	6	3	37	17	+20	36
5	Bala Town	20	9	6	5	30	23	+7	33
6	Prestatyn Town	20	8	3	9	32	31	+1	27
7	Airbus UK B'ton	21	6	7	8	31	35	-4	25
8	Afan Lido	20	5	7	8	22	30	-8	22
9	Port Talbot Town	20	5	4	11	22	33	-11	19
10	Aberystwyth Town	21	4	6	11	26	36	-10	18
11	Newtown	21	5	1	15	26	57	-31	13
12	Carmarthen Town	21	3	1	17	17	50	-33	10

Newtown deducted 3 points
Top six/bottom six split after 22 games

21
January 2012

Sunday, 1 January 2012

2012 Recipe
Ingredients

- 150ml/5fl oz bile

- 75g/2½oz jealousy

- 100g/3½oz unsalted loneliness.

- 275g/10oz soft porn

- 2 free-range Tories, heavily beaten

- One welfare state, broken into pieces

- 2 tbsp frustration

- 100g/3½oz anxiety

- 450ml/16fl oz sleaze

- 22 large tsp lies

- 550g/1lb 4oz paranoia

- 52 bottles of whiskey

- ½ tsp boredom

- 2½ tsp ground lazy monarchs

- 525g/1lb 3oz hatred, grated

- 150g/5½oz depression, chopped

- 500,000,000 Union Jacks to decorate

Method

For the 2012 cake, watch your carers preheat the oven to 160C/325F/Gas 3 if you can afford such an appliance on slashed benefits.

Instruct carers to grease and line a 26cm/10in cake tin because you're a useless piece of shit that can't do anything for yourself.

Get a pair of fully-functioning hands to mix all of the ingredients for the cake, except the lies and paranoia, together in a bowl until well combined. Stir in the lies and paranoia.

Spoon the mixture into the cake tin and bake for 1 hour 15 minutes, or until a skewer inserted into the middle comes out dripping with bile.

Ask an employee – as you have no friends – to remove the cake from the oven and set aside to cool for 10 minutes, then carefully chisel the cake from the tin and set aside to act as a landing pad for flies in your skanky kitchen.

Eat while watching *Man Vs Food* on Dave, or *Bob's Full House* on Challenge.

Feel guilty for eating cake when other disabled people with different, less crippling disabilities and plenty of money are training for Paralympic glory.

Vomit.

News Round-Up

After winning their last four games and topping the table at the mid-season break, it was no surprise that Bangor City's Nev Powell landed the manager of the month award for December. City beat Bala Town 2-1 at home before overcoming Prestatyn Town 5-3 in the last match to be played at Farrar Road.

A 2-1 win at Port Talbot Town and a 5-0 romp in the seasonal return against Prestatyn at Bastion Gardens speaks volumes for Powell's motivational skills, following a Welsh Cup exit at the hands of Llanelli in the first match of the month.

Meanwhile, Matthew Rees of Neath was named player of the month for December. A change of management at the Gnoll put Kristian O'Leary in charge of team affairs and his unbeaten run since taking over can be put down in great part to the form of central defender Rees.

Joining from near-neighbours Port Talbot in the summer, Rees quickly made himself a regular in the Eagles' back four, turning in some stirring performances and his form during December was highly consistent.

***

Carmarthen Town reorganised their management team by appointing Mark Aizlewood as their new manager to support recently-appointed player-coach Neil Smothers.

This is the third time that the 52-year-old Aizlewood has been associated with the Old Gold, after previously serving the club as coach, academy director and assistant manager.

EVERY SILVER LINING HAS A CLOUD Nathan Lee Davies

"We welcome Mark back to Richmond Park. He knows we face a big battle ahead to avoid relegation, but our executive committee is sure that he is up to the task," said chairman Gareth Jones.

Newport-born Aizlewood, joined his hometown club in 1975, before progressing to Luton Town and Charlton Athletic. In 1986, the solid defender won his first Welsh cap and went on to make 39 international appearances in all.

He also played for Leeds United, Bradford City, Bristol City, Cardiff City, Merthyr Tydfil, Aberystwyth Town and Cwmbran Town before hanging-up his boots in 2002. In total, he made 499 Football League appearances and 81 (+18) in the Welsh set-up.

***

Bangor City goalkeeper Lee Idzi has confirmed that he will remain with the club until the end of the season. The Welsh semi-professional international was rumoured to be departing for Australia after the festive period but managed to negotiate a contract with Manly United that runs from April to August.

"I'm joining Manly United near Sydney, which is one division below the A-League, so it's a great opportunity for me," he said.

"Manly were happy for me to stay longer with Bangor City as we're top of the league. I'm really pleased that they were flexible.

"I'm really enjoying my time with Bangor and the club is really going in the right direction. It will also be great to play at the new stadium in Nantporth. It looks excellent and the pitch is in perfect condition."

***

EVERY SILVER LINING HAS A CLOUD Nathan Lee Davies

Aberystwyth Town dropped closer to the relegation zone after having one point deducted for fielding an ineligible player.

Youth player Alex Samuel came on as a 77th minute substitute in the 2-0 defeat at Llanelli's Stebonheath Park on October 8.

"The FAW found Alan Morgan's team guilty of fielding a player who had not been registered correctly as per FAW Rules 51.3 and 51.3.1," said a statement.

"The fact that the player had not been correctly registered resulted in him being ineligible and the penalty was imposed by a Welsh Premier League commission on December 15.

"The club had the right of appeal to the FAW but chose not to do so."

***

Airbus UK Broughton turned to Northwich Victoria manager Andy Preece as the man to succeed Craig Harrison as their director of football.

The 44-year-old former Bury boss, who scored 125 goals in 387 Football League appearances, has signed a three-year deal. He will be joined at the Airfield by Andy Morrison and Darren Ryan.

"It's a long-term project and we can do it in stages," said Preece.

"We haven't been in that position at clubs we've been at before because they've always had problems financially.

"This club's on a stable footing with the potential to be a force in the Welsh Premier and the immediate goal is to put out a team that can finish in seventh position this season.

"I spoke to Stewart Roberts and he told me about the plans and what could be achieved if we're successful. If things go well, there's no reason why we can't qualify for Europe over the next couple of years," he added.

"If we do that, we can move on again and look to be challenging at the top of the league.

"This club is set up really well. It has a good base and just needs to be built on."

**

Kristian O'Leary has been appointed Neath manager on a full-time basis after guiding the side to four wins and two draws while in caretaker charge.

"The club are delighted with the new professional ethos that he has instilled during his short period in charge," said a Neath statement.

"Training is now well structured and preparations for games are thorough and well thought-out."

Neath, one of the league's biggest spenders, have been continuing amid a backdrop of financial uncertainty over recent weeks.

Chairman Geraint Hawkes has been forced to place his business, FG Hawkes, into administration, but the club say that all outstanding tax issues have been addressed.

"As a club we have endured some challenging times recently which have been well documented, however, the board, management, players, sponsors, and supporters have all pulled together and worked tremendously hard to ensure that the club is in a position to drive forward in a strong and united manner," continued the statement.

"Appointing Kris is a key factor in this process and we are excited as a club about the future."

***

The Football Association of Wales unveiled its strategic plan and vision for the future of Welsh football at the St David's Hotel in Cardiff Bay.

The audience heard from the chief executive of the FAW, Jonathan Ford, the First Minister, Carwyn Jones and the newly appointed national team manager, Chris Coleman.

Ford said: "The strategic plan we are launching is a manifestation of a lot of hard work from a lot of people.

"The message has been clear on the badge for years. "Gorau Chwarae Cyd Chwarae" or "Best Play is Team Play". Our messages are clear; greater team work, better communication, a longer term perspective through evolution and winning more.

"Included in our vision of success is a Welsh way of playing and qualification for a major tournament.

"It is also important to be progressive and promote a forward thinking, modern and high profile FAW."

The FAW was delighted to receive the backing and endorsement of the First Minister, Carwyn Jones.

In relation to the WPL, the strategy promises to help clubs' improve European results, consider a salary cap and reintroduce drug testing.

The event was supported by the League secretary John Deakin and his successor, Gwyn Derfel.

***

EVERY SILVER LINING HAS A CLOUD Nathan Lee Davies

The Super 12 had now reached its mid-season split and there were doubts in some quarters about the appeal of such a limited format, which results in a number of repetitive fixtures for many clubs.

Port Talbot chairman Andrew Edwards was particularly frustrated after the Steelmen booked a place in the quarter-finals of the League Cup by beating Carmarthen Town over two legs. Their prize was another two-legged clash with close neighbours Afan Lido, who they also played in the Welsh Cup third round.

It is a scenario that does not please Edwards, who is also a WPL representative on the FAW panel.

"Our double header against Lido will bring the number of games we will have played against each other this season to seven and it's not good," he told the *South Wales Evening Post*.

"Something has to be done about it."

Manager Mark Jones agrees: "Seven games against Lido and six against Carmarthen is ridiculous and the fans will get bored with it."

Aberystwyth Town and Lido will also have played each other six times come the end of the season, as will Neath and Llanelli.

WPL table as of 14/01/12

Pos	Team	P	W	D	L	F	A	GD	Pts
1	Bangor City	22	16	2	4	53	28	+25	50
2	TNS	22	15	4	3	52	24	+28	49
3	Llanelli	22	14	3	5	47	23	+24	45
4	Neath	22	12	7	3	43	20	+23	43
5	Bala Town	22	11	6	5	35	25	+10	39
6	Prestatyn Town	22	8	4	10	33	37	-4	28
7	Airbus UK B'ton	22	6	7	9	32	37	-5	25
8	Port Talbot Town	22	6	4	12	26	37	-11	22
9	Afan Lido	22	5	7	10	24	35	-11	22
10	Aberystwyth Town	22	4	6	12	27	38	-11	17
11	Carmarthen Town	22	4	1	17	19	51	-32	13
12	Newtown	22	5	1	16	26	62	-36	13

Newtown deducted 3 points
Aberystwyth Town deducted 1 point
Top six/bottom six split after 22 games

22
February 2012

Sunday, 12 February 2012

I turned 35 years old today. How did that happen?

It was supposed to be a joyous occasion, with friends and family showering me with attention and gifts. So, when I received my first text message of the day, I was rather disappointed to discover that my mum had caught a sickness bug and would be unable to make it to the local Indian restaurant for my birthday curry. When this news was followed by a similarly apologetic notification of my brother-in-law's projectile vomiting, I began to get nervous. There was obviously a bug going round and I was bound to catch it as my immune system is next to useless.

When will my luck ever change?

I've been anxious all day as I've got tickets to watch Noel Gallagher and the High Flying Birds live in concert at the MEN Arena tomorrow evening. I'll be accompanied by my friend Michelle. We've been looking forward to the gig for ages, so I couldn't afford to take any chances and decided to postpone the meal in favour of self-imposed quarantine – making an exception only for my sister and two-year-old niece. Not only did this allow my sister to escape her diseased husband for a couple of hours, but it also meant that I could get my hands on some birthday presents. These included the complete collection of *Carry On...* films on DVD, a Wrexham Lager pint glass and a pair of socks that confirmed my status as "Number One Uncle".

I spent the afternoon writing about Port Talbot Town and was only interrupted when one of my dearest friends phoned. Without fail, Valerie always remembers my birthday and sends a card that shows she understands and appreciates me more than most people. This is usually accompanied by a telephone call where the conversation always races but never falters.

EVERY SILVER LINING HAS A CLOUD Nathan Lee Davies

We met at the University of Nottingham. She was on a year-long exchange programme from the University of British Columbia, and I went to visit her in Vancouver, during my stint as a student across the pond. We've stayed in touch ever since. Of course, I was initially attracted to her blonde hair and big boobs, but as our friendship flourished, I realised my feelings ran deeper than surface appearances. I'm sincerely happy that she's now settled in Oxfordshire with a decent bloke and two lovely children.

Lately, I've been lucky enough to recreate this type of friendship with fellow divorcee Michelle, a former classmate during my time at sixth-form college, with whom I was reunited after my Scottish nightmare. We have loads in common, she makes me laugh uncontrollably like no other, is more attractive than she realises and I could fall in love with her in a heartbeat if I let myself.

The fact that I won't let my feelings escalate to an inappropriate level with either of these beautiful ladies is both a tribute to them as people I respect, and indicative of my twisted perception of sex as a dirty and loveless act. Surely, friendship and sex need to be kept apart? Is it really possible to cum on someone's face and continue to enjoy a dignified and respectful relationship? I obviously haven't found the right person to build a complete partnership with yet, as in my experience, sex spoils even the strongest of unions. I'd hate five minutes of grunting and groaning to devalue special bonds.

Besides, if it was possible to combine bedroom activities and remain bosom buddies, don't you think I'd have tried it by now?

Anyway, I'm beginning to waffle, so I'm going to say good night, take some Indian Brandy to settle my excitable stomach and fall asleep to the strains of "The Death of You and Me".

Monday, 13 February 2012

You've guessed it...

I woke at 2am with stomach cramps and it wasn't long before I started spewing my guts up. I was still gagging eight hours later and knew I'd have to let Michelle down. I was gutted, more for her sake than mine, and encouraged her to go without me, but she didn't. Apparently, it wouldn't be the same without me.

I'll sleep well this evening, safe in the knowledge that there's more to life than sex – at least until the next time I'm horny.

News Round-Up

Aberystwyth Town parted company with manager Alan Morgan by mutual consent after a humiliating, but hardly surprising, Welsh Cup exit at the hands of Cefn Druids of the Huws Gray Alliance. This proved the final straw for the Seasiders' board.

Chairman Tony Bates said: "From a financial point of view it was a devastating blow to be knocked-out of the Welsh Cup.

"It has been a really disappointing season for the club. Relegation is a real threat, as it looks as though two clubs will be relegated this season, with two clubs likely to come up.

"It would be a devastating loss to the supporters and the town if the club was to be relegated, especially given the amount of work that is put in off the field at the club to maintain Welsh Premier status."

Aberystwyth-born Morgan joined the Seasiders as manager in November 2009 after leaving Bangor City. He led the Black & Greens to a fourth place finish in his first season and qualified for the Europa League play-offs a year later.

To help revive the club's flagging fortunes, ex-Carmarthen Town boss Tomi Morgan has been brought in as successor to his namesake.

"We are delighted that Tomi has agreed to take over after Alan's departure," says club chairman Tony Bates.

"He served the club with great distinction in the past, and his experience in the Welsh Premier League speaks for itself.

"I am also very glad to have some local involvement in the management team once again. It was the ideal opportunity for Tomi to come back, and he will have the full support of the board in his role as first-team manager."

Morgan was awarded the UEFA Pro Licence in October 2010.

***

Llanelli boss Andy Legg has argued that money must be spent on improving pitches if the WPL is to flourish. His outburst followed the Reds' crashing out of the Welsh Cup after a 5-4 penalty shootout defeat at Bala.

The sides were tied at 1-1 after 120 minutes of football, played on a quagmire at Maes Tegid. This made passing football impossible and both teams were forced into a long-ball game.

Bala had worked hard on the pitch to make sure the game could go ahead. They plan on making a substantial investment during the summer in an attempt to bring the surface up to scratch.

Maes Tegid is not the only venue in the Welsh top flight with a poor playing surface, and Legg believes it is impossible to raise the standard of the league until the issue of sub-standard pitches is addressed.

"Our product is on the grass and that's where money should be spent," said the Reds manager to the *Llanelli Star*.

"We've always had a good pitch, but we spent money on it last summer because rain would often lead to games being called off.

"We've got to look at pitches at other clubs.

"Going back over a decade, when John Lewis was in charge at Ebbw Vale, he told me the league would never improve until the pitches improve, and I think he's right."

EVERY SILVER LINING HAS A CLOUD Nathan Lee Davies

Bala called in consultants to conduct a pitch survey, which concluded that the main drainage at Maes Tegid is actually in good working order, but the problem lies with the top 6-8cm of the surface not allowing sufficient drainage to take place – thereby retaining too much moisture. This is also affecting grass root development.

"The club hopes to receive recommendations for improvement in the near future and to implementing as much of the recommendations as possible from the survey," said a statement from the Lakesiders.

***

Carmarthen Town have answered a cry for help from the newly-formed Wales Football-Tennis Association.

"The request for help arrived by email at Carmarthen Town's online shop. Futnet (www.futnet.eu) is played with a football over a tennis net by teams of one to eight players," explained club shop administrator Celia Kirkby.

"They are running a tournament for unemployed adults and underprivileged youngsters in February – but they have no kit. We were asked if we could we help with any surplus old kit.

"Our storeroom contains a collection of kits from previous seasons, examples of which are being displayed in the clubhouse, but a quantity has been parcelled up and sent to the Futnet organisers, who are going to name one of their teams after Carmarthen Town AFC."

Old Gold president Jeff Thomas said: "Carmarthen Town is delighted to be able to help another Welsh sports group as part of our community programme and wishes Wales Futnet every success in this new venture. We will be proud to see the Old Gold colours being worn at Futnet tournaments and tours."

WPL table as of 19/02/12

Pos	Team	P	W	D	L	F	A	GD	Pts
1	Bangor City	25	19	2	4	57	29	+28	59
2	TNS	25	17	4	4	59	26	+33	55
3	Neath	25	15	7	3	48	21	+27	52
4	Llanelli	24	14	3	7	47	26	+21	45
5	Bala Town	24	11	6	7	35	28	+7	39
6	Prestatyn Town	25	8	4	13	34	44	-10	28
7	Airbus UK B'ton	24	7	7	10	36	38	-2	28
8	Afan Lido	24	6	8	10	27	37	-10	26
9	Port Talbot Town	24	6	5	13	28	40	-12	23
10	Aberystwyth Town	24	4	8	12	30	41	-11	19
11	Carmarthen Town	24	5	2	17	22	53	-31	17
12	Newtown	24	5	2	17	27	67	-40	14

Aberystwyth Town deducted 1 point
Newtown deducted 3 points

23
Place Your Bets

EVERY SILVER LINING HAS A CLOUD Nathan Lee Davies

> Plunge boldly into the thick of life, and seize it where
> you will, it is always interesting.

> Goethe

Jerry Farr was diagnosed with Friedreich's Ataxia at the age of nine, but unlike me he remained determined, positive, focused, energetic, loving and well-adjusted throughout his life. Speaking to Ataxia UK following his sad passing in 2007, Jerry's family paid tribute to a remarkable man:

"He might not have been able to walk, but in the last ten years he globe-trotted on holidays to numerous countries — Brazil, China, Australia, New Zealand, South Africa amongst others — and as he travelled he made more great friends. It seemed to us that he lived for those holidays and the thought of more of them was probably what kept him going.

"Jerry went white-water rafting and paragliding. He did a bungee jump in New Zealand which gave him such a massive thrill. All of these images we treasure — images of an incredible man rising above the perceived constraints of his disability."

It must be nice to have money.

***

Jerry must've been a likeable guy as his family and friends decided to launch a travel fellowship in his memory to pay tribute to his spirit of adventure, which it was hoped would live on through the experiences of others.

Sufferers of Ataxia, who wanted to broaden their horizons through travel, could suddenly dare to dream. On offer was a maximum of £3,500, to cover all the pre-agreed costs of a trip for a single person, and up to £6,500 if accompaniment by a carer was required. The destination and purpose of the trip was entirely up to the entrant, provided it was outside British shores.

This was too good an opportunity to pass up…

I chose to apply to go on a trip of a lifetime to Las Vegas, which is a city I've always dreamt of visiting and regret not experiencing during my time as a student in the United States, many moons ago.

This proposal wouldn't automatically result in a fortnight of debauchery – though the gambling and classy call girls do appeal – as my application touched on my desire to marvel at the natural wonder of the Grand Canyon, get my kicks on historic Route 66 and take cultural excursions to the Tomb of King Tut at the Luxor, the Bellagio Gallery of Fine Art and even the Atomic Testing Museum. For God's sake, I'd even go to the Nevada State Railroad Museum if it meant getting my hands on the prize money. Even though I never met him, I'm sure Jerry would've approved of such an epic adventure.

I completed the application form in shamelessly arse-licking style and refrained from swearing over four sheets of A4, which was a new record. Nevertheless, I still felt the dull paperwork needed something extra to mark it out from the competition. Sacrificing time on the book, I set to work on an accompanying scrapbook that included various photographs of my changing faces over the years, paragraphs of text outlining my life story and details of my dream trip to visit the neighbouring states of Nevada and Arizona.

I used themed scrapbook paper and sprinkled the pages with stickers and other embellishments to produce an attractive and informative application that was fit to win any competition, especially one in which there were only eight entries the last time I unsuccessfully entered. With the bad luck I'd been experiencing and the high standard of application I'd created, surely it was time for good fortune to shine down on me for once?

EVERY SILVER LINING HAS A CLOUD Nathan Lee Davies

***

I'd bought my silver jump suit, shades and coiffured wig and spent hours quivering my lips in the mirror, but I still had a heavy heart. Instead of performing as a wheelchair-bound Elvis in front of thousands of adoring fans at the MGM Grand, I'd be slurring "Heartbreak Hotel" into a karaoke microphone after a few pints too many at a near-empty pub on the outskirts of Wrexham.

For a minute there, I was silly enough to think my luck could change.

Bangor City 1 TNS 3

Corbett Sports Welsh Premier League
Saturday, 10 March 2012
17:15

Nantporth Stadium / Stadiwm Nantporth
Attendance: 746

Bloody Bangor City...

The Citizens had been based at Farrar Road since 1919, but after making me endure a bladder busting afternoon at this shambolic old ground, the powers that be decided to sell the historical site to Asda and relocate across the city to a new home overlooking the Menai Straits. As a result, I have to drag my arse to north-west Wales yet again and write another chapter for this book when the final manuscript really should already be in the hands of my publisher. It'd better be worth it, especially after all the fuss they made about leaving fortress Farrar back in December.

"There have been happy memories [at Farrar Road] for the last 65 years I've been involved with this club," said Bangor City's honorary president, Gwyn Pierce Owen.

"My father used to take me here at the age of 12.

"He used to carry me over the turnstile and that was the last time I'd see him for the next 90 minutes.

"I'd just get lost amongst the crowd. It was thrilling.

"There was no room for us to stand. We used to sit between the touchline and the perimeter fence."

EVERY SILVER LINING HAS A CLOUD Nathan Lee Davies

As well as being club president, Owen has served as chairman, director and even found time to prove himself as a world class referee – but first and foremost he is a Bangor City fan.

"We've done so well. We've been to Europe eight or nine times, winning the Welsh league championship on three occasions since I've been involved, beating teams like Yeovil, Boston and Barrow.

"I was looking at it [Farrar Road] the other day, but it's like me now, a bit worn and decrepit, it is about time we moved now," accepted the club president.

As well as such sickeningly sentimental tributes, there were nostalgic blogs aplenty from dedicated fans, who were determined to remember and respect the past before making a success of the move to Nantporth.

S4C showed the final match at Farrar Road – a 5-3 thriller against Prestatyn – and included miserable montages of footage of this soon-to-be-demolished blight on the landscape, with melancholy musical accompaniment. It was a tear-jerker for some, a blessed relief for others.

On 24 January 2012, Bangor City started life at Nantporth with a 6-1 win over Caernarfon Wanderers in the North Wales Coast Challenge Cup. More than 1,200 fans saw Chris Jones net the first ever goal at the new stadium with a volley from a Les Davies cross.

The first game at Nantporth in the WPL took place on 4 February 2012. It was a repeat of the club's farewell to Farrar Road and a victory over north Wales coast rivals Prestatyn. On this occasion the Citizens recovered from a goal down to beat the Seasiders 2-1. I would've gone but it was the beginning of February and the weather was particularly vicious, with bitingly cold, sub-zero temperatures and relentless rain coupling to increase the appeal of S4C's live coverage. I wasn't the only one to feel this way as the landmark match attracted a disappointing crowd of 709.[1]

Instead, I waited until 10 March 2012 to visit Nantporth for Bangor City's top of the table clash with TNS. It promised to be a mouth-watering affair that would have a big say in the destiny of the WPL crown as although the Citizens were top, only a point separated the two sides. It was all to play for, but I wasn't looking forward to it as I was still traumatised from my visit to Farrar Road and was not convinced that they'd got the design of their new stadium right, judging by what the S4C cameras and the amateur photography of various webmasters had suggested.

The incomplete ground was opened with an 800-seat main stand and a further 400 on the opposite side of the pitch. The club had also submitted plans to increase the seating capacity to the current 1,500 minimum needed for staging European ties. I was more concerned that I could see no sign of accessible disabled areas and feared another afternoon of struggle.

I needn't have worried.

I arrived at the neat and tidy ground with two hours to spare before kick-off and was immediately heartened by the sight of disabled car park spaces at either side of the main stand. I could see that things had improved straight away. There were no supporting beams of wood needed to stop this structure from toppling over, and I'd already passed through a large club park that sits next to a floodlit, all-weather, 3G training pitch.

With ages to go before the match started I wondered how we were going to fill the time, when my dad revealed his grand plan – Wales

---

[1] Single, middle-aged men that wear slacks may be interested to note that the honour of scoring the first WPL goal at Nantporth went to Prestatyn player-manager Neil Gibson.

were playing Six Nations rugby against Italy in Cardiff and we could watch them chasing eggs from the comfort and splendour of the Bangor clubhouse with other proud and patriotic Welsh supporters. I was overjoyed.

The main stand houses a stylish bar area that is kitted out with tables and chairs, adorned with club memorabilia and is home to three wall mounted televisions that I ignored while concentrating on the matchday magazine. I'm glad to report that this hadn't altered in style or substance since the issue I'd enjoyed at Farrar Road, back in 2011. My only problem with this edition, or any other multi-page publication for that matter, is that I no longer have the necessary dexterity to leaf through pages. As you can imagine, this makes the whole reading process very frustrating. It's agony for a former bookworm to visit a library or a well-stocked second-hand book store and be surrounded by tempting titles that I know I'll never be able to open with useless fingers that can only claw. I've invested in a kindle to solve the problem, but it's not the same.

While the brick shithouses did their stuff on the televisions around me, my sausage fingers grabbed at a sheet of A4 paper that was lying on a nearby table. It was an advertisement/order form for a commemorative book to celebrate "City's glorious time at Farrar Road". To subscribe to this dubious tome cost £50 and although fans would be able to bask in the glory of the "many achievements at that special stadium", they'd have to pay £25 for a limited edition, signed copy. The book, produced by the club and its supporter's club, was to be called *Farewell Farrar Road*. If it had been called *Good Riddance Farrar Road*, I might have invested in a copy.

There was a warm round of applause and some loud cheering as Wales moved another step closer to the Grand Slam with a 24-3 victory over the Italians. Thankfully, this meant it was now time to leave the social club, turn our attentions to a different sport and discover where, if anywhere, the stadium designers had decided to plonk disabled spectators. Provision for the physically challenged is usually an afterthought so, as usual, I expected the worst as I followed a steward through freshly carpeted corridors towards my viewpoint for the afternoon.

I was led to an opening at the top of the main stand and positioned myself in line with the centre circle next to a sponsorship-clad logo board that players and managers would be interviewed in front of after the game. This was perfect. Not only would I be watching this crucial encounter from an ideal vantage point at the back of a busy covered stand, but I could also let my imagination run free, by pretending to be quizzed against a familiar backdrop.

I wasn't expecting to call upon such fantasy to occupy my thoughts though. Even if the game, between the top two teams in the national league, didn't live up to the pre-match hype then my position allowed me an unbeatable view of Nantporth and the surrounding beauty. On the horizon it's possible to see the Menai Straits between picturesque woodland, Thomas Telford's Menai Suspension Bridge and the distant coastline of Anglesey. In the foreground, the Menai Straits side of the ground is overlooked by epic trees and is home to two separate prefabricated stands to seat 400, a towering television gantry and hard standing. The areas behind both goals are simply uncovered hard standing, with just a single step of terracing, but plenty of room to expand in the future.

The 800-seat main stand is the dominant structure. It was just as well that I entered from the back as it's a raised seating area that is accessible from pitch-side via flights of stairs. The roof of the stand doesn't cover some of the blue seats on the flanks, while a picky person would moan about the thin floodlight columns at the front that slightly impede what would otherwise be a perfect view. Oddly, the dressing rooms are situated at the back of the stand – as they were at Newtown – but at least in this case the players are somewhat protected from angry supporters by a dividing wall and a concertina cover that stretches out onto the pitch.

EVERY SILVER LINING HAS A CLOUD Nathan Lee Davies

Overall, I was suitably impressed with the ground as I was comfortable, dry and looking forward to using the nearby disabled toilet at half-time. Nantporth may not have been totally completed but improvements were in the pipeline and small additions were being made on a weekly basis. My visit coincided with the unveiling of a small portacabin that was home to the club shop. It was also good to hear that a refreshment stall for hungry supporters was now fully operational.

It seems to me that the key word to be associated with Nantporth is "potential". There is plenty of scope for adding extra stands, or shelter for those who prefer to stand, but such improvements will depend, not just on the ambitions of the club, but on how well they are supported by their fans. The current set up is fit for purpose, but if the ground is to grow and blossom into a flagship football facility, as envisioned by Bangor chairman Dilwyn Jones, then City's loyal fan base will also need to grow substantially.

This will only happen if Nev Powell's men continue to succeed and develop on the pitch, but based on the opening 45 minutes this is a lot to ask of a part-time outfit. TNS totally ripped City's shoddy defence apart with thoughtless, yet decisive, long balls.

The foreigners were quick out of the blocks and only good work from Lee Idzi in the Bangor goal kept them at bay on three occasions in the opening seven minutes. Idzi's hapless defenders then left him to deal with a misplaced header from Dave Morley, but he slid out of his goal to clear the danger as Draper threatened to capitalise. Bangor had been warned.

Subsequently, it came as little surprise when, on 18 minutes, a through ball from Evans found Draper, who coolly rounded Idzi before stroking the ball into the net to the delight of the few wearing green and white. To be fair, these fans were creating what little atmosphere there was and had even bought along a drum to beat annoyingly throughout the game. The Saints were asking all the questions and Idzi came to the Blues' rescue again on the half-hour by palming a Tom Roberts shot onto his crossbar. City's best effort in the first half came from Alan Bull's counter attack down the right. His cross to the far post was met with a volley by Les Davies, only for the shot to go straight to TNS keeper Paul Harrison.

This was as good as it got for Bangor. They fell further behind on 38 minutes when a long ball forward from ex-City defender Phil Baker was lobbed home by man-of-the-match Aeron Edwards. This was followed, in the 41st minute, by Draper's 19th league goal of the season after another long-ball from Baker. The game was effectively over and I hadn't even enjoyed a half-time pie.

You may recall that the single redeeming feature about my trip to Farrar Road was the gorgeous pie I'd consumed in ramshackle surroundings. I was hoping that the club had stuck with the same caterers, so I could indulge myself in another delicious serving. Imagine my disappointment then when I was told that they'd run out of hot food and could only offer crisps or chocolate bars. I could understand if my request had come late in the day, but the referee had only just blown the half-time whistle and the stadium was hardly a sell-out. I was most disgruntled and let everyone on Twitter know about it.

Whatever was said by Nev Powell and his coaching staff at the interval certainly did the trick as within 90 seconds of the restart a Chris Jones cross-cum-shot was palmed away by Harrison in the TNS goal, only for Neil Thomas to fire the loose ball into the roof of the net. The passionate home fans went wild and urged their team forward. If City had shown as much determination and effort in the opening period then they wouldn't have been in such a desperate situation, but unfortunately the element of fortune they needed to accompany their increased endeavour, failed to materialise. This was highlighted on 56 minutes when Peter Hoy agonisingly hit the post from a Les Davies lobbed pass.

EVERY SILVER LINING HAS A CLOUD Nathan Lee Davies

TNS did carry some threat when Idzi got down well to prevent Alex Darlington from finishing the game as a contest, but after their first half efforts the visitors were now content to defend in depth. Chris Jones was inches wide with an 18-yard snapshot and then headed just wide from a Chris Roberts cross, but the pressure came to nothing and waned as the part timers began to tire. In the end, TNS could've added a fourth, but Roberts just failed to get enough on Draper's by-line cross.

The weekend previously, the Citizens had succumbed to Neath at Nantporth in remarkably similar circumstances. In both matches against title rivals they had trailed 3-0 at the interval and scored their solitary goal within two minutes of the restart. All this meant they were now licking their wounds in second place as the invaders from Shropshire regained top spot with just five games remaining.

***

After a blissfully relieving visit to the plush disabled toilet, there was just time to pop back to the social club and enjoy S4C's post-match analysis – even if it was incomprehensible – as well as highlights of all the weekend's WPL action.

The large windows in the social club overlook the ground and, through these, it was possible to see John Hartson and Malcolm Allen giving their views on the game, while simultaneously watching them on television screens 100 yards away. As gobbledegook was showered upon replays of Greg Draper's earlier brace, I was fending off advances from a drunken Bangor fan, who seemed determined to buy me a pint of lager. I declined his kind offer as I was eager to find a chip shop on the way home and make up for my lack of half-time sustenance.

The problem was that my new found friend wasn't taking no for an answer. He was too busy shaking my hand and telling me how people like me were an inspiration to listen to my polite refusal of even a half. In the end I escaped by bamboozling him with a series of puzzling questions that keep me awake on lonely nights and bent his addled mind:

What was the best thing before sliced bread?

What colour does a Smurf turn when you're choking him?

Why does the BBC keep broadcasting *Last of the Summer Wine*?

My new admirer retired to the corner of the room with his pint and quietly sat in deep contemplation, but before I could celebrate my freedom and concentrate on listening to Nev Powell and Craig Harrison – both English speakers – I was accosted by an army of patronising well-wishers. My dad had been telling anyone who'd listen about the book I was writing and though I was happy to be making him proud, I could've done without the extra pressure brought about by questions regarding the publication date, format and how much I had left to write. I had a completion date in mind, but now that I could see light at the end of a creative tunnel I was beginning to doubt the artistic merits of my work.

I refused several other pints and offers to recount the "glory days" at Farrar Road before making for the exit with the weight of expectation on my shoulders. How could I celebrate finally completing my journey when I still had six chapters left to write, hours of research to conduct and reams of re-writing, editing and meticulous spell-checking to perform?

As the car pulled away from Nantporth, I received a text. It was from Joanna – the latest occupant of my heart and star of some vividly sordid sexual fantasies. My worries and concerns were replaced with excitement and affection as I opened the enticing electronic envelope.

It's over. Well done. Can't wait to read the book ☺ xx

I broke out in a sweat...

Bangor City
Nantporth

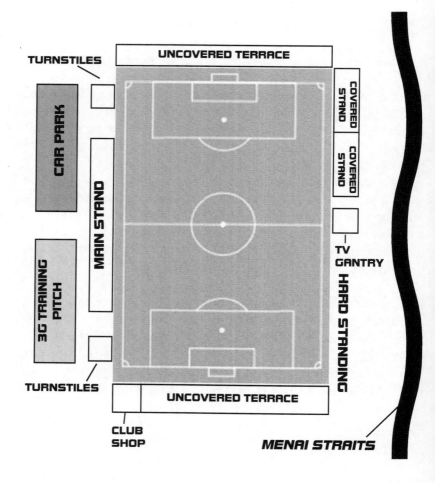

24
March 2012

Thursday, 29 March 2012

Be who you are and say what you feel, because those who mind don't matter and those who matter don't mind.

The above utterance is often incorrectly attributed to Dr. Seuss. According to Wikiquote, it was actually coined by Bernard Mannes Baruch (19 August 1870 – 20 June 1965) – an American financier, stock market speculator, statesman, and presidential advisor. After his success in business, he devoted his time toward advising Democratic presidents, Woodrow Wilson and Franklin D. Roosevelt on economic matters.

While working as an advisor to FDR, Baruch was asked by Igor Cassini, a popular society columnist for the *New York Journal American*, how he handled the seating arrangements for all those who attended his dinner parties. The full response was "I never bother about that. Those who matter don't mind, and those who mind don't matter." This anecdote has since become part of a larger expression, which has been commonly [and incorrectly] attributed to Dr. Seuss, even in print, but without citation of a specific work.

No matter who actually formulated the words, I'm reminded of the quote after recent events. I decided to allow Valerie and Michelle read my diary entry for February before publication. They are mentioned by name, so I thought it was only fair to check that there were no objections to what I'd written.

Valerie didn't mind. Michelle did.

The book hasn't even been published and it's causing upset and controversy – so much so that I appear to have lost a friend. According to Michelle, what I wrote was "shocking", "disrespectful" and "inappropriate" and as a result she has cancelled future trips

EVERY SILVER LINING HAS A CLOUD Nathan Lee Davies

we'd planned together. She also objects to being called a "divorcee" as she is trying to look to the future and leave the past where it belongs. Fair enough, but as her marriage has been legally dissolved, she remains a divorcee.

Unfortunately, she has read my ramblings all wrong and focused on my blunt crudeness, rather than the deeper thoughts that lurk beneath the surface. I was merely making the point that she was such an important friend to me and that I didn't intend on sullying our relationship with sexual thoughts or advances. I've apologised for any upset caused and changed her name to protect her identity, but it's been a fortnight since we last spoke and I'm not expecting any calls or texts from her soon.

I'll never understand women. I'm obviously disappointed at losing a close friend, with whom I'd shared many smiles, but on the bright side, it's given me something to moan about within this empty diary space.

Life goes on.

HOMER SIMPSON: I will never understand women if I live to be forty.

BART SIMPSON: Big if.

The Simpsons
"Marge Gamer"
2007

News Round-Up

Kristian O'Leary picked up his first manager of the month award just three months after taking the reins at Neath, while TNS striker Greg Draper lifted the player of the month prize.

Former Swansea City favourite O'Leary has transformed the fortunes of the Eagles since succeeding Terry Boyle and Peter Nicholas in November.

The full-timers are unbeaten this year, with five wins from six, and have established themselves as serious title contenders with away victories at TNS and Bangor City.

Their unbeaten run – in all competitions – stretches back to October.

Meanwhile, player of the month Draper hit six goals in five games during January and February. This prolific run included a hat-trick against Newtown in a 5-0 romp at Park Hall.

The 22-year-old competed in New Zealand's 2008 Olympic campaign as a teenager, before receiving his sole senior cap in a World Cup qualifier against Fiji.

Draper has played for Canterbury United, Wellington Phoenix, Melbourne Knights and Team Wellington.

He spent season 2010-11 with Basingstoke Town, where he hit 15 goals from 28 appearances, before joining TNS in June 2011.

***

There was bad news for fans of Prestatyn Town as president Mike Walsh and his brother, vice-president Sean Walsh, formally stepped down from their roles at the club. The duo had been the club's main sponsors since 2007, but they indicated that they no longer wish to carry on in their posts.

"There is no doubt that without their wholehearted support, both financially and behind the scenes, the club would not be where it is today and their input over the past five years has been immense," read a statement on the club website.

"As a club we are grateful to Mike and Sean for everything they have done but regretfully accept their decisions to step down. The search for a new main sponsor will begin immediately."

***

When I first read news of a "WAG probe" into the Welsh Premier League, I imagined that the wives and girlfriends of the players involved in the national league had designed and launched a new sex toy.

THE WAG PROBE

This fabulous realistic penis vibrator combines a soft outer skin texture on a rigid and veined shaft. The combination delivers a truly sensational experience. You can enjoy this realistic vibrator both in and out of the water as it is fully waterproof and submersible. It delivers low to high multi-speed vibrations controlled by a dial knob at the base of the shaft. This superb dildo vibrator has a 7' inch insertable length including a widening base for added stimulation.

Free batteries supplied.

Unfortunately, the WAG probe referred to was not a new fun stick for females, but a dry and dull investigation into the WPL by the Welsh Assembly Government's Communities, Equality and Local Government Committee.

The inquiry will, amongst other things, look to the future of the League and analyse its format, development of players and media coverage.

Such a move could open the possibility of sanctions from world football's governing body FIFA, which has previously suspended national organisations for perceived political interference.

But while a spokesman for the FAW could only say it was "aware that the inquiry is taking place", it is understood that they're not worried about it.

The FAW has spoken to the committee and even assisted it with who it should speak to as part of its inquiry, content that it will not be obliged to act on any of its findings.

Fans were urged to contribute to the inquiry. I would've, but I had a book to write.

***

Airbus UK Broughton chief, Andy Preece, is the latest figure to speak out against the poor standard of some pitches in the WPL.

Preece is a recent recruit to the Welsh scene, after 25 years playing and managing in the English pyramid. In an interview with http://backpagefootball.com, he doesn't hide his disappointment.

"Against Bala and against TNS, the pitches for both of those games weren't the best.

EVERY SILVER LINING HAS A CLOUD Nathan Lee Davies

"As a player, I wouldn't have been keen to play on that [Park Hall] every week. Personally, I'm not in favour, I think football should be played on grass.

"I think it gives too big of an advantage to the team who has that surface and, although the surfaces have improved over the years, still lots of our lads came off with burns and cuts on their legs.

"Saying that, I'd much prefer to play on the 3G at TNS than a couple of the pitches that we've played on recently, that have been of a very poor quality.

"That's the one thing that's surprised me about Welsh football.

"If you're going to improve the standard of football, and the standard of players going through for the Welsh national team, then I think that the improvement needs to go, a bit more, into the grounds.

"Then you'll attract better quality players, you'll get better quality football and, ultimately you'll get better quality players pushing for the national team."

***

Neath FC has been hit with new cash demands, despite having paid off a huge tax bill. Revenue and Customs asked the High Court to dismiss a winding-up petition against the club, after it paid a £65,000 tax debt – only for lawyers for Barclays Bank to then request that they take over as petitioner in respect of an alleged unpaid debt. The amount of money in question has not been revealed.

Lawyers for the club said that they were not in a position to admit that the debt was owed to the bank. A spokesperson for the FAW said that the governing body had been in touch with the club and is confident the matter will be resolved in the coming weeks.

EVERY SILVER LINING HAS A CLOUD Nathan Lee Davies

***

UEFA's executive committee rejected a FAW proposal that Welsh clubs playing in the English pyramid system should be allowed a route into Europe by winning the Welsh Cup.

UEFA's ruling is a blow to the FAW, who wanted to offer Welsh clubs competing in the English league pyramid, including Swansea City, Cardiff City, Wrexham, Newport County, Colwyn Bay and Merthyr Town, the carrot of Europa League qualification to persuade them to play in the Welsh Cup.

Newport, Wrexham and Merthyr entered this season's Welsh Cup, but their future participation may now be in some doubt without the lure of European qualification.

"We accept the decision and as an association we'll move on to strengthen the profile of the competition as it exists at the moment," said FAW spokesman Ian Gwyn Hughes.

"I think everybody would accept since the likes of Cardiff and Swansea ceased playing in the Welsh Cup the profile has dropped.

"But it's up to us as an association to improve the strength and the profile of the competition with the clubs that play in it."

To soften this disappointing news UEFA gave reassurances that any of the Welsh clubs – realistically Swansea or Cardiff – would qualify for Europe should they finish high enough in the English top flight, or win the FA Cup or League Cup.

***

It's that time of year again when European hopefuls cover their backs by appointing coaches with the requisite paperwork to "manage" clubs in Europe. Subsequently, Bala Town have appointed Pro Licence holder Allan Bickerstaff, as head coach, while Colin Caton becomes director of football. Bickerstaff has assistant managerial experience with spells at Airbus and Porthmadog before managing at Rhyl from June 2008 until July 2009. He was also WPL manager of the season that term. More recently, he managed at Llandudno Town for a 3-month spell and has since been working for the Welsh Football Trust in Denbighshire.

WPL table as of 31/03/12

Pos	Team	P	W	D	L	F	A	GD	Pts
1	TNS	29	21	4	4	68	30	+38	67
2	Bangor City	29	20	3	6	65	37	+28	63
3	Neath	29	17	8	4	55	26	+29	59
4	Llanelli	28	15	4	9	53	33	+20	49
5	Bala Town	28	13	7	8	44	34	+10	46
6	Prestatyn Town	29	8	4	17	36	55	-19	28
7	Airbus UK B'ton	28	9	8	11	44	44	0	35
8	Afan Lido	28	7	11	10	36	42	-6	32
9	Port Talbot Town	28	7	7	14	33	45	-12	28
10	Aberystwyth Town	2.8	5	10	13	37	46	-9	24
11	Carmarthen Town	29	7	2	20	28	65	-37	23
12	Newtown	29	6	4	19	34	76	-42	19

Newtown deducted 3 points
Aberystwyth Town deducted 1 point

25
April 2012

Thursday, 5 April 2012

It's one of my many bugbears – ignorant members of the public who park in disabled parking bays without the requisite blue badge.

According to the Welsh government (http://wales.gov.uk), you may be eligible for a badge if:

- your Consultant Ophthalmologist has signed a Certificate of Vision Impairment for you and you provide this to support your application

- you are able to show that you have a permanent and substantial disability which means you are unable to walk or have considerable difficulty walking

- you can provide a recent award letter from Disability and Carers Services (DCS) showing that you have been awarded the Higher Rate Mobility Component of Disability Living Allowance (HRMCDLA)

- you can provide an award letter from the Service Personnel and Veterans Agency to show you receive War Pensioner's Mobility Supplement (WPMS) or that you receive a guaranteed payment under tariffs 1-8 of the Armed Forces Compensation Scheme (AFCS) and have been certified as having a permanent and substantial disability which causes an inability to walk or very considerable difficulty in walking

- you have a severe disability in both upper limbs, regularly drive a car but have difficulty or cannot use parking meters and similar equipment

- you have a child under the age of three who needs to be accompanied always by bulky medical equipment or needs to have access to a motor vehicle in case they need emergency medical treatment

Nowhere here does it say that you're entitled to park in a space assigned for disabled people if you're a an unemployed, single mum nipping into Tesco for some fags, or a young professional poser driving a sports car bound for Boots to purchase some moisturiser for a smug, smarmy face that is asking for a good punch.

I was glad to learn that new plastic blue badges – with extra security features – are being introduced in Wales to help tackle abuse of parking for disabled drivers. The badges will be harder to forge, or use fraudulently, as police and parking wardens can check them on the spot against a national database if they suspect abuse.

Welsh government ministers say the badges will be free, unlike some in England and Scotland. The current handwritten card badges will be replaced by plastic, electronically-printed photo ID versions as disabled drivers renew them over the next three years.

A UK government report has highlighted widespread abuse of the system, which creates problems for disabled people and costs £46m a year in parking fee evasion.

Transport Minister Carl Sargeant said: "When people abuse blue badges, or use disabled parking spaces they're not entitled to, they are seriously affecting the quality of life of those individuals who legitimately carry badges.

"Blue badges allow people in genuine need to live independent lives, and by invading blue badge spaces, other drivers are actually causing not just great inconvenience to the disabled person, but also physical pain."

EVERY SILVER LINING HAS A CLOUD Nathan Lee Davies

This is a step in the right direction, but in my opinion, it doesn't go far enough. Too many people still qualify for a blue badge with around 230,000 in circulation in Wales. I've seen people displaying the correct paperwork yet performing cartwheels and handstands while I continue a frustrated search for available spaces. Surely, it should be tougher for people to get their hands on these passes in the first place? I'd also like to see more people fined for improper use of a blue badge.

Unfortunately, I'm not running the country and don't have enough of a social conscience to spend time campaigning for the rights of others. As long as I can get my moisturiser from Boots I'm happy enough to carry on moaning...

***

When I talk about improper use of blue badges I'm not talking about a jobsworth fining me £50 because my badge had expired without my knowledge. If I'd been alerted to the problem then I would've renewed the paperwork immediately, but instead the car park attendant slapped a £50 notice on the windscreen of my wheelchair accessible van. I later confronted the Euro Car Parks official and lamented that my disability hadn't expired but – along with a letter of appeal to head office – it made no difference and the fine stood.

My mate, Andy Evans, hit on an excellent idea to settle the fine with 1p coins. I was all for it, but unfortunately they only accepted debit cards or cheques.

News Round-Up

Manager of the month for March was Carl Darlington of The New Saints.

TNS remained unbeaten throughout the month. This fine run included away wins against Bangor City (1-3) and Neath (0-1). The Saints also secured victories over Bala Town (3-2) and Prestatyn Town (2-1) at Park Hall.

They rounded off a successful month by convincingly beating Bala 4-0 to reach the Welsh Cup final.

Meanwhile, player of the month for March was Carl Evans of Afan Lido. The defender won many personal accolades from opposing clubs throughout March and notched the equaliser against local rivals Port Talbot Town in the last match of the month at the GenQuip Stadium.

***

The final round of Welsh Premier League matches saw much excitement at the top and bottom of the table. S4C took their cameras to Park Hall, where leaders TNS took on second place Bangor City in a repeat of last season's title showdown.

The full-timers had "home" advantage on this occasion and took full advantage with a mesmerising performance that made a mockery of the fact that the Citizens only trailed the foreigners by two points ahead of the game. The visitors were simply outclassed by an outfit with the potential to dominate Welsh football for years to come.

It was all over bar the shouting before I'd even opened my first Budweiser as Greg Draper ran through to beat the offside trap and net calmly within four minutes.

EVERY SILVER LINING HAS A CLOUD Nathan Lee Davies

Christian Seargeant's goal from a 25-yard free-kick on seven minutes meant City had a mountain to climb.

Worse was to come as Greg Draper scored his second on 26 minutes. I didn't bother watching the rest as the championship trophy was clearly leaving the country for the next twelve months at least.

Apparently, Ryan Fraughan added a fourth in the second half. Alex Darlington could even afford to miss a penalty before a second spot-kick was converted by hat-trick hero Greg Draper to seal a 5-0 romp.

I switched the television back on at six o'clock and saw fans wearing England tops and green wigs celebrating on an artificial surface.

I reached for my sixth Budweiser...

***

On the same day, Rhys Griffiths claimed a seventh consecutive Welsh Premier Golden Boot with a brace as Llanelli hammered Neath 1-5 at the Gnoll.

In a game of no significance, the Reds were five goals to the good against the hapless Eagles by half-time, with Stuart Jones, Lloyd Grist and Chris Venables adding to Griffiths' goals. Lee Trundle scored a second half consolation for the home side.

It's the sixth time that Griffiths has won the accolade with Llanelli after first landing the trophy with Port Talbot in season 2005-06.

The season ended on a sad note at Bastion Gardens as Prestatyn midfielder Gareth Wilson and Bala's Peter Doran were taken to hospital following a clash of heads, six minutes from time.

Both sides had earlier been reduced to 10-men with Rhys Owen (Prestatyn) and Ross Jefferies (Bala) sent-off. Bala won the game 2-1. Former seaside favourite Lee Hunt scored the winner on 76 minutes.

In the bottom six, Airbus UK Broughton claimed a Europa League play-off spot after a 1-2 win at Afan Lido – striker Jon Bathurst scored both goals for the Wingmakers. Carl Payne was on the scoresheet for the hosts.

Aberystwyth clawed their way to safety with a heart-stopping 3-2 home win over already relegated Newtown, but it took a highly controversial goal to seal the win. Andy Jones was ruled to have turned a Geoff Kellaway cross into his own net, but the Robins claimed the ball had not crossed the line.

Despite winning 1-0 with a Corey Thomas goal at Port Talbot, Carmarthen Town finished in the bottom two on goal difference from Afan Lido and could be relegated if Haverfordwest can maintain second spot in Welsh League Division One.

***

Of course, we must remember that the WPL is still in its infancy and is dogged by administrative and structural headaches. As a result, final league standings were still far from decided...

One thing was known for sure – Connah's Quay Nomads would be taking their rightful place in the WPL. The club gained their domestic licence at the beginning of the month and then clinched the Huws Gray Alliance title for the second successive season. As discussed earlier, Mark McGregor's men were cruelly denied promotion at the end of 2010-11 when they failed to gain the domestic licence on appeal. Prior to their relegation in 2010, Nomads had enjoyed 18 unbroken seasons in the top flight since the inception of the league in 1992.

EVERY SILVER LINING HAS A CLOUD Nathan Lee Davies

The 2012 licensing process was just as controversial. At the initial licensing meeting, the majority of Welsh Premier clubs received their licences along with Llandudno Town and Porthmadog from the Alliance and Haverfordwest County from the Welsh League.

The two clubs that missed out on their licence were Neath and TNS, who both had the chance to appeal. This was seen by many as a mere formality, despite the demotion of Rhyl in 2010 due to financial irregularities.

Neath were also denied a UEFA licence, while all the other WPL clubs received their European passports.

The appeals panel granted a domestic licence to TNS as well as the successfully restructured Rhyl – who finished second in the Huws Gray Alliance – but Bridgend Town's appeal was rejected. However, it was the decision to refuse both the FAW domestic and UEFA licences to Neath that sent shockwaves throughout the game in Wales.

After a season of well-publicised financial difficulties, which has included a winding-up petition at the High Court, the Eagles lost their place in the WPL despite finishing in third position. Club officials were obviously angered as is reflected in the following statement that appeared on their website:

> As a club we cannot begin to describe how we feel regarding the decision of the licensing authority not to renew Neath FC's domestic and European licence. We feel that the club has done everything it could to satisfy the requirements and are bitterly disappointed.
>
> There has been a major investment at the Gnoll to bring the facility up to the required standard stipulated by the League of Wales and FIFA, and to not have a team participating in the Welsh Premier and the possibility of

EVERY SILVER LINING HAS A CLOUD Nathan Lee Davies

European competition is nothing short of disastrous.

It is no secret that we have faced more than our fair share of challenges both on and off the pitch this year. The loss of our main sponsor early in the campaign triggered off a chain of events which seriously affected the day to day running of the club. The negative press coverage both through local media and the so-called Welsh football channel [S4C] has resembled more of a comedy show. The way that the club's off-field issues have been focused on, rather than the football it's played and the value and interest it has brought to the League, has done nothing but fan the flames.

We could have decided back in October not to continue, however we struggled on against severe adversity. The business model on paper was sustainable. However, when over half your crowds disappear and a number of sponsors withdraw its always going to be difficult. We have played some wonderful football this year both at home and away and have swelled the coffers of the other Premier clubs on the road. Unfortunately, Neath FC has been the talking point for all the wrong reasons.

We would like to thank the players, coaching staff, sponsors, volunteers and fans who have invested their time, energy and money these last three seasons. These individuals have stuck together in our quest not only for success, but more importantly stability and our clubs long term future. We will always be grateful and indebted to them.

Neath's ambition should have been embraced instead of shunned by the dad's army, back bencher committee members who only have their own agendas at heart. The way these individuals "run the league" is nothing short of shambolic. A total impartial structure must be established if the league is to flourish. Serious investment needs to be made by the governing body. Without outside reliance the league cannot produce a product that is both attractive to supporters and marketable from a commercial perspective. We tried and were making progress if it had not been for events which were out of our control.

Through all this we survived and made it to the end of the season and have been already making plans for the next. We must now assess where the future of Neath FC now lies as we try to come to terms with today's ruling. This is a travesty.

This rash and emotive statement is the sort of thing you'd expect to find in an angry teenager's diary, who thinks the world is against him and takes no responsibility for his own actions. The demise of this newly formed club had nothing to do with financial mismanagement, or operating beyond meagre means, according to this rant. Instead the finger of blame is directed towards the FAW, local media and S4C.

The FAW's licensing appeals panel was obviously unconvinced that the club's business model was sustainable, after a season that saw business problems for one of their main backers, players going unpaid, and the club facing a winding-up petition. Although it may seem bizarre that a team can be relegated after finishing in third place, I think it's fair enough as the FAW and WPL are imposing licence rules to help clubs maintain stability, structure and organisation. In such an environment, the competing clubs will eventually flourish on strong foundations. Only a fool builds on sand...

You have to feel sorry for the players though – some of whom gave up day jobs to play for the club on a full-time basis. They weren't to know that the ambitious project would turn sour in much the same way as similar collapses at Barry Town and Rhyl.

All this means a reprieve from relegation for the 11th-placed club, Carmarthen Town, while bottom-club Newtown will also escape the drop if Haverfordwest County fail to gain promotion from the Welsh League. Neath will also be ineligible to participate in the end-of-season Europa League play-offs, with eighth-placed Aberystwyth Town now playing at Airbus UK Broughton in the first round game next month.

After all was done and dusted, the clubs with a domestic licence for 2012-13 were Aberystwyth Town, Airbus UK Broughton, Afan Lido, Bala Town, Bangor City, Carmarthen Town, GAP Connah's Quay (promoted), Haverfordwest County (Welsh League), Llandudno Town (Huws Gray Alliance), Llanelli AFC, Newtown AFC, Port Talbot Town, Prestatyn Town, Rhyl FC (Huws Gray Alliance) and The New Saints.

The future for Neath remains uncertain.

***

Before recounting the next news item, taken from the BBC website, I have taken a deep breath and bitten off my own tongue, so my words, blinded by pain, cannot get me in trouble.

After clinching the WPL title, TNS chairman Mike Harris announced his belief that his club should be allowed to play in the FA Cup next season.

He feels they should join Welsh exile sides Newport, Wrexham and Merthyr, who played in the English league pyramid, FA Cup and the Welsh Cup this year.

"We thought it only fair... that we try to compete in the competitions they compete in as well," said Harris.

"We're not the unique ones in this – I would imagine a couple of other Welsh Premier clubs have applied as well."

The FAW invited the six Welsh clubs playing in the English system to participate in this season's Welsh Cup following a 16-year absence.

Swansea City, Cardiff City and Colwyn Bay turned down the chance, but Blue Square Bet Premier clubs Wrexham and Newport, plus Toolstation Western League side Merthyr accepted and could all be eligible to play in the Welsh Cup again next season.

Wrexham, Newport and Merthyr also played in the FA Cup and Saints feel that if those clubs can enter both knock-out competitions then they have a right to enter the FA Cup as well.

However, the entry requirements for next season's FA Cup state that new entrants must have played in the FA Trophy or FA Vase the previous season to be considered. The artificial pitch at Park Hall could also fall foul of regulations.

Applications to play in the Football Association's knock-out competitions had to be in by the 1st of April and Saints have applied for entry into both the FA Cup and the FA Trophy.

No other Welsh Premier clubs have applied to the FA for entry.

Harris contends that having the exiled clubs back in a Welsh club competition should pave the way for other Welsh-based clubs to enter the FA Cup.

He said: "Obviously [with] the inclusion of the exile clubs like Wrexham, Newport, Merthyr in our club competition, we thought it only fair and equal that we should try to compete in the competitions they compete in as well.

"The Welsh Cup and the FA Cup have similar status, both get into Europe.

"I don't quite see the English system as a higher platform; I see it as an equal platform, but with a bigger population and bigger crowds.

"Yes we're a business and as a business [the FAW have] included the likes of Wrexham and Newport into our competition which gives them an advantage because they play in the FA Cup.

"To balance that off and so we can compete on equal terms, we've chosen to take the decision to compete in the FA Cup.

"We've clearly stated we have no interest in the English place in Europe should we win the competition.

"We've declared that we don't want that place and we wouldn't want to be considered if we won the competition to qualify for that place, just like we hope that the FAW wouldn't give one of our cherished places to an English-playing club if they were to win the Welsh Cup.

"I spoke to several chairmen probably four or five months ago and I believed several other clubs were going to take the same approach.

"I'm not sure what they ended up doing. I wouldn't be surprised if there's not three or four other clubs who've applied as well.

"Football is a business and currently Welsh Premier clubs are having to compete against teams that have access to money playing in competitions over the border, such as Wrexham, such as Newport, such as Merthyr.

"So to balance that up we should be able to compete in the same competitions as them. It's just simple, equal rights."

I'm saying nothing...

***

The excellent www.welsh-premier.com featured an end of season review of crowd figures, which found that regular attendances dropped by 7.4% in 2011-12 – one of the largest falls ever recorded in the 20-year history of the Welsh Premier League.

The average attendance at the 192 games was 314, compared with 339 in 2010-11, with five clubs – Aberystwyth Town (1.8%), Bala Town (19.4%), Newtown (6.2%), Prestatyn (6.2%) and The New Saints (27.9%) – showing an improvement.

The biggest fall came at Neath, where the number of spectators through the turnstiles at the Gnoll plummeted by 32.2%. There were also significant decreases at Carmarthen Town (9.9%) and Bangor City (8.8%) despite a league record attendance of 2,593 for the last game at Farrar Road against Prestatyn.

Apart from that fixture, the only other four-figure attendance was at Park Hall when 1,468 watched TNS play Bangor in the title decider.

The Citizens were again the best-supported club both at home (727) and away (436) while Llanelli had the lowest home average of 205, an 8.7% fall on last season.

The Reds also attracted the lowest gate of the season, just 95 for the visit of Bala Town.

Attendances at the festive games were generally lower than in previous years, while the loss of Easter local derbies for most clubs

– since the advent of the 12-club league – has also had an effect.

Overall 60,291 spectators' watched Welsh Premier games compared with 65,107 in the previous campaign. The mid-season split seems to have had a negative effect on attendances with average crowds of 337 before the winter break and only 311 in the second phase.

***

Llanelli manager Andy Legg has backed calls for the Welsh Premier League to switch to a summer football season. FAW chief Jonathan Ford and WPL secretary John Deakin both support the move, designed to attract crowds.

Only 95 were at Llanelli's home match against Bala last month and the Reds boss insists the playing season must be shifted, in order to improve attendances.

"For the Welsh Premier League I think it's the only forward," he said.

"We've tried cutting the league down to 12 teams and introducing play-offs and crowds haven't got better – they've got worse. Now it's time to give this a try."

Llanelli have been hit hard by Swansea's promotion to the Premier League, with many people preferring to watch Brendan Rodgers's side either at the Liberty Stadium or in pubs.

"We can't compete with that and it's the same for the north Wales clubs," said Legg.

"When Caernarfon got relegated, there were 52 people watching the game and the chairman told me it broke his heart because four coach loads of people had left the town to watch Liverpool or Everton.

"In the summer, football fans might come to our games."

EVERY SILVER LINING HAS A CLOUD Nathan Lee Davies

***

Prestatyn Town are the latest Welsh Premier club to investigate the possibility of installing an artificial playing surface.

"The club realises the income potential an artificial pitch can provide and while it is still a controversial topic with some players and supporters, more and more non-league and semi-pro clubs are looking into the possibilities," said a statement from Bastion Gardens.

Town vice-chairman Mark Jones will lead a feasibility study into the idea. The expected cost of laying a 3G surface would be around £400,000 and, although a good portion of that sum may be grant-funded, the Seasiders say they may still have to find some of the money themselves.

The New Saints are now in their fifth season of football on the artificial surface at Park Hall and have staged European ties at the ground, while Newtown have already expressed their interest in a similar project.

"Although I am an old-fashioned football purist who believes games should be played at 3 o'clock on a Saturday on a grass pitch with player's boots only allowed to be black and white, I understand the need for change and the sound business sense an artificial surface makes to a club like ours in the current economic climate," said Jones.

"A 3G facility could be used seven days a week, 52 weeks a year and is both an income generator and a cost saver.

"We would save on expensive training pitch hire, ground maintenance overheads, the losses incurred by postponed games and make money on pitch hire, due to the increased number of games we would be able to stage.

EVERY SILVER LINING HAS A CLOUD Nathan Lee Davies

"The pitch could be opened up for community use, lower league teams with poor grass surfaces may like to consider relocating on a season-long hire commitment and we could better accommodate our reserves, under-19s, academy and ladies sides, as well as run more summer soccer schools and coaching initiatives for young people and adults.

"All this would generate revenue in hire fees, through the turnstiles, over the bar, in the snack bar, in the club shop – the potential is enormous. For a small club like ours it is the way forward, like it or not, and it really would help put the club where we want it to be – at the heart of the community with facilities that everybody can access and enjoy," Jones added.

Town officials will now meet with Welsh Football Trust bosses to find out what kind of grant aid is available to help meet the cost.

The Trust's Kevin Moon said: "I can confirm I have registered Prestatyn Town's interest. At the moment I am compiling a report of potential projects which will form part of a longer term funding strategy and will visit the club shortly after the Easter break to discuss the project in more detail."

***

It was interesting to read that the chief of the FAW was complaining that football doesn't get the same level of funding as rugby.

Jonathan Ford said his sport was much more popular in Wales than rugby, yet there was far from a "level playing field" between the two.

He made the comments as he gave evidence to a panel of AMs, looking at improving the Welsh Premier League.

Ford said the Welsh rugby team enjoys more perks than their football counterparts, such as not having to qualify for the World Cup.

EVERY SILVER LINING HAS A CLOUD Nathan Lee Davies

He called on the Welsh Assembly to give more cash to the sport, promising that the investment would "halve their health budget" by improving fitness levels.

Ford said: "Don't get me wrong, I love rugby. But when you actually look at the hard facts and the numbers behind it, in football clubs versus rugby clubs alone we've got something like 1,500 clubs, rugby has got 323.

"The numbers absolutely are totally different. And if you look at the numbers of players, we outstrip on a three-to-one basis.

"Even in live games alone, of course adding Cardiff and Swansea, you get considerably more people watching football than rugby.

"Yes, rugby has got some fantastic opportunities. I'd love to be playing France, Italy and England every year in the equivalent of a Six Nations. The money we would make on the back of that would put football in Wales in a very different place.

"I'd love [the football team] to be able to just to turn up to the World Cup every four years, but we can't.

"We have to compete with 209 other countries for 32 places. The Wales rugby team just turns up to the Rugby World Cup because they are one of the founder members.

"There are many more people that participate in and watch football, yet the money on a proportionate basis is not equal with what we should get versus rugby.

"It's not quite a level playing field."

During a committee hearing in the Senedd, Ford said the WPL had come on "leaps and bounds" since its formation in 1992.

EVERY SILVER LINING HAS A CLOUD Nathan Lee Davies

However, it is dwarfed by the English Premier League which has attendances of up to 75,000 per match and commands television rights worth billions due to its global audience.

This season the WPL had an average attendance of 314 per match and the total number of spectators who turned up to watch games came to 60,291 – not even enough to fill Manchester United's Old Trafford stadium.

But FAW officials insist the "chasm" between the Welsh system and the English pyramid has begun to close and that its coaching system was winning plaudits from across Europe. However, Ford said Wales lags behind the other home nations in terms of investment.

"We are building a national development centre in Newport," he said.

"It's a huge outlay for which we do not have the resources. Our turnover is just under £10 million per year. We are putting good percentages into infrastructure but it is just scratching the surface.

"The problem we've had over those years is that none of our funds have been matched to any great degree.

"Northern Ireland recently announced an investment in their infrastructure of £36 million.

"The sport in England, through the Football Foundation, receives around £30 million, going into grassroots football. In Scotland they take money from people's estates [when they die intestate] which is reinvested into sport.

"I can quote so many examples of governments working very closely with sporting bodies to ensure that money is invested. Forgive me, but there is very little from the Welsh Government going into sporting infrastructure. It needs to change."

Ford said that unless money was spent, national team matches would have to be played in south Wales for the foreseeable future.

In the past, Wales have played games at Wrexham's Racecourse ground.

However, he said the stadium – the only north Wales stadium to host the national team – needs at least £500,000 to bring it up to scratch.

The FAW chief also added that he would like to see more Welsh Premier League football teams have artificial, or 3G, pitches.

He said they could prove lucrative to clubs as they could be leased out during the week and used for local sides.

Ford and WPL Secretary John Deakin, who also gave evidence today, added that they are both in favour of Wales' football season being switched to the summer.

Doing so, they said, could improve WPL teams' progress in European competitions in the future.

League Cup

Afan Lido claimed the League Cup for the third time in their history, with a penalty shoot-out win over Newtown at Aberystwyth's Park Avenue.

Keeper Craig Morris was Lido's hero – saving spot kicks from Kieran Mills-Evans, Nicky Rushton and Shane Sutton to take the cup back to the Marston's Stadium.

The Aberavon outfit had come close to winning the game inside normal time, after a deft side-footed pass from Danny Thomas had set-up Mark Jones to fire them in front after 42 minutes.

EVERY SILVER LINING HAS A CLOUD Nathan Lee Davies

Some resolute defending denied Newtown many clear-cut openings, but, in the second minute of stoppage time, Sutton's shot was blocked by a defender and Rushton drove home the rebound to set-up an additional 30 minutes.

Anthony Finselbach twice came close to restoring Lido's lead in the first period of extra time. He had keeper Nick Thomas scrambling across his line with a threatening volley, and later saw his drive hit the top of the crossbar.

But Newtown found their second wind in the final stanza. Sutton headed over from a free-kick and Rushton lobbed Morris only to find the top of the net as the Robins kept pushing. Bernard McNally's men almost sealed their comeback at the death, but Callum Wright was left with held his head in his hands as he fired a good chance inches over with almost the last kick of the game.

This miss proved costly as Andy Dyer's men edged home in a tense shoot-out.

Lido's previous wins in the competition were back in 1993 and 1994, when they beat Caersws and Bangor City respectively.

[*League Cup final results table overleaf*]

Season	Winner	Score	Runner-up	Venue
1992-93	Afan Lido	1 - 1	Caersws	Park Avenue, Aberystwyth
	Afan Lido won 4-3 on penalties			
1993-94	Afan Lido	1 - 0	Bangor City	Park Avenue, Aberystwyth
1994-95	Llansantffraid	2 - 1	Ton Pentre	Latham Park, Newtown
1995-96	CQ Nomads	1 - 0	Ebbw Vale	Recreation Grnd, Caersws
1996-97	Barry Town	2 - 2	Bangor City	Park Avenue, Aberystwyth
	Barry Town won 4-2 on penalties			
1997-98	Barry Town	1 - 1	Bangor City	Farrar Road, Bangor
	Barry Town won 5-4 on penalties			
1998-99	Barry Town	3 - 0	Caernarfon T	Park Avenue, Aberystwyth
1999-00	Barry Town	6 - 0	Bangor City	Park Avenue, Aberystwyth
2000-01	Caersws	2 - 0	Barry Town	Park Avenue, Aberystwyth
2001-02	Caersws	2 - 1	Cwmbran T	Park Avenue, Aberystwyth
2002-03	Rhyl	2 - 2	Bangor City	Belle Vue, Rhyl
	Rhyl won 4-3 on penalties			
2003-04	Rhyl	4 - 0	Carmarthen T	Latham Park, Newtown
2004-05	Carmarthen T	2 - 0	Rhyl	Latham Park, Newtown
2005-06	TNS	4 - 0	Port Talbot T	Park Avenue, Aberystwyth
2006-07	Caersws	1 - 1	Rhyl	Park Avenue, Aberystwyth
	Caersws won 3-1 on penalties			
2007-08	Llanelli	2 - 0	Rhyl	Latham Park, Newtown
2008-09	TNS	2 - 0	Bangor City	Latham Park, Newtown
2009-10	TNS	3 - 1	Rhyl	The Airfield, Broughton
2010-11	TNS	4 - 3	Llanelli	Park Avenue, Aberystwyth
2011-12	Afan Lido	1 - 1	Newtown	Park Avenue, Aberystwyth
	Afan Lido won 3-2 on penalties			

WPL table as of 21/04/12

Pos	Team	P	W	D	L	F	A	GD	Pts
1	TNS (C)	32	23	5	4	75	31	+44	74
2	Bangor City (EL)	32	22	3	7	72	45	+27	69
3	Neath (R)	32	18	8	6	60	36	+24	62
4	Llanelli	32	18	5	9	63	37	+26	59
5	Bala Town	32	14	7	11	48	41	+7	49
6	Prestatyn Town	32	8	4	20	41	63	-22	28
7	Airbus UK B'ton	32	10	9	13	48	50	-2	39
8	Aberystwyth Town	32	8	10	14	45	50	-5	33
9	Port Talbot Town	32	8	9	15	39	51	-12	33
10	Afan Lido	32	7	11	14	40	55	-15	32
11	Carmarthen Town	32	10	2	20	33	67	-34	32
12	Newtown	32	7	5	20	44	82	-38	23

(C) = Champions (EL) = Europa League (R) = Relegated
Newtown deducted 3 points
Aberystwyth Town deducted 1 point

<u>26</u>
May 2012

Tuesday, 29 May 2012

I woke up in a positive and determined mood. I'd reached the final stages of my book and I was about to take the final step towards becoming a published author. Creativity was soaring through my veins and I felt back to my prolific best. My diary was free, as usual, so I had the whole day to dedicate to my potential bestseller.

I'm currently aiming for a June 2012 completion date so that the book can be published soon after.

Today, I'm looking forward to starting the proof reading process with the end, most definitely, in sight...

***

To: nathandavies01@hotmail.com
Subject: Book

Hi Nathan
I have been proof reading the first few chapters of your book and would like to draw your attention to the following websites:

http://www.informatics.sussex.ac.uk/department/docs/punctuation/node14.html

http://english.stackexchange.com/questions/37856/do-you-need-a-comma-before-a-subordinating-conjunction-like-if

http://www.grammar-monster.com/index.html

***

http://www.grammar-monster.com/lessons/commas_before_conjunctions.htm

When a word like 'and', 'or' and 'but' (called <u>conjunctions</u>) joins two standalone sentences, you should put a comma before it.

***

Fuck. I wasn't taught that in school.

Does it really matter?

Of course it does.

I thought you were a free spirit.

I can be but the basics should be right.

In that case, shouldn't you be using speech marks here?
.
You are an utter cunt. Did you know that.

EVERY SILVER LINING HAS A CLOUD Nathan Lee Davies

Question mark.

Arseholes like you are the reason why I'm gonna have to delay publication of the book and waste six months of my life on punctuation.

I'm surprised you care.

I'm a man of contradictions. While I couldn't give two shits for your opinion, I am determined not to give u a reason to judge me. Don't u think I am judged enough?

U? Really? You're not texting.

Do one knob rot, but before u do... PUNCTUATE THIS.

***

,,,,,,,,,,,,,,,,,,,,,..
....
,,
,,
,,,
????????????????????????????????????
??????????????????????????????????????
?????"''',,,,,,,,,

A relative clause—also called an _adjective_ or _adjectival_ clause—will meet three requirements.

- First, it will contain a subject and verb.

- Next, it will begin with a <u>relative pronoun</u> [*who*, *whom*, *whose*, *that*, or *which*] or a <u>relative adverb</u> [*when*, *where*, or *why*].

- Finally, it will function as an <u>adjective</u>, answering the questions *What kind? How many? or Which one?*

http://www.chompchomp.com/terms/relativeclause.htm

. . . .
' ' ' ' ' ' ' ' ' ' '
. . . .
' '

. . . . ------ . . . .
. . . .;;;;;;;;;;;;;;;(.)?????!!!!!----
,,,,,,,,,,SERIAL COMMA

. . . .,,

Let's eat Roger.
Let's eat, Roger.

Punctuation was important to Roger.

383

There are four types of comma: the listing comma, the joining comma, the gapping comma and bracketing commas,,,
,,,
,,,
,,,

Subordinate clauses, which can't stand alone, have three main purposes in life. A subordinate clause can describe nouns and pronouns; describe verbs, adverbs, and adjectives; or at act as the subject or object of another clause,,,
,,,
,,,
,,,
,,,

There are no rules – it's all subjective.

Says who?
....
,,,
,,,
,,,
,,,
....
,,,

A semi-what?

....The question that you brought up wouldn't address your question because "if" is not one of the <u>coordinating conjunctions</u>, but it is a subordinating conjunction. The words that introduce each are:

Coordinating Conjunctions: and, but, or, yet, for, nor, so (a helpful acronym is FANBOYS)

Subordinating Conjunctions: after, although, as, as if, as long as, as though, because, before, even if, even though, if, if only, in order that, now that, once, rather than, since, so that, than, that, though, till, unless, until, when, whenever, where, whereas, wherever, while

EVERY SILVER LINING HAS A CLOUD Nathan Lee Davies

The definition of a subordinating conjunction is:

Subordinating Conjunction (sometimes called a dependent word or subordinator) comes at the beginning of a Subordinate (or Dependent) Clause and establishes the relationship between the dependent clause and the rest of the sentence. It also turns the clause into something that depends on the rest of the sentence for its meaning.

*He took to the stage **as though** he had been preparing for this moment all his life.*

***Because** he loved acting, he refused to give up his dream of being in the movies.*

***Unless** we act now, all is lost.*

However, in these examples, there is a short bridge between the first half and the second half. The bridge is known as a 'transitional phrase'. There is always a comma *after* a transitional phrase.

- 1

- £

- "

- —

- @

- ?

- =

I'm a writer. Full stop. I need an editor.

EVERY SILVER LINING HAS A CLOUD Nathan Lee Davies

Your saviour can be found on Sanderman Street, Dundee, DD3 7JY, Scotland.

Which side of the street?

Silly question, I'm not going to recommend a retard.

'>>>
'>>>
'>>>
'>>>

An Arab, wanting to earn some money, decided to hire himself out as a handyman-type and started canvassing a wealthy neighborhood. He went to the front door of the first house and asked the owner if he had any jobs for him to do.

"Well, you can paint my porch. How much will you charge?"

The Arab said "How about £50?"

The man agreed and told him that the paint and other materials that he might need were in the garage. The man's wife, inside the house, heard the conversation and said to her husband: "Does he realize that the porch goes all the way around the house?" The man replied, "He should, he was standing on it."

A short time later, the Arab came to the door to collect his money.

"You're finished already?" he asked. "Yes," the Arab answered," and had paint left over, so I gave it two coats."

Impressed, the man reached in his pocket for the money.

"And by the way," the Arab added, "it's not a Porch, It's a Ferrari..."

'>>>
'>>>

,,

I'll get my coat – the dark blue one.

....
....
....
....
....

Panda walks into a bar...

```
N  I  E  T  S  D  P  T  L  D  O  E  R
W  I  L  D  E  C  B  L  X  I  S  K  E
L  M  K  H  E  B  R  E  W  C  S  I  T
Y  A  X  P  L  U  D  O  J  K  T  D  S
T  N  G  V  A  H  M  F  R  E  O  P  A
C  U  B  N  R  N  V  C  F  N  O  U  C
R  T  J  L  I  Y  R  B  G  S  H  S  L
E  I  G  S  E  D  S  E  A  T  S  U  U
B  U  Q  R  A  A  L  L  P  N  C  D  M
R  S  A  B  F  O  V  E  T  A  T  I  R
U  C  O  M  M  A  A  E  I  F  P  L  O
H  Y  E  L  T  R  A  H  S  F  Y  O  S
T  M  N  O  S  A  E  R  T  R  U  S  S
```

EATS, SHOOTS, LEAVES, TRUSS, THURBER, ROSS, MULCASTER, SOLIDUS, HARTLEY, HEBREW, PAPERNAPKIN, MANUTIUS, COMMA, FIELDING, DICKENS, WILDE, STEIN, CAREY, UPDIKE, YOB, TREASON.

***

EVERY SILVER LINING HAS A CLOUD Nathan Lee Davies

After months of chopping and changing, I've come to the conclusion that I don't like punctuation and detest rules. I've had invaluable help from a fully qualified academic who ensured my work was accurately punctuated, but I can now see that flooding my writing with squiggles and marks detracts from the natural flow that I'm looking for.

Punctuation is important and can serve to clarify, but it can also be easily overdone. I am now in a healthy position, thanks to editorial assistance, that allows me to delete and ignore commas and semi colons without fear of being labelled ignorant.

It is all about opinions and I sympathise with James Thurber – a humorist for the *New Yorker* in the 1930s – who fought with his editor, Harold Ross, about the overuse of commas.

> From one casual of mine he picked this sentence. "After dinner, the men moved into the living room." I explained to the professor that this was Ross's way of giving the men time to push back their chairs and stand up. There must, as we know, be a comma after every move, made by men, on this earth.

At the end of the day, I've done things my way. If you've got a problem then you know what you can do.

On with the news.

News Round-Up

Andy Dyer has quit as manager of Afan Lido less than a week after lifting the League Cup, his first major trophy in management.

Dyer, who joined the Martson's Stadium outfit last summer, told www.welsh-premier.com: "It's a shame really, Lido are a fantastic little club, but it is impossible for me to carry on.

"Many people said we were relegation favourites at the start of the season, but we have survived and won a cup.

"I am disappointed to be leaving, but I can't take them any further within the resources available," added Dyer, who says he is keen to continue in management either in south Wales or over the Severn Bridge.

Meanwhile, there are rumours that the financial situation at Lido, where wages have gone unpaid for several weeks, may be considered by the FAW this week.

***

Newtown were reprieved from relegation after Taffs Well claimed second place in the MacWhirter Welsh League.

The Wellmen needed to win by two clear goals against already-relegated Caerau (Ely) to leapfrog Haverfordwest County – who have the requisite FAW domestic licence – into the second promotion place. They did not balk at the challenge and recorded a comfortable 1-5 victory at Cwrt-yr-Ala.

Founder members of the League of Wales in 1992, Newtown stay-up and retain their unbroken 20-year membership of the league, despite a three-point deduction and finishing bottom of the WPL, nine points adrift of Carmarthen Town.

With Neath's failure to gain a domestic licence, no club will lose its membership of the WPL on sporting merit this season. This means Huws Gray Alliance champions Gap Connah's Quay are the only promoted outfit to complete the 12 club line-up for 2012-13.

Welsh Cup

Since 1995, only clubs from the Welsh league system have been eligible to represent Wales in Europe. Welsh clubs playing in the English league pyramid – Cardiff City, Swansea City, Wrexham, Newport County, Colwyn Bay and Merthyr Tydfil – were barred by the FAW from entering the Welsh Cup after pressure from UEFA.

Despite this, in April 2011 the FAW controversially invited the six Welsh clubs playing in the English pyramid to participate in the 2011-12 Welsh Cup. This led to a whole load of internal arguments as discussed in Mark Pitman's excellent blog entry "Welsh Premier let down by Exiles return", which can be found at www.markpitman1.com. These issues were only really resolved in March 2012, when UEFA ruled that Welsh clubs playing in an English league cannot qualify for Europe through the Welsh Cup.

This decision had not been reached when Swansea City, Cardiff City and Blue Square Bet North side Colwyn Bay turned down the FAW's invitation, but Blue Square Bet Premier sides Newport County and Wrexham along with Merthyr Town (formerly Merthyr Tydfil) of the Toolstation Premier League, chose to enter regardless. Unfortunately, they all fielded weakened teams and made early exits.

Meanwhile, the competition – in its 125th season – was taken seriously by some clubs, including The New Saints and Huws Gray Alliance outfit Cefn Druids, who competed in the final at Bangor City's Nantporth.

EVERY SILVER LINING HAS A CLOUD Nathan Lee Davies

The hot favourites from Shropshire didn't disappoint and clinched their second WPL and Welsh Cup double with a 2-0 victory over the part-timers. Early goals from Greg Draper (14') and Alex Darlington (15') sealed the win, but the Druids emerged with considerable credit after limiting any further damage against the full-timers and still have the lucrative consolation of a place in the Europa League.

The New Saints' director of football Craig Harrison celebrated his second major trophy, less than five months after arriving at Park Hall.

"I'm glad we didn't win the treble because where do you go from there?" said an elated Harrison.

"I couldn't even have dreamt about this but it's not about me, it's about the lads who go out on the pitch.

"It was a good performance and a professional performance.

"Cefn Druids played very well and they'd already beaten three Welsh Premier teams on the way to the final."

S4C's man of the match Steve Evans added: "We definitely should have scored more goals, but their keeper has made four or five world class saves.

"But we went about it professionally and got the job done in the first half.

"But all credit to them, what a run they have been on and now they're in Europe as well."

Ancients' manager Huw Griffiths praised his players.

"The wind was a lot stronger than it appeared and it was difficult for us in the first half," he said.

"In the second half we pushed them back a bit, created some chances, and if just one of them had gone in I believe it could have been a different game.

"Credit to TNS though, they did their job in the second half, stopped us from scoring.

"They did enough and it was a very professional showing from them – they are a very good team.

"The feeling in the dressing room is positive," he added.

"We've got the NEWFA Cup final a week on Tuesday and it's important we focus on that.

"We're bringing the good times back to Druids – that's the important thing. We'll learn from today and hopefully have more days like this."

[*For a full list of previous Welsh Cup final results, visit the Welsh Football Data Archive at* www.wfda.co.uk]

UEFA Europa League play-offs

Aberystwyth Town went into the final game of the season with the very real threat of relegation hanging over them, but after benefitting from the demotion of Neath, the Black and Greens moved within two games of European qualification by beating Airbus UK Broughton at the Airfield.

Wyn Thomas scored the only goal of the game on 55 minutes to send Aber into the play-off semi-finals where Llanelli laid in wait. Andy Parkinson's left-wing flag kick was headed across goal for Thomas to fire home the only goal of the game at the far post.

EVERY SILVER LINING HAS A CLOUD Nathan Lee Davies

Aberystwyth arrived at Stebonheath Park on the back of four successive victories and gave fourth-placed Llanelli a scare, despite playing with 10 men for virtually the whole of the game. Michael Walsh was harshly dismissed in the fifth minute by referee Bryn Markham-Jones for a challenge on Ashley Evans, but the Seasiders battled well with the defence expertly marshalled by former Llanelli centre back Wyn Thomas.

Neither side could break the deadlock over 90 minutes, so the game went into extra-time. As players began to tire, a defensive mix-up from Aber proved decisive. Liam James squared a suicidal back pass to Sion James, who slipped to allow sub Jordan Follows – who'd spent much of the season on loan at Park Avenue – to drive home the winner in the 108th-minute.

In the other semi-final, Bala Town beat Prestatyn by the odd goal at Maes Tegid. The home side got off to a dream start when Ian Sheridan tucked away the opening goal in the third minute, but they failed to make the best of their first half chances and allowed Dave Hayes to restore parity on the half hour.

The big-spending Lakesiders were back in front early in the second half, through former Seaside favourite Lee Hunt, and held on for the win, although the visitors had a shot cleared off the line late-on.

As Llanelli had finished the regular season above Bala in the table, they had home advantage in the play-off final. Only 318 fans bothered to turn up.

The hosts got the perfect start when seven-time Golden Boot winner Rhys Griffiths converted Jason Bowen's fourth-minute cross. The lead was eventually doubled when Lloyd Grist's free-kick took a deflection to defeat keeper Terry McCormick.

EVERY SILVER LINING HAS A CLOUD Nathan Lee Davies

Bala's European dreams seemed to be in tatters, but with fifteen minutes left to play Lee Hunt latched onto Stephen Brown's right-wing cross.

With time running out, Llanelli's Craig Richards produced a vital save from Hunt, at point blank range, before smothering the follow-up from substitute Stephen Brown. Bala's Connolly was then denied by the woodwork from a 20-yard set-piece that rattled the bar, but Llanelli held out for the remaining minutes to book a European ticket for the seventh successive season.

Llanelli boss Andy Legg was delighted with the afternoon's work and paid special credit to his shot stopper:

"I thought that goalkeeper Craig Richards was outstanding, and we owe him a great deal of credit, because the double save he made towards the end was terrific, not to mention those he made in the first half.

"It really is a team effort that has got us through, everything is done together, there's no individual here, and the lads can be proud of themselves this season. They've got more points than they did last year, finished in the same place and they've qualified for Europe again, so they deserve a pat on the back."

***

[Information about the women's WPL can be found overleaf]

Women's Welsh Premier League

The third season of the Women's WPL was the last campaign to feature a play-off championship final between northern and southern Conference winners. From next term a 12-team national league will be contested.

The clubs contesting the 2011-12 season included Aberystwyth Town, Caernarfon Town, Llanidloes, Northop Hall and Wrexham in the north, with the southern set-up comprising of Caerphilly Castle, Newcastle Emlyn, Swansea City, Trefelin and UWIC.

Northern Conference

Pos	Team	P	W	D	L	F	A	GD	Pts
1	Wrexham Ladies (Q)	8	6	1	1	30	13	+17	19
2	Llanidloes Ladies	8	4	1	3	21	11	+10	13
3	Caernarfon Town Ladies	8	4	1	3	19	14	+5	13
4	Aberystwyth Town Ladies	8	4	1	3	15	13	+2	13
5	Northop Hall Girls	8	0	0	8	7	41	−34	0

Southern Conference

Pos	Team	P	W	D	L	F	A	GD	Pts
1	UWIC Ladies (Q)	8	6	1	1	19	5	+14	19
2	Swansea City Ladies	8	4	3	1	16	9	+7	15
3	Trefelin Ladies	7	2	2	3	12	17	−5	8
4	Caerphilly Castle Ladies	8	1	2	5	9	16	−7	5
5	Newcastle Emlyn Ladies	7	0	4	3	11	20	−9	4

The final took place at Victoria Park, Llanidloes with Wrexham facing UWIC. The Wrexham men had missed out on promotion back to the Football League just a few weeks earlier, despite amassing 98 points in the Blue Square Premier. Their female counterparts also threw away the chance of glory with a 0-3 defeat to a bunch of students.

EVERY SILVER LINING HAS A CLOUD Nathan Lee Davies

The teams that will comprise the league in 2012-13 are: Aberystwyth Town Ladies, Caernarfon Town Ladies, Caerphilly Castle Ladies, Cardiff City, Cardiff Met Ladies (formerly UWIC), Llandudno Junction Ladies, Llanidloes Ladies, Newcastle Emlyn Ladies, Northop Hall Girls, Swansea City Ladies, Trefelin Ladies and Wrexham Ladies.

The Champions will represent Wales in the UEFA Champions League.

Now that I've finished my WPL tour maybe I should resolve to be less arrogant, more accepting of the woman's game and actually attend a match. I'll think about it, but if the FAW had the foresight to demand that goalscorers perform a seductive striptease then I'd be there every week...

***

The New Saints started work on the second stage of an ambitious project, which will eventually see their Park Hall home become a 3,000-seater stadium.

Construction began on a cantilever stand behind the goal at the opposite end of the stadium from Burma Road, which will provide an additional 500 seats.

The stand will have the capability to be extended to 1,000 seats. Provision has also been made for the addition of hospitality boxes at the back of the structure.

An extension to the road at the side of the Venue leisure centre will allow direct access into the new stand, which is scheduled for completion by June 18.

I haven't even finished this bloody book and my publisher is talking about future updates to reflect ground improvements...

***

EVERY SILVER LINING HAS A CLOUD Nathan Lee Davies

Eight feeder league clubs have been invited to participate in a new competition next season.

The new and as-yet unnamed competition is to be played under floodlights, on a straight knockout basis, replacing the much-maligned League Cup. Cambrian & Clydach, Taffs Well, Haverfordwest County and Bryntirion Athletic from the Welsh League will take part, along with the clubs that finished in the top four places behind champions Gap Connah's Quay in the Huws Gray Alliance. This will bring in Rhyl, Buckley Town, Porthmadog and Penrhyncoch.

Further details have yet to be revealed.

***

Tomi Morgan was named WPL manager of the month for April after guiding relegation-haunted Aberystwyth Town into the play-offs.

The Black and Greens won three games and lost once during the month; with victories coming against Afan Lido at the Marston's Stadium, Airbus UK Broughton at Park Avenue, and a dramatic 3-2 success over Newtown on the final day of the league season.

Ryan Fraughan is the player of the month after a string of scintillating displays as The New Saints marched to a WPL and Welsh Cup double.

The 21-year-old arrived at Park Hall in January, on loan from Stockport County, and hit three goals in nine (+1) appearances.

***

The WPL team of the season, as voted for by each of the 12 managers, has been announced and it should come as no surprise that the line-up included five players from The New Saints. Central defender Steve Evans, wingback Chris Marriott, midfielders Aeron Edwards and Craig Jones, and leading scorer Greg Draper are all named in the starting eleven.

One surprise absentee was seven-time Golden Boot winner, Rhys Griffiths who was edged out by Bangor City's burly frontman Les Davies, who hit 16 league goals in 2011-12.

The starting eleven is completed by goalkeeper Lee Idzi (Bangor City), defenders Kai Edwards (Neath) and Stuart Jones (Llanelli), as well as midfielders Mark Jones (Bala Town) and Chris Jones (Neath).

The substitute nominations were: Lee Kendall and Jack Lewis (Neath), Michael Johnston (Bangor City), Alex Darlington (The New Saints) and Chris Venables and Rhys Griffiths (Llanelli).

Each manager was asked to select his best starting eleven and a substitute bench, comprising of a goalkeeper, two defenders, two midfielders and one striker.

***

Afan Lido announced the appointment of Paul Reid as the club's new manager for the 2012-13 season.

Reid – the first-team coach at rivals Port Talbot Town during 2011-12 – replaces Andy Dyer, who left the club after one successful season that saw Lido finish tenth in the WPL and lift the League Cup.

"Afan Lido Football Club is delighted that Paul has accepted the role as first team manager. A former player at the club, Paul has vast football experience, from playing over 550 Football League games – Swansea City (20), Leicester City (162), Bradford City (89), Huddersfield (77), Oldham (93) and Bury (110)," said a club statement.

EVERY SILVER LINING HAS A CLOUD Nathan Lee Davies

"[He has] a great understanding of the Welsh Premier League, as a former player (Afan Lido and Carmarthen) and also as a successful coach with Port Talbot Town over recent seasons.

"Paul was our first choice to take over the reins. He has already spoken to a number of players and is happy with the way the squad is taking shape and relishing the challenge of management. Over the coming weeks, Paul will be finalising his back room together with strengthening his squad.

"The club would like to add [...] their unreserved thanks to former manager Andy Dyer and all his staff for all their hard work and effort over the last twelve months, resulting in a creditable 10th place finish in our first season back in the Welsh Premier League and winning the League Cup. The club would like to wish them all the best in the future."

***

As well as clinching a WPL and Welsh Cup double, The New Saints have also won the FAW Fair Play Award.

Launched at the beginning of the 2011-12 season, the aim of the FAW Fair Play Award is to encourage a reduction in on-field misconduct and to promote the FAW fair play code. In addition, the award aims to promote the positive ideology it wishes the football community to adopt.

Winners in the Huws Gray Alliance were Llanrhaeadr Ym Mochnant, with Bryntirion Athletic claiming the prize in MacWhirter Welsh League Division One.

Each League winner wins £1,000.

EVERY SILVER LINING HAS A CLOUD Nathan Lee Davies

The New Saints	2	53	55	234
Airbus UK Broughton	7	49	56	268
Newtown	4	56	60	268
Carmarthen Town	3	64	67	286
Bala Town	4	62	66	294
Neath	6	58	64	296
Bangor City	3	67	70	302
Aberystwyth Town	10	49	59	304
Port Talbot Town	7	58	65	308
Afan Lido	6	63	69	322
Llanelli	6	66	72	332
Prestatyn Town	6	68	74	342
	64	713	777	3,556

***

The writing had been on the wall for a long time, but as May drew to a close Neath FC was officially wound-up at London's High Court.

An official receiver will now ensure debts are paid, where possible, by selling any assets available and then bring business to a close following a decisive petition by Barclays Bank. The decision led to an honest outburst from club secretary Tony Melding, who hit out at the running of the club and the sacking of manager Andrew Dyer at the end of 2010-11.

After the Eagles were wound-up in the High Court – and speaking for the first time since the club's failure to gain either the FAW domestic or UEFA licences – Melding told www.welsh-premier.com that developments had left him with no other option than to resign his position as secretary.

"Whilst I have no desire to oversee the Official Receiver coming in and slamming nails into the coffin of the club that I have built up over the last 10 years, I will remain in contact with the players and manager Kris O'Leary to ensure that I can do everything to ensure that they are all dealt with as well as possible by the club," Melding said.

"Kris has done a fantastic job since he took over in November, under severe pressure and restrictions, and that is testament to his qualities as a manager and a person.

"I am deeply hurt and shocked that people have let this happen today and feel that certain decisions taken in the last 12 months have been made out of self-interest and not for the good of the club.

"The sacking of Andrew Dyer has proved to be catastrophic to the club and the resultant appointments equally so.

"One of the regrets that I will take away from the last 10 years is that I didn't see the sacking of Andrew for all that it was and should have.

"I would like to give thanks to the many great people I have met and worked with over the last 10 years – there are way too many to mention individually.

"But a sad day for Neath FC is not going to be about me but that of the history of the club that has been lost today, but not lost on certain individuals who could not care – 10 years in the building, 10 months in the undoing."

Meanwhile, a statement on the club's official website said: "The collapse of the club's main sponsor in October 2011 caused untold financial problems, however against all odds and due to the hard work and determination of everyone involved we continued until the end of the season.

"The recent decision by the FAW not to grant the club its domestic and UEFA licences for next season was another huge blow to us and unfortunately one that we were unable to recover from.

"Our priorities lie with providing as much support and assistance as we can to all the players and staff who are currently employed by the club."

***

Cefn Druids received the green light from UEFA to participate in the 2012-13 Europa League.

UEFA licensing regulations do not permit clubs from outside the top division to undergo the annual UEFA licensing process, but allows the scope for clubs outside the elite to apply for a special licence, should a specific situation occur. This scenario occurred when the Druids lost against WPL champions TNS in the Welsh Cup final.

Druids' licensing officer John Henry Davies and secretary Mark McKean have been working hard with the FAW to ensure that the standards required by UEFA are met by the Huws Gray Alliance club. UEFA general secretary Gianni Infantino confirmed the positive decision in writing to the FAW's chief executive Jonathan Ford.

"After assessing the submitted documentary evidence to demonstrate compliance with the set criteria, the UEFA administration has decided that special permission to participate in the 2012-13 UEFA Europa League is granted." wrote Infantino.

"We are delighted that Cefn Druids have been given the green light. The fact that Druids have been proactive with licensing over several years has certainly helped them with their submission and they thoroughly deserve their place in the Europa League. We wish them a favourable draw and every success." a spokesman for the FAW added.

**

I'm trying my best to finish this damned book, but I'm being hindered by WPL member clubs that continue to inconsiderately create stories that I think will be of interest to my readers. I've got to draw the line somewhere though, so you'll have to go online if you want to read all about the latest transfer news, the League's new three-year deal with S4C or new WPL secretary Gwyn Derfel's belief that the future includes installing artificial pitches for all clubs.

However, I'll make an exception for the Welsh Premier League's annual awards, which were unhelpfully presented on Saturday, 9 June 2012 at the Marine Hotel, Aberystwyth.

The player of the season prize went to Bala Town captain Mark Jones while Neath's Kai Edwards picked up the young player of the season award. Unsurprisingly, manager of the season was TNS head coach Carl Darlington after he guided the full-timers to the WPL and Welsh Cup double.

The inaugural Welsh Premier women's player of the season award was won by Chloe Bassett of UWIC Ladies. The 21-year-old midfielder is a former Plymouth Argyle player. She signed for UWIC when she joined the university in September 2009.

Bassett, a 3rd year student in the capital city, was instrumental in UWIC's play-off final win against Wrexham Ladies at Llanidloes Town last month and, as well as scoring a goal in the 3-0 win, she was voted player of the match.

I've just seen a picture of Bassett accepting her award and would like to invite her to north Wales, where I'd be only too happy to help her celebrate her achievement.

Corbett Sports Welsh Premier League 2011-12
Final League Table

Pos	Team	P	W	D	L	F	A	GD	Pts
1	TNS (C)	32	23	5	4	75	31	+44	74
2	Bangor City (EL)	32	22	3	7	72	45	+27	69
3	Neath (R)	32	18	8	6	60	36	+24	62
4	Llanelli (EL)	32	18	5	9	63	37	+26	59
5	Bala Town	32	14	7	11	48	41	+7	49
6	Prestatyn Town	32	8	4	20	41	63	-22	28
7	Airbus UK B'ton	32	10	9	13	48	50	-2	39
8	Aberystwyth Town	32	8	10	14	45	50	-5	33
9	Port Talbot Town	32	8	9	15	39	51	-12	33
10	Afan Lido	32	7	11	14	40	55	-15	32
11	Carmarthen Town	32	10	2	20	33	67	-34	32
12	Newtown	32	7	5	20	44	82	-38	23

(C) = Champions (EL) = Europa League (R) = Relegated
Newtown deducted 3 points
Aberystwyth Town deducted 1 point

27
Injury Time

EVERY SILVER LINING HAS A CLOUD Nathan Lee Davies

Women shouldn't be allowed mobile phones if they never intend on answering them. I'd just reached four answering machines – two with personally recorded messages and, worse still, two standardised greetings from faceless phone operators with digitally precise pronunciation. It really was most frustrating as I had something worth listening to for once.

I'd just finished writing my first book and wanted to share my joy with someone. Month after arduous month I'd been locked away in my home office, declining trips to the pub, shunning family gatherings and becoming something of a recluse. Now that I'd finally written my last line and was free from my self-imposed shackles, I found that no one was available to listen to my reflections.

There was only one, premium rate, option remaining.

***

Hi, you've got through to Anal Amateurs.

Before we continue I must inform you that all calls are recorded and cost 36p per minute plus network extras. Callers must be 18 or over and have the bill-payers permission. If you're calling from a mobile we may send free promotional messages that are filthy in nature. To avoid embarrassment – should your girlfriend ever check your phone – send STOP to 83222.

It's time for some naughty adult fun with our sexy selection of girls. We've got them all, from barely legal 18 year olds to horny housewives or even glamorous grannies. They've all got one thing in common – a burning desire to give you the wank of a lifetime. There'll be plenty of chances for you to shoot your load as quickly, or as slowly, as you like. We're sure to have your dream fantasy figure waiting to take your call, so simply unzip your trousers, relax and enjoy.

EVERY SILVER LINING HAS A CLOUD Nathan Lee Davies

If you know the extension number of the girl you'd like to speak to, press 1.

If you'd like to listen to a selection of girls currently waiting for your call, press 2.

If you want to be connected to the first available girl, press 3.

[3]

You are about to be connected to one of our girls. If, at any time during the conversation, you wish to return to the main menu press the star key.

Please be patient while we try to connect you.

[5 second pause]

Please be patient while we try to connect you.

[5 second pause]

Please be patient while we try to connect you.

[5 second pause]

ALEXI: Hi, who's come to play?

NATHAN LEE DAVIES: Hi, my name's Nathan, what's yours?

A: I'm Alexi. I'm 26-years-old with blond hair, 38DD boobs...

NLD: Yeah, yeah I know. I bet you've got long legs, a pert bum and a winning smile as well.

A: Got it in one.

EVERY SILVER LINING HAS A CLOUD Nathan Lee Davies

NLD: I bet I know what you're wearing.

A: Have a guess.

NLD: You've either just finished showering and wrapped yourself in a soft, fluffy towel, or you've had a hard day at the office and are dying to get out of those stockings and suspenders.

A: It was a lovely shower.

NLD: Thought so.

A: I'm just drying myself off, passing the towel over my inner thighs.

NLD: Really?

A: Yeah. I wish you were here now so I could sit on your face.

NLD: Would you tell me that you loved me as well.

A: Eh?

NLD: Eric Idle.

A: Who?

NLD: Monty Python.

A: I haven't got a clue what you're on about babe.

NLD: Google it.

A: Later. I'm dripping wet at the moment. Have you got your cock out?

NLD: No, no, no. I've finished with all that. I'm 35-years-old.

EVERY SILVER LINING HAS A CLOUD Nathan Lee Davies

A: That doesn't matter. We get all ages on here. Yesterday, I made an 82-year-old cum.

NLD: You must be very proud of yourself. Make sure that nugget takes pride of place on your CV.

A: Why've you called then?

NLD: Simply because my "friends" don't know how to use a mobile phone and I'm excited to tell someone, anyone, that I've finished my book.

A: Oh, well done hun. I've just finished reading *Look who it is!*, by Alan Carr.

NLD: Never mind. Worse things happen at sea.

A: It was good.

NLD: Anyway, I meant I've finished writing my first book.

A: Really?

NLD: Yeah, that's what I do. I'm a writer.

A: That's great. What's the book about?

NLD: It's a journey of self-discovery around Welsh Premier League football grounds.

A: OK.

NLD: Don't get too excited.

A: I don't like football.

EVERY SILVER LINING HAS A CLOUD Nathan Lee Davies

NLD: You don't need to like football to enjoy the book. Each chapter is split into two sections – part an autobiographical look back at my life so far and part about my visits to football grounds.

A: That's the bit I won't like.

NLD: I've tried to inject it with plenty of humour.

A: I bet you're not as funny as Alan Carr...

***

I ended the conversation abruptly. I'm not paying 36p per minute to be insulted, plus I don't like writing dialogue, so it was best all-round to end the call, even if it did mean being left alone with a bulge in my jeans.

I needed a cold shower, but with no carer on hand for another couple of hours, I had to quash my basic desires.

After flushing my SIM card down the toilet to prevent another hefty phone bill, I scrolled through the latest electronic version of *When Saturday Comes* and settled on an article entitled "Mistaken Identities", by Scott Johnson. The article focused on events at the inventively named Cardiff City Stadium, where the popular Malaysian owners had tried to push their own country's colours and symbols on the Welsh club's kit.

Apparently, owner Vincent Tan and chairman Dato Chan wanted to revolutionise the once proud club by settling the historical Langston debt, building a state-of-the-art training headquarters, increasing the capacity of their soulless home to 35,000, and providing substantial funds for manager Malky Mackay in the transfer market.

EVERY SILVER LINING HAS A CLOUD Nathan Lee Davies

Predictably, there was a catch. In return for this investment, Cardiff's traditional playing strip of blue shirt, white shorts and blue socks would be changed to a red-black-red combination. This kit would also feature a redesigned badge that would see the bluebird replaced by a mighty Welsh dragon.

Initially, supporters were aghast and outraged at such a ridiculous proposal that was designed to create a "fusion of cultures" between Malaysia and Wales – red is a shared national colour and the dragon is an important symbol for both countries. In the Far East, red is associated with vibrancy, good luck and happiness, while blue is linked to funerals and death. It should therefore be no surprise that Manchester United, Liverpool and Arsenal have established themselves in the lucrative Asian market while Chelsea and Manchester City have, so far, failed.

Tan was offering to pump in excess of £100m into the club and elevate it into a new stratosphere, but was it worth sacrificing the club's identity to secure such a deal? Initially, the majority of fans thought it wasn't and signed an online petition in protest as well as organising a march from Cardiff Central railway station to the ground. In the end, this rally was not needed as within 48-hours the plans were scrapped. This seemed to be a victory for the vocal masses.

However, as Johnson points out in his well-balanced article, the negative reaction seemed to cause offence to Tan and it was assumed that the original offer of investment had been withdrawn. This could hardly be seen as good news to pragmatists, especially when it's considered that Cardiff's annual wage bill is 88% of the club's turnover, £1m was being lost every month, and total debts were thought to have reached £70m.

Unfortunately, by the time this piece had been published in *When Saturday Comes* there had been further developments. Johnson's warning that the new kit and badge couldn't be ruled out in the future was proved to be accurate. Despite reaching a compromise that would see Cardiff retain blue home shirts for 2012-13, with a red away strip, Tan and his cronies didn't let the matter lie.

Just weeks after the initial furore had died down, the unseemly proposals re-emerged and were implemented with an apparent disregard for the fan base. The lure of filthy lucre was too great for the directors of the club, whatever the sacrifice, and Cardiff wore red home shirts from the beginning of 2012-13. The famous bluebird, which once represented the club so proudly, no longer soars majestically on the club badge but has been reduced to the size of a moth and is trapped underneath a dominant red dragon and a generic new slogan – Fire and Passion.

An astonishing number of fans have accepted that this is progress and the only way forward for the club, but I'll never understand such soulless and unprincipled individuals, who are prepared to sacrifice identity for meaningless and empty success. I used to have a soft spot for Cardiff City and favour them over their rivals from Swansea, but now I wish them nothing but failure in their unseemly new guise.

It's clear that I'm out of touch with modern football as I seem to have spent the last 20 years moaning about one thing or another – unimaginative new grounds, commercial overload, spiralling admission prices, absurd wage demands from pampered prima donnas, et cetera. I could go on, but I want this book to be published in my lifetime. The general idea is that I've become disillusioned with the once beautiful game as a whole.

In researching this section, I read a blog entry by Phil Stead on his award-winning *Ffwtbol* site entitled "Losing My Religion". As a Cardiff City fan, he was distraught about what was happening to the club he loves, but still managed to write articulately about the situation. Discussing the powerlessness of supporters in the face of the "corrupt, immoral, dispassionate business" that football has become, he defiantly notes:

EVERY SILVER LINING HAS A CLOUD Nathan Lee Davies

> I need you to know that for many of us, success and superiority have never been the guiding principle of our devotion. All we need from our football is community, companionship, and a focus for our shared obsession. That's why small clubs playing rubbish football hold just as much, if not more appeal than a multi-million pound corporation with incredible players, but a synthetic identity.

Stead has hit the nail on the head, but I'm afraid the days of such simplistic, community focussed football are a thing of the past – in the higher echelons of the English system at least.

If only there was an alternative...

***

The Welsh Premier League is a breath of fresh air that has reignited my interest and passion for football.

You are probably startled by that last sentence, considering that I've moaned and groaned to such an extent throughout this volume. Indeed, the book was originally going to be called *Final Whistle* and be more of a fond farewell to the game I loved before capitalists took complete control.

However, while watching some abysmal football in ill-equipped stadiums I realised that I was rather enjoying myself. I'd gone back to basics to rediscover what I'd been missing for over a decade – a certain brotherhood and spirit fused by a shared enthusiasm for a simple game. If you can go to matches at this level with an open mind, stop yourself from making unfair comparisons with the English leagues and just take things as you find them, then you're guaranteed to make friends, laugh a lot and even be entertained by ever-improving playing standards.

EVERY SILVER LINING HAS A CLOUD Nathan Lee Davies

A typical afternoon in the WPL will include approachable players and managers, characteristic grounds, welcoming smiles wrapped in genuine best wishes, amateurish programmes written by passionate and dedicated people, homemade refreshments from locally sourced ingredients and the delight of enjoying all this for as little as £10.

If I could freeze time and keep the competition as it is – with the obvious exception of TNS – then I would, but supposed progress and development seems to be the order of the day. Clubs are striving for bigger and better things, but the self-inflicted combustion of Neath should serve as a warning to other clubs that they must live within their modest means by not irresponsibly overstretching themselves. It's concerning to see that certain clubs seem to be going down a similar route and it appears likely that the Eagles won't be the last club to self-destruct in the search for manufactured glory.

Why try to run before you can walk?

Organic growth will take time, but it looks to be the best way forward for all involved. However such progression is made, it's crucial that developments on the field are mirrored by the launch of fresh and exciting all-inclusive community projects to maintain and expand the family feel that clubs currently nurture so well. I'd hate to return to the WPL in twenty years' time to find elusive, stressed-out management teams and prima-donna players going about their business in half-empty plastic bowls, while sitting next to grumpy strangers, reading a glossy brochure full of impeccable spelling, noshing on stale, standardised refreshments and parting with the best part of £100.

That'd be my idea of hell...

***

EVERY SILVER LINING HAS A CLOUD Nathan Lee Davies

Old Wales is dead. The Wales of stereotype, leeks, daffodils, look-you-now boyo rugby supporters singing Max Boyce songs in three-part harmony while phoning mam to tell her they'll be home for tea and Welsh cakes has gone... So where does it leave us? Free to make up, reinvent, redefine our own versions of Wales, all three million definitions if necessary, because the Wales I know is bilingual, multicultural, pro-European, messed up, screwed up and ludicrously represented in the British press... So old Wales is dead and new Wales is already a possibility, an eclectic self-defined Wales with attitude.

Edward Thomas
"A Land Fit for Heroes (Max Boyce excluded)"
The Observer
20 July 1997

Throughout this book you've been reading the thoughts and opinions of a confused individual who was born and raised in old Wales, but matured and developed in a constantly evolving global village that has twisted and changed everything he once took as gospel.

Things were much simpler back then as everything was black and white.

GOOD	BAD
Wales	England
Labour	Conservative
Neil Kinnock	Margaret Thatcher
Rugby	Cricket
Hetrosexuality	Homosexuality
Tom Jones	Cliff Richard
Coal Miners	Royalty
Beer	Wine

EVERY SILVER LINING HAS A CLOUD Nathan Lee Davies

These straight-forward days are a thing of the past, but despite a healthy acceptance of the homosexual community, I can't shake off the remainder of my pre-dated ideas as I was brought up well. My intellectual capacity allows me to limit my hatred of England to its representative sports teams, which is handy because most of my friends are English, but I've never been as unhappy as I was during summer 2012, as brainless idiots waved Union Jacks at anything and everything.

Orchestrated by the BBC, the bleating masses thoughtlessly celebrated the Queen's Diamond Jubilee, the Olympic Flame as it headed for London and Roy Hodgson's average England side during Euro 2012. A cringe-worthy few months also meant having to endure face painters at Wimbledon, the loss of five Welsh traitors to Team GB and patronisation throughout the Paralympics.

To top it all, these events took place under a Conservative-led coalition and I still wasn't receiving any good news from www.isthatcherdeadyet.co.uk, despite daily checks (I finally opened the champagne in April 2013).

There is no escaping my deeply ingrained left-wing beliefs as, like it or not, this is part of who I am. It's also true that, despite my best efforts, some of the outdated thoughts that I've inherited continue to linger in my writing. I'm conscious that I've been guilty of pedalling stereotypes at times, and for that I'm truly sorry but hopeful that you've taken them in the light-hearted manner they were intended. In addition, TNS have been picked on unfairly and, while I'll never agree with the way in which the club has been artificially manufactured and relocated, I'd like to apologise for any anti-English jibes that may have caused offence to those of you who neglected to take my words with a pinch of salt, as instructed prior to chapter one.

My journey has highlighted the fact that I'm trapped in a lonely middle ground between the romantic Wales of the past and the dynamic, multicultural society we now live in. If my travels have taught me anything, it's now clear that I can personally define my own identity as a Welshman. For too long I've listened to stereotypes and believed that to qualify as a true Welshman I had to be a fluent Welsh speaker that enjoyed rugby, sang in a male voice choir and shagged sheep. Like thousands of others I took cultural icon Max Boyce far too literally and saw him as the embodiment of being Welsh instead of an over-rated comedian who deals in stereotypes. Boyce's 20th century ideals can not be imposed on a 21st century man living in revolutionary times.

I'm trying to become more open, accepting and tune into contemporary trends but realise that to be true to myself I must fuse these new ideas with unfashionable beliefs from the past to create a unique individual who isn't like everybody else. I started this tour looking for a sense of belonging and familiarity that I was missing from my life and to a degree I found it but, of much greater importance, I ended up finding myself.

***

It'll take time to form this new and exciting Welsh identity, but at least I'm working on it. I've got all the essential ingredients – pride and passion from previous generations mixed with the openness and optimism that characterises the contemporary melting pot. While this mixture settles and congeals, I need to address that other aspect of my identity that needs thought and attention – my disability.

The problem is that I'm not willing to give it the head-space required and am happy to carry on struggling like a square peg outside the round hole of society. I'll carry on moaning and groaning in an entertaining manner from this lonely and isolated space I inhabit, sandwiched between the mainstream and segregation, in the hope my words might help, in some small way, to irritate the conscious of the status quo and conquer a few of the obstacles preventing acceptance in the wider community. I'm aware that my efforts probably won't make a blind bit of difference, but I'm going to have some fun trying.

In the meantime, I've decided to return to my spiritual home to see some familiar faces. I just needed to sort one or two things out first...

The disabled section at the Racecourse runs along the front of the Mold Road Stand and offers a poor view with inadequate shelter from the rain. The stand roof does not cover the first few rows of seats, so if it rains, everyone scurries to the back of the stand, while fans in chairs – who are often more susceptible to illness from cold, damp conditions – are left to be pissed on.

Something also had to be done about the lack of away travel opportunities for those in wheelchairs. I always found it demoralising not to be able to join others on away trips, merely because I couldn't get on a standard coach. Frustratingly, alternatives have never been provided. With the Wrexham Supporters Trust now in control of the club, I feel that more effort needed to be made to include disabled fans into the mainstream body of support.

I shared my views on the Red Passion website and got a favourable reaction that resulted in a meeting at the Racecourse in one of the executive boxes. In attendance were George Powell, the WST's disabled supporters' representative; Ann-Marie Brown, representing current ground owners Glyndwr University; and Lee Jones, former Prestatyn puppet and current Football in the Community manager at the club.

Also at the meeting were some blokes trying to set up a disability football project with the club, and a fellow supporter. The meeting kicked-off with discussions revolving around creating opportunities for those with learning difficulties or physical handicaps to access the sport in the area. This is not something that I'm particularly interested in, so my mind drifted back to Upton Park, 1992.

EVERY SILVER LINING HAS A CLOUD Nathan Lee Davies

I'll never forget that day in the East End of London. With time running out, it seemed that the lower league strugglers from north Wales were heading out of the FA Cup after a gutsy performance against top flight rivals. Cue heroics from Lee Jones who plundered an equaliser – following an exquisite 80-yard pass from Gareth Owen – to force the fourth round tie to a replay.

The pint-sized striker has certainly been on a different journey to me since that day, but here we were breathing the same air again. This time I was the one wearing the Wrexham shirt and he was spruced up and confident in a suit. He seemed a nice guy, but I was worried about how he'd react to my chapter from Bastion Gardens when I referred to him as a "puppet". I suppose I'm going to have a lot of such worry over the coming months...

The conversation opened up and I was able to deliver my agenda to surprisingly receptive ears that promised decisive action.

"Bloody hell lad. You've done alright for yourself. You've come through that door and in five minutes you've got your cover and a mini-bus to away games," said Jones in recognition of my negotiating skills.

"I know it's great, but listen Lee, I need a word..."

***

The meeting broke up, but before I made my way home, I took some time to admire the personalised brick that I had built into the Mold Road Stand – for a fee of £30 – back in 1999.

Nathan Lee Davies
Cymru Am Byth

As I was gazing at the brick in all its glory, I couldn't help but think that maybe a more appropriate inscription might've been:

Nathan Lee Davies
Wrexham Forever

<u>28</u>
Full Time

EVERY SILVER LINING HAS A CLOUD Nathan Lee Davies

It was one of those glorious days when jumpers, jeans and coats are discarded and women stay cool in tight t-shirts, short skirts and little else. Subsequently, I'd made a rare foray into my back garden with half the contents of my office to keep me occupied.

I'd been neglecting my correspondence while writing this book, so I parked my wheelchair in the cooling shade of an old oak tree and fired off a succession of emails and old-fashioned letters to the older generation – my concentration only broken when nature called. My bungalow is hidden underneath a busy dual carriageway, but I find the constant hum of traffic, combined with the faint whiff of exhaust fumes, to be reassuring and conducive to a productive few hours of writing.

As I put the finishing touches to an anti-monarchy rant of epic proportions in a letter to the local rag, I was distracted by a tired bag of air that was carried over my garden fence by a random gust of summer wind. As it fluttered towards my feet, I noticed that the faded red inflatable looked strangely familiar, with its final revolution confirming that I had indeed seen this balloon before.

Those of you who've been paying attention may remember that this very same slippery bladder of chemicals – unmistakable due to its distinctive markings – had escaped confinement from a Ford Cortina at Alderhey Children's Hospital before I was diagnosed with

EVERY SILVER LINING HAS A CLOUD Nathan Lee Davies

Friedreich's Ataxia. Back then, I couldn't make out the translation as it floated skywards but vowed to remember the symbol and discover its true meaning. Of course, I never did, but now that I'd finally cracked the code, I could only appreciate the rich irony.

I picked up the dishevelled, weather-beaten scrap of foil from a barren flower bed. It was desperately clinging onto the final remnants of helium in the vain hope and deluded belief that it was still attractive enough to brighten a birthday, anniversary or any other special event with the sickeningly optimistic message emblazoned upon it.

I unfastened the Wrexham AFC badge that I'd pinned to my polo shirt that morning and hovered the sharp fastener inches above the doomed balloon. A nightmarish sequence of images raced through my mind, including haunted depictions of evil hospital staff laughing manically while wielding oversized needles, Highland cows dressed in lingerie and an eerie care home full of poisonous snakes with human faces. Each gruesome scene overlapped the next and featured neon crash test dummies chanting the bible backwards over a harrowing recital of Radiohead's obscure cacophony of electronic beats, while gorgeous models made love to one another beneath vibrant green clouds that spat out purple question marks.

Only I could stop such haunting hallucinations. I lowered my hand and pierced the balloon.

I breathed a deep sigh of relief...

Obituaries

It's not all been fun and laughter.

Back in September 2011, I read the tragic news that much-travelled goalkeeper Mark Ovendale had died at the age of 37 after a battle with cancer.

The shot stopper was born in Leicester in 1973. He began his football career with Northampton Town before moving to Barry Town in 1995.

"Gloves" played 145 games for Barry Town between July 1995 and April 1998. He later returned to the club for a brief spell in 2003.

In three seasons, he played in 112 League of Wales games for the club, of which only four were lost. During this spell he managed to keep 61 clean sheets.

From September to December 1995, he also played a total of 1,086 minutes in the League of Wales without conceding a goal.

Ovendale played in the UEFA Cup and Champion's League for Barry, including games against Aberdeen and Dynamo Kiev. He also won three League titles, one Welsh Cup and one League Cup.

In addition, this experienced campaigner made 181 Football League appearances for Northampton Town, Bournemouth, Luton Town and York City.

Tiverton Town, Carmarthen Town and Newport County also called on his services. The journeyman later had a coaching role at Wimborne Town, where he made a handful of appearances.

A tumour had been discovered in Ovendale's left calf in 2010. The cancer eventually spread to his back.

This proud family man is survived by his wife, Rhianon, and four children, Jacob, Evan, James, and Maisy-Mai.

TRIBUTES

Barry Town club secretary David Cole:
"He was one of our full-time players when we were dominating the League of Wales.

"He was undoubtedly one of our best, and it wasn't long before a Football League side came in for him.

"He had a huge impact on the team.

"His defence had great confidence in him, and he was a really nice guy, really friendly."

Former Bournemouth team-mate Mark Stein:
"Mark will be remembered as being a good goalkeeper, who worked tirelessly to become a better one.

"He was popular in the changing room but also had a dry sense of humour when he decided to open his mouth!

"What people didn't see was that he had a heart of gold and would always put others before himself, which is rare.

"I would like to send my condolences to all his family after he lost his determined battle to overcome his illness."

Former Tiverton Town boss Martyn Rogers:
"First of all he was a very good goalkeeper and he was the life and soul of the dressing room.

"It is tragic that someone so young and talented is no longer with us. It is difficult to come to terms with. Mark was a Football League goalkeeper with great awareness and to have him at Tiverton was a big signing at the time.

"He certainly showed his worth in the two seasons he was with us and he was well-liked by everyone.

"He had a good rapport with the supporters.

"I had heard he had some form of cancer, but you obviously don't hear everything that is going on.

"It really is heartbreaking. It is a particularly hard time for his family and children and our thoughts are with them."

Wimborne Town chairman Ken Stewart:
"We are all deeply shocked. He was very professional and well-liked and our thoughts go out to his family."

Alan Walker-Harris, who was coached by Mark while at Wimborne:
"He was very dedicated to what he wanted to do with football and anything he did.

"He was quite an infectious person who had a very positive outlook on everything and always tried to keep his thoughts positive.

"Even when it was serious, he was always laughing and joking. He was determined and he kept telling me he wasn't going to let it beat him."

Mark John Ovendale
1973 – 2011

After completing my tour of the Welsh Premier League, and while I was writing my experiences for this book, I was shocked and saddened to learn about the passing of former FAW general secretary Alun Evans, on 12 November 2011. The 69-year-old had been suffering from a long illness.

Born in Porth, Evans took over from Trevor Morris as FAW secretary in 1982 and continued until 1995, when he was succeeded in the role by David Collins. Evans taught economics and geography before moving into sports administration and was heavily involved with the Universities Athletic Union. He was well-respected in Europe and the wider world, serving on FIFA's disciplinary committee at the 1994 World Cup.

Known for his forthright views and abrasive manner, Evans was instrumental in the controversial formation of the Welsh Premier League – launched as the League of Wales – and was a strong leader of FAW policies, who didn't suffer fools gladly. By all accounts he wasn't a popular man and was roundly criticised by the public and media, while pressing forward with his long-term vision.

Ultimately and undoubtedly, Evans proved to be a resilient and valuable visionary, who showed unlimited amounts of dogged determination and energy in making his dream of a national competition in Wales become a reality. For this, he deserves our upmost gratitude and deserves to be remembered with respect and admiration.

TRIBUTES

From League Secretary John Deakin:

"It was well known that Alun Evans had suffered declining health in the past few years, which was doubtless exacerbated when he fell and broke his hip three weeks ago, resulting in him being hospitalised. He was In the Heath Hospital in Cardiff, when he passed away as a result of a stroke at the early age of 69. Despite his failing health, his death was a personal shock to me as when I visited him, together with my colleague Jan Hoskin, only a week before his death, we found him in excellent spirits and looking much better than had been the case in recent months.

"I have known Alun since I moved to Wales in 1983, being then a well-established Football League referee and obviously wanted to develop my career and he was a great help to me. When I was due to finish refereeing in 1992, I applied for the job of secretary of the new League of Wales and Alun was secretary of the panel that appointed me.

"The Football League of Wales had been his dream throughout his tenure as chief executive of the Football Association of Wales, and when the competition was founded in August of 1992, it was the culmination of his ambition for Welsh domestic football. The history of the preparations for that date were fraught with conflict, with clubs that wanted no part of the project being vociferous in their opposition and desire to remain in the English system. Alun bore the brunt of the furore and was subjected to significant and often unfair public and media abuse. However, he stuck to his guns, and he can rightly be identified as the founder of the competition that is now in its twentieth season.

"He continued as chief executive until 1995, after which he maintained his interest in the League and served on the council of the FAW as the clubs representative until 2007, in his final three years holding office as chairman. He carried out those duties with dignity and enthusiasm, and it was a considerable personal shock to me when he lost his position on the council in the triennial elections of that year.

"Alun was a complex character and I certainly had my moments with him over the years, but his enthusiasm and commitment to Welsh football could not be questioned. He was well respected in Europe and the wider world and served on FIFA's disciplinary committee at the 1994 World Cup in the United States. The contribution that he made to football in Wales, when viewed with hindsight, will be considered to be both visionary and valuable.

"Let the success of the Welsh Premier League continue to be his epitaph in the years to come."

From League historian Mel Ap Ior Thomas:
"Alun was a good friend and his devotion to Welsh football was second to none. The Alun I knew was passionate about football, domestically and globally, and we had many a long debate about football in Wales and how its future should be guaranteed. I did not agree with everything he said, but I can say that I agreed with 98% at least!

"I am proud that I appeared for the FAW in the High Court in the months leading up to the formation of the then League of Wales and [...] one thing this case did prove was that [Evans] was committed to setting-up a national league [for Wales]. He received abuse for his dedication to this cause, none more so than from the southern based press, but he once told me that it was totally worth it in the end."

Alun E. Evans
1941-2011

November 2011 was a bad month for Welsh football as following the death of Evans came the news that Wales manager Gary Speed had been found dead at his home in Chester.

Initially, it was thought that a deeply depressed Speed had intentionally committed suicide by hanging himself in his garage. However, an inquest later reached a narrative verdict and stated that the cause of death was by "self suspension". It was ruled that there was insufficient evidence to determine whether it was intentional as he may have intended to make a "dramatic gesture" and then "nodded off to sleep".

I don't want to delve any further into the exact events of 27 November 2011. Instead, I think it's more appropriate to celebrate Speed's achievements in the beautiful game. He starred for Leeds United, Everton, Newcastle United, Bolton Wanderers and Sheffield United, in a playing career that spanned 22 seasons. As a model professional, Speed maintained extraordinary fitness levels throughout his career, escaped serious injury, avoided suspensions and consistently delivered cultured, energetic and committed performances, which meant he was often the first name on the team sheet. As a result, he held the record for the most appearances in the Premier League at 535, until it was surpassed by David James. At the time of his death, only James and Ryan Giggs had played in more Premier League matches than Speed.

If we factor in matches played at Football League level and add cup competitions, Speed made a staggering 840 domestic appearances. In addition, he won 85 full international caps – scoring seven goals – between 1990 and 2004 to become the most capped outfield player for Wales.

In 2010, he moved into management with Sheffield United, but after only a few months in the Bramall Lane hot-seat he was unveiled as the new Wales manager, following the departure of John Toshack.

Speed was also made an MBE in the 2010 Birthday Honours, for services to football.

I never knew the man personally, but I watched him in action from the stands on many occasions and always held him in high regard. I wasn't the only one, judging by the mass outpouring of grief that followed news of his death, but the most touching and revealing tributes came from those who worked alongside Speed and classed him as a friend. I have therefore chosen to end this obituary with a selection of heartfelt tributes paid by politicians, former colleagues and close friends. Their words illustrate – more than mine ever could – that we lost far more than an ex-professional footballer, who was having a promising stab at international management. Gary Speed was a genuinely decent human being, who still had a great deal to offer...

TRIBUTES

Downing Street spokesman:
"The Prime Minister [David Cameron] was deeply saddened to hear of the death of Gary Speed, who was greatly respected by football fans across the country both as a player and manager. The Prime Minister's thoughts are with his family and friends on this very sad day for fans everywhere, especially in Wales."

Richard Scudamore, the Premier League's chief executive:
"This is truly tragic news and the thoughts of all of those associated with the Premier League are with Gary's family and friends.

"Gary was a wonderful ambassador for our league, and indeed all of football, but more than that he was a decent man widely respected throughout the game and beyond.

"Gary will go down in history as one of our iconic players, he was a stand-out professional of the modern game and I'm sure all football fans across Britain will be deeply saddened at his untimely passing."

Phil Pritchard, the president of the FAW:
"It's been a tremendous shock to us all. Obviously Louise [Speed's wife] and the family are foremost in our thoughts. It takes a lot of taking in.

"The tributes to him are endless – we are going to miss him tremendously in Welsh football, the world of football is going to miss him. I've already had a personal communication from Mr Blatter, the president of FIFA, and from Mr Platini [the president of UEFA]. That's the respect that he has.

"He really was such a nice genuine guy – I'm sorry in my heart that it's happened to Welsh football, but I really do feel for the family as they'll be absolutely devastated. A very close family is Gary's and he always kept his family life to himself. I'm sure that they will need the time to grieve."

FIFA President Sepp Blatter in the aforementioned letter to FAW president Phil Pritchard:
"Gary Speed was a hugely talented player and a great servant for both club and country, who will be greatly missed. He will always be remembered as a model professional and a fantastic ambassador for the game.

"Having attended the [qualifying] draw for the 2014 FIFA World Cup, it was clear to all there that he was a man who exuded enthusiasm and passion for the game.

"I would like to offer my deepest condolences on behalf of FIFA and the worldwide family of football to you, the Football Association of Wales, his wife Louise and their two sons, as well as Gary Speed's friends and family. I hope the knowledge that we are all thinking of them can provide some solace in this time of deep sadness."

Robin van Persie on Twitter:
"I heard the sad news about Gary Speed, great footballer my condolences and sympathies to his family."

Gary Neville:
"It's absolutely devastating. My career and his crossed many times, I played against him many times. Everyone that I know that knew him couldn't say enough good things about him. We think of football as being important, but it's not really."

Alan Shearer, who spent six years with Speed at Newcastle United:
"Gary was a magnificent person – bright, fun and a wonderful family man – who lit up every room he walked into. I am proud to have been his friend and will miss him dreadfully."

Graeme Souness:
"I can't say that I knew Gary, but the little that I do know about him came from Dean Saunders, who used to room with him. He was a deep thinker, a thoughtful intelligent man."

Howard Wilkinson, who managed Speed at his first club Leeds United:
"It's such a loss. I cannot begin to try to understand what his parents are thinking. I knew his mum and dad, and particularly his dad very well. I've met a lot of people in my time, a lot of sportsmen. Gary had none of those things which we associate with sportsmen. He was ordinary as a bloke, very nice, very genuine, very honest, very hardworking.

"He was a joy to manage. I think I played Gary in every position apart from goalkeeper, and never even once did his face change or did he seem annoyed when I told him. He had a terrific sense of loyalty and commitment to the people around him.

"This is a genuine loss to the world."

Kenny Dalglish:
"He was a smashing lad and was really well respected. We don't know the circumstances obviously, and there'll be a lot of people who are saddened at what's happened, but I think the most important people at this particular moment in time is his wife and kids – they must be absolutely devastated. It's at times like this that the football becomes a wee bit irrelevant.

"He was a very respected man in and around football, not only for his ability but as a person. I signed Gary for £5million from Everton and he did a fantastic job for us at Newcastle, during the time I was there and after I'd left as well."

Bobby Gould, former Wales boss:
"He was a great pro. He would play anywhere for you – left back, left wing, centre of midfield, wide left. It's such a tragedy. People are just stunned.

"I saw John Hartson earlier. The big man just cried and cried. We cuddled each other. He's gone home [from the Liberty Stadium where a match between Swansea City and Aston Villa went ahead in difficult circumstances only hours after Speed's death. The match was dedicated to his memory]. That is his respect towards Gary to say "I can't work this afternoon". Speedo was his pal. They were buddies. Gary was the ultimate professional."

Mark Bowen, Welsh team-mate of Speed's and later coach of the national side:
"I'm totally stunned and devastated, you feel completely numb. It goes without saying that the plaudits for the man himself will come thick and fast.

"I played with him and I knew him as a colleague for many years. He was captain of Wales when the likes of Mark Hughes and Ian Rush were still playing and I think that tells you a lot about the man he was. I can't put into words what a fantastic guy he was.

"In that short space of time [as Wales manager] he showed the talent he had for working with the players. He had such a bright, fantastic future to look forward to in football but that is secondary [...] it's about his family and his boys."

Speed's former Wales team-mate Robbie Savage on Twitter:
"He was upbeat on phone yesterday we were laughing together, talking football and dancing he was a great teammate and a great friend."

Speed's former Wales team-mate Ryan Giggs:

"I am totally devastated. Gary Speed was one of the nicest men in football and someone I am honoured to call a team-mate and friend.

"Words cannot begin to describe how sad I feel at hearing this awful news. It goes without saying my thoughts are with his family at this tremendously sad time."

Speed's former Wales team-mate John Hartson:

"Speedo was probably one of the nicest people I have ever known, irrespective of football, and everybody loved him. He was like a brother and captain for 10 years. Craig Bellamy, Robbie Savage, me and Ryan Giggs were around the same age and all came through together.

"I remember him as a wonderful player, a great leader and someone who led by example. If you were in the bar he was the first at the bar, if he was in the golf course he was right in amongst it, he was the first on the training ground and the last off it.

"He had two great feet, a tremendous engine and always scored goals. He had a knack of getting headers as well and was a tremendous header of the ball.

"It's difficult to talk about him as a footballer before you talk about him as a man. That's what he will be judged on. For everyone in Wales, it's a sad, sad loss especially to the family and two boys and his wife."

Gary Andrew Speed MBE
1969-2011

In April 2012, Welsh football mourned the passing of Eddie May, who died in his sleep, aged 68.

May was born in Epping, but this burly central defender – who developed his skills with Dagenham and Southend United – was to become a much-loved figure in Welsh football after starring in successful Wrexham and Swansea sides in his 13-year playing career.

However, May will be best remembered for his stint as Cardiff City manager, during which the Bluebirds won the 1992-93 Division Three title. Cardiff also won the Welsh Cup that season with a 5-0 win over Rhyl and went on to beat Manchester City 1-0 in the FA Cup in 1994.

He also managed Newport County, Torquay United, Brentford and Highlanders in Zimbabwe, as well as enjoying spells in Iceland, Ireland, Kenya, Norway, Qatar, Pakistan, Saudi Arabia, Uganda, Malawi and South Africa.

May succeeded John Lewis as Barry Town boss in March 1995, as the club began their professional era but left after only six months.

In 1998, he was set to join Haverfordwest County but instead became manager of Finnish outfit FinnPa, before eventually joining the New Bridge Meadow outfit later that same year as director of football. He then left to manage Merthyr Tydfil in December 1998 but returned after only one day.

May joined Llanelli in August 2004, but his tenure lasted only four months; a disastrous nine-match losing start to the campaign saw Nick Tucker arrive from Taffs Well to take over in mid-October.

In October 2009, he took up the position of manager of Porthcawl Town in Welsh League Division Two, leaving the club in January 2010.

TRIBUTES

Jason Perry, who captained Cardiff City under May:
"Eddie was somebody who had great man-management skills. He made everyone feel loved and got players thinking they were important to him and to the team. He was someone who instantly commanded respect and who respected others, he was a very loyal man and somebody you wanted to work for.

"In many ways he was well ahead of his time, he brought in methods which were different back then and many of them are still being used today. The brand of football that he got us to play and the quality of players he brought in really helped to bring the crowds back to capacity. He knew how to get the best out of people and because of that we had some great success."

Lennie Lawrence, who worked with May at Charlton Athletic:
"I can't speak highly enough of him, he worked at a lot of clubs at a lot of levels and he was a truly honest man. There were no airs and graces about him at all — it was always black and white. He was a fantastic man. Eddie really was larger than life.

"I knew him before I got the Charlton job in 1982, so I didn't think twice about working with him. I knew he would complement me perfectly and he helped me a great deal through some difficult years. We had a good working relationship and he was a good man."

Former Wrexham team-mate Mickey Thomas:
"He was a big man both on and off the pitch and he was someone we all looked up to. He cut a very imposing figure in so many ways and he was so well respected in the football world.

"It was a massive shock when I found out and I'm sure it was the same for fans all over Wales because he was loved in the north just as much as he was in the south."

Former Swansea City team-mate Alan Curtis:

"I'm really shocked and saddened by the news. He was instrumental to the club and made a big contribution to every game he played. He bought a wealth of experience that was vital for the development of myself and other young players at the time – he was a huge influence both on and off the pitch."

Cardiff City's chief executive Alan Whiteley:

"On behalf of everyone at the club I would like to pass on our sincere condolences to Eddie May's family at this sad time. We will be honoured to collectively show our respects and appreciation to a man who will forever and rightly be remembered as an integral part of modern Cardiff City history. He will be sadly missed by all."

Edwin Charles May

1943-2012

As I was nearing my deadline for this book, I learnt that former WPL defender Captain Stephen James "Steve" Healey had been killed in action on vehicle patrol in the Nahri Saraj District of Helmand province, Afghanistan.

An officer with the 1st Battalion The Royal Welsh, Healey started his football career as a professional with Swansea City before being loaned to Llanelli in 2001.

After being released by the Swans, he decided he wasn't likely to have a long career in football, so quit the professional game to resume his education.

Despite not having any A-Levels, Swansea University accepted him on a degree course in sports science, based on his experience as a footballer.

Healey remained in the national league after leaving Llanelli and joined Port Talbot Town in 2003. After a couple of seasons at Victoria Road, he moved to Cardiff Grange Harlequins for their one and only season in the top flight (2005-06).

He made a total of 46 starts in the national competition and also appeared for Bridgend Town, Goytre United and Barry Town.

He continued to play football for the Army and also for Garden Village.

Captain Healey leaves behind his father John, mother Kerry, brother Simon and girlfriend Thea.

TRIBUTES

Major Ian Lawrence, a spokesman for Task Force Helmand:
"It is with great sadness I must inform you that a soldier from 1st Battalion The Royal Welsh has died of wounds sustained in an IED strike while on a mobile patrol in the Nahri Saraj District of Helmand Province. The thoughts and prayers of all in the Task Force are with his family and friends at this sad time."

Swansea City Football Club:
"Swansea City Football Club are saddened to hear of the death of former defender Stephen Healey. The 29-year-old served his apprenticeship at the Swans, before playing for Llanelli and Port Talbot Town in the Welsh Premier League. Everyone at Swansea City Football Club would like to offer their condolences to Stephen's family and friends at this difficult time."

Captain Healey's family:
"Stephen was all you could wish for in a son, brother, uncle and friend. He will be sadly missed by us all. He managed to do more in his 30 years than most people do in a lifetime."

Captain Healey's girlfriend, Thea:
"Stephen will always be in my heart. I will miss him so much. He was my love, my life, my everything. Now he rests in peace. He was living the life he wanted with his men."

Captain Stephen James Healey
1982-2012

Postscript

EVERY SILVER LINING HAS A CLOUD Nathan Lee Davies

So, 2012-13 has been and gone and my bloody book has still not been published. The hold-up can be attributed to a number of factors — chiefly my anal pretentions — but in the meantime, TNS have won a second successive WPL title, Carmarthen Town captured the freshly formatted League Cup and Prestatyn Town were crowned Welsh Cup winners for the first time in their history.

Meanwhile, Swansea City qualified for the Europa League after lifting the Capital One Cup, the pride of Asia purchased promotion to the Premier League and Gareth Bale was awarded the PFA Young Player of the Year, the PFA Players' Player of the Year and the FWA Footballer of the Year awards. Then there was Wrexham...

We reached Wembley for the first time in our history to win the worthless FA Trophy and booked a return trip to the sterile "home" of football for the Blue Square Premier play-off final. Unfortunately, things didn't go according to plan and our fan-owned club was defeated by a bunch of south Walian cretins, who were partly funded by a personal fortune.

There's no justice in this world — a fact proven by the sad demise of Llanelli AFC in April 2013. The former Welsh Premier champions were wound up at London's High Court over a mere £21,000 tax debt. Lawyers for the club, which formed in 1896 and were founder members of the league in 1992, said the debt's size had been disputed since last August. However, HMRC said no attempt was made to pay £3,000, which was undisputed.

Llanelli finished 11th in the league and had fended off three winding up attempts in an uncomfortable last six months.

Carmarthenshire MP Jonathan Edwards said the news was a "tragedy" for local football.

EVERY SILVER LINING HAS A CLOUD Nathan Lee Davies

"As a football supporter from Carmarthenshire this is a sad day. It is a tragedy when something like this happens to a football club like Llanelli, because the club is such a vital cog in the local community.

"It is has a huge impact when any club like this goes to the wall. We just hope now that the club can reform quickly and work their way back up the Welsh pyramid. This is also bad news for all concerned as such clubs produce local talent who work their way up to Premiership level."

It should also be noted that Barry Town AFC – seven times champions of Wales – is no more. Inexplicably, former owner, Stuart Lovering, decided to simply walk away from the debt-free club without recognition or thought to the loyal and dedicated band of supporters, who have run and funded the club since 2011. The story really is jaw-dropping and further details of a shocking injustice can be found at http://forzabarry.blogspot.co.uk. I wish the newly-formed Barry Town United AFC every success in the future.

The mass media keep telling us that 2012-13 was a year to cherish for Welsh football, but the loss of two former championship winning clubs, the concentration of filthy lucre amongst the privileged few and Wrexham's failure to regain their rightful place in the Football League, mean I'm left scowling underneath dark and depressing rain clouds with little hope for the future.

Corbett Sports Welsh Premier League 2012-13
Final League Table

Pos	Team	P	W	D	L	F	A	GD	Pts
1	TNS (C)	32	24	4	4	86	22	+64	76
2	Airbus UK B'ton (EL)	32	17	3	12	76	42	+34	54
3	Bangor City	32	14	9	9	65	53	+12	51
4	Port Talbot Town	32	13	8	11	51	52	-1	47
5	Prestatyn Town (EL)	32	11	7	14	62	79	-17	40
6	Carmarthen Town	32	10	7	15	36	50	-14	37
7	Bala Town (EL)	32	17	5	10	62	41	+21	56
8	CQ Nomads	32	12	5	15	62	69	-7	40
9	Newtown	32	10	7	15	44	54	-10	37
10	Aberystwyth Town	32	9	10	13	40	59	-19	37
11	Llanelli (R)	32	10	6	16	41	68	-27	36
12	Afan Lido	32	8	3	21	43	79	-36	27

(C) = Champions (EL) = Europa League (R) = Relegated
Connah's Quay Nomads deducted 1 point

* Further details of the 2012-13 WPL season can be found by consulting the links in the acknowledgement section at the beginning of this book.

Nathan Lee Davies
May 2013

Appendix A

What is Friedreich's ataxia?

Friedreich's ataxia (also called FA or FRDA) is a rare inherited disease that causes nervous system damage and movement problems. It usually begins in childhood and leads to impaired muscle coordination (ataxia) that worsens over time. The disorder is named after Nicholaus Friedreich, a German doctor who first described the condition in the 1860s.

In Friedreich's ataxia the spinal cord and peripheral nerves degenerate, becoming thinner. The cerebellum, part of the brain that coordinates balance and movement, also degenerates to a lesser extent. This damage results in awkward, unsteady movements and impaired sensory functions. The disorder also causes problems in the heart and spine, and some people with the condition develop diabetes. The disorder does not affect thinking and reasoning abilities (cognitive functions).

Friedreich's ataxia is caused by a defect (mutation) in a gene labelled FXN. The disorder is recessive, meaning it occurs only in someone who inherits two defective copies of the gene, one from each parent. Although rare, Friedreich's ataxia is the most common form of hereditary ataxia, affecting about 1 in every 50,000 people in the United States. Both male and female children can inherit the disorder.

What are the signs and symptoms?

Symptoms typically begin between the ages of 5 and 15 years, although they sometimes appear in adulthood and on rare occasions as late as age 75. The first symptom to appear is usually gait ataxia, or difficulty walking. The ataxia gradually worsens and slowly spreads to the arms and the trunk. There is often loss of sensation in the extremities, which may spread to other parts of the body. Other features include loss of tendon reflexes, especially in the knees and ankles. Most people with Friedreich's ataxia develop scoliosis (a curving of the spine to one side), which often requires surgical intervention for treatment.

Dysarthria (slowness and slurring of speech) develops and can get progressively worse. Many individuals with later stages of Friedreich's ataxia develop hearing and vision loss.

Other symptoms that may occur include chest pain, shortness of breath, and heart palpitations. These symptoms are the result of various forms of heart disease that often accompany Friedreich's ataxia, such as hypertrophic cardiomyopathy (enlargement of the heart), myocardial fibrosis (formation of fiber-like material in the muscles of the heart), and cardiac failure. Heart rhythm abnormalities such as tachycardia (fast heart rate) and heart block (impaired conduction of cardiac impulses within the heart) are also common. About 20 percent of people with Friedreich's ataxia develop carbohydrate intolerance and 10 percent develop diabetes. Most individuals with Friedreich's ataxia tire very easily and find that they require more rest and take a longer time to recover from common illnesses such as colds and flu.

The rate of progression varies from person to person. Generally, within 10 to 20 years after the appearance of the first symptoms, the person is confined to a wheelchair, and in later stages of the disease individuals may become completely incapacitated.

Friedreich's ataxia can shorten life expectancy, and heart disease is the most common cause of death. However, some people with less severe features of Friedreich's ataxia live into their sixties, seventies, or older.

How is Friedreich's ataxia diagnosed?

A diagnosis of Friedreich's ataxia requires a careful clinical examination, which includes a medical history and a thorough physical exam, in particular looking for balance difficulty, loss of proprioception (joint sensation), absence of reflexes, and signs of neurological problems. Genetic testing now provides a conclusive diagnosis. Other tests that may aid in the diagnosis or management of the disorder include:

- electromyogram (EMG), which measures the electrical activity of muscle cells,

- nerve conduction studies, which measure the speed with which nerves transmit impulses,

- electrocardiogram (ECG), which gives a graphic presentation of the electrical activity or beat pattern of the heart,

- echocardiogram, which records the position and motion of the heart muscle,

- blood tests to check for elevated glucose levels and vitamin E levels, and

- magnetic resonance imaging (MRI) or computed tomography (CT) scans, tests which provide brain and spinal cord images that are useful for ruling out other neurological conditions.

How is Friedreich's ataxia inherited?

Friedreich's ataxia is an autosomal recessive disease, meaning individuals only develop symptoms if they inherit two copies of the defective FXN gene, one from their father and one from their mother. A person who has only one abnormal copy of the gene is called a carrier. A carrier will not develop the disease but could pass the gene mutation on to his or her children. If both parents are carriers, their children will have a 1 in 4 chance of having the disease and a 1 in 2 chance of inheriting one abnormal gene that they, in turn, could pass on to their children. About one in 90 Americans of European ancestry carries an abnormal FXN gene.

In 1996, an international research team identified the Friedreich's ataxia gene on chromosome 9. The FXN gene codes for production of a protein called "frataxin." In the normal version of the gene, a sequence of DNA (labeled "GAA") is repeated between 7 and 22 times. In the defective FXN gene, the repeat occurs over and over again—hundreds, even up to a thousand times.

This abnormal pattern, called a triplet repeat expansion, has been implicated as the cause of several dominantly inherited diseases, but Friedreich's ataxia is the only known recessive genetic disorder caused by the problem. Almost all people with Friedreich's ataxia have two copies of this mutant form of FXN, but it is not found in all cases of the disease. About two percent of affected individuals have other defects in the FXN gene that are responsible for causing the disease.

The triplet repeat expansion greatly disrupts the normal production of frataxin. Frataxin is found in the energy-producing parts of the cell called mitochondria. Research suggests that without a normal level of frataxin, certain cells in the body (especially peripheral nerve, spinal cord, brain and heart muscle cells) cannot effectively produce energy and have been hypothesized to have a build-up of toxic by-products leading to what is called "oxidative stress." It also may lead to increased levels of iron in the mitochondria. When the excess iron reacts with oxygen, free radicals can be produced. Although free radicals are essential molecules in the body's metabolism, they can also destroy cells and harm the body. Research continues on this subject (see section on "What research is being done?").

Can Friedreich's ataxia be cured or treated?

As with many degenerative diseases of the nervous system, there is currently no cure or effective treatment for Friedreich's ataxia. However, many of the symptoms and accompanying complications can be treated to help individuals maintain optimal functioning as long as possible. Doctors can prescribe treatments for diabetes, if present; some of the heart problems can be treated with medication as well. Orthopedic problems such as foot deformities and scoliosis can be corrected with braces or surgery. Physical therapy may prolong use of the arms and legs. Advances in understanding the genetics of Friedreich's ataxia are leading to breakthroughs in treatment. Research has moved forward to the point where clinical trials of proposed treatments are presently occurring for Friedreich's ataxia.

What services are useful to Friedreich's ataxia patients and their families?

Genetic testing is essential for proper clinical diagnosis, and can aid in prenatal diagnosis and determining a person's carrier status. Genetic counsellors can help explain how Friedreich's ataxia is inherited. Psychological counselling and support groups for people with genetic diseases may also help affected individuals and their families cope with the disease.

A primary care physician can screen people for complications such as heart disease, diabetes and scoliosis, and can refer individuals to specialists such as cardiologists, physical therapists, and speech therapists to help deal with some of the other associated problems. Support and information for families is also available through a number of private organizations. These groups can offer ways to network and communicate with others affected by Friedreich's ataxia. They can also provide access to patient registries, clinical trials information, and other useful resources.

What research is being done?

Within the Federal government the National Institute of Neurological Disorders and Stroke (NINDS), a component of the National Institutes of Health (NIH), has primary responsibility for sponsoring research on neurological disorders. As part of this mission, the NINDS conducts research on Friedreich's ataxia and other forms of inherited ataxias at its facilities at the NIH and supports additional studies at medical centers throughout the United States. Several nonprofit organizations also provide substantial support research (see the section on "Where can I get more information?").

Researchers are optimistic that they have begun to understand the causes of the disease, and work has begun to develop effective treatments and prevention strategies for Friedreich's ataxia. Scientists have been able to create various models of the disease in yeast and mice which have facilitated understanding the cause of the disease and are now being used for drug discovery and the development of novel treatments.

Studies have revealed that frataxin is an important mitochondrial protein for proper function of several organs. Yet in people with the disease, the amount of frataxin in affected cells is severely reduced. It is believed that the loss of frataxin makes the nervous system, heart, and pancreas particularly susceptible to damage from free radicals (produced when the excess iron reacts with oxygen). Once certain cells in these tissues are destroyed by free radicals they cannot be replaced. Nerve and muscle cells also have metabolic needs that may make them particularly vulnerable to this damage. Free radicals have been implicated in other degenerative diseases such as Parkinson's and Alzheimer's diseases.

Based upon this information, scientists and physicians have tried to reduce the levels of free radicals, also called oxidants, using treatment with "antioxidants." Initial clinical studies in Europe suggested that antioxidants like coenzyme Q10, vitamin E, and idebenone may offer individuals some limited benefit. However, recent clinical trials in the United States and Europe have not revealed effectiveness of idebenone in people with Friedreich's ataxia, but more powerful modified forms of this agent and other antioxidants are in trials at this time. There is also a clinical trial to examine the efficacy of selectively removing excess iron from the mitochondria.

Scientists also are exploring ways to increase frataxin levels through drug treatments, genetic engineering and protein delivery systems. Several compounds that are directed at increasing levels of frataxin may be brought to clinical trials in the near future.

Armed with what they currently know about frataxin and Friedreich's ataxia, scientists are working to better define fraxatin's role, clarify how defects in iron metabolism may be involved in the disease process, and explore new therapeutic approaches for therapy.

About the Author

Nathan Lee Davies lives in Wrexham, north Wales with his right hand.

There is not much to write here that you won't have already discovered from the proceeding pages. Davies has been brutally frank, funny and revealing to entertain the majority on a base level. However, intelligent readers will be able to see beyond the self-deprecating humour, anger and bitterness to the frustrating isolation of living in modern day Britain with a disability.

This is his first book.

For contact details, updates to this volume, and news of future projects, visit http://nathanleedavies.wordpress.com.